Water Women Wisdom

**Now is the time
for the feminine
to come forward**

Native American
and Daoist Prophecy

Water Women Wisdom

Voices
from the
Upper Mississippi

Water * Women * Wisdom

Written & Illustrated by
Nancy Scheibe

Singing River Publications, Inc.
Ely, Minnesota

Published by:

Singing River Publications, Inc.
PO Box 72
Ely, MN 55731
www.singingriverpublications.com

Book design by Dorie McClelland, Spring Book Design
Cover design by Amy Kirkpatrick
Printed in Canada

ISBN-10: 0-9789870-1-2
ISBN-13: 978-0-9789870-1-5

In Loving Memory of

Mom
Myrtle Grout

Auntie Chuck
Charlotte Miller

Grandmother
Helen Grout

Grandmother
Maude Turgeon

Sartell Gathering
Participant, Melanie

Dedicated to women who touch my life

Mother-in-Law
Jean Scheibe

Step-Mother
Maxine Grout

Auntie
Joyce Nelson

Sister
Diane Grout

Daughter
Sara Jo Dickens

Daughter
Naomi Scheibe

Contents

Maps

Acknowledgments

It takes a community to make an expedition such as this happen. Following are the people and organizations who contributed to the success of this venture. It is with deep gratitude their names are listed.

Individuals

LouEzza Bradely, Barbara Berglund, Bob Bicking, Loretta Bodey, Kristi Broderick, Karen Casey Elliot, Bill and Melissa Collins, Dan Crealy Jr., Jeanne & Erin Dahl, Sara Jo & Doug Dickens, Deborah Dora, Sue Duffy, Mark & Dianna Ellerbroek, Andrea Gregorson, Heidi Favet, Linda Ganister, Brian & Jayne Grout, Cis Hager, Sarah Hansen, Joany Haag, Paula & Andy Hill, Wade & Heather Jeske Pharr, Rebecca Kali, Gil Knight, Juliette Looye, Lydia McKlusky, Joyce Nelson, Emily Quick, Pat & Dave Romprtl, Alice Rueter, Jean Scheibe, Naomi Scheibe, Doug Scheibe, Sandy Scheibe, Rev. Dorothy Tatem Watson, Debbie Tiffany Quick, Janet Twohey, Nancy Jo Tubbs, Barb VanHauer, Gordy Wansura, and Kari Wenger

Organizations

Artic Transect 2004, Will Steger, Ely, MN; American Family Insurance, Jim Ridinger, Edina, MN; Arbonne International, Chicago, IL; Music Outfitters, Ely, MN; Cascade Designs, Winona, MN; Chota, Knoxville, TN; Ely Chiropractic, Ely, MN; Garden Lake Resort, Ely, MN; Hand Done Tee-Shirts, Ely, MN; Kangas Realty, Ely, MN; Piragas Northwoods Company, Ely, MN; PJ's Hair, Ely, MN; Stokes Bay Resort, Ely, MN

Organizations and individuals that assisted in bringing this book to print.

Individuals

Sara Jo Dickens, Heidi Favet, Heather Jeske Pharr, Alanna Johnson, Christine Moroni, Lisa Pekuri, Naomi Scheibe, Barbara Smith, Nancy Jo Tubbs

Organizations

Jack Pine Bob Cary Enterprises, Ely, MN, Spring Book Design, West St. Paul, MN, and Kirkpatrick Design, St. Paul, MN

Water Women Wisdom

Mission

While journeying the waters of the Mississippi, the Water Women Wisdom venture celebrates the value, power and sacred abilities of women by giving the Grandmothers a voice, gathering their truths, and sowing those seeds far and wide.

Grandmother is a term that embraces women age 50 and older, regardless of whether they have had children or grandchildren. It is a term of great respect in the Native American culture.

Women of all ages are invited to join us at a Gatherings of Grandmothers, or to travel with us on the water. The goal is to keep paddling and to hold sacred gatherings to collect the Grandmother's wisdom, until we reach the Gulf of Mexico.

To view photos from
Water Women Wisdom
expeditions go to:

www.waterwomenwisdom.com

Preface

All of us are called to do things in our lives. It comes like a persistent thought or yearning that tugs at you until you take action. You don't always know or understand what it is that you are doing but you follow the inner direction because you must. Those words sum the beginning of this expedition for me. This book was an expedition in itself and a labor of deep love. I consider it a great honor to have been called to do this work and grateful that I answered the call.

Portraying the inspiration, honesty and passion of the women's wisdom, my unfolding personal experiences, along with the story of the expedition down the river into one cohesive book was challenging. Each of these components could stand alone—yet their interconnection required they be presented together. On the following pages the women's wisdom that was not included in the body of the text is found on the pages with the shaded border. The story of the expedition and my personal reflections are on the remaining pages. I recommend reading the sections separately.

Some of the names of the women speaking have been changed at their request. The last names have been omitted to protect their privacy.

The appendix at the back of the book has a full listing of the women who contributed.

Maps at the back of the book provide a better perspective of the areas through which this expedition passed.

Poem & Song

I would like to repeat a poem by e. e. cummings.

Thank you God for this most amazing day,
For the blue true dream of sky,
For the weeping greenery of trees,
For everything which is natural
Which is infinite,
Which is yes.
—Paula

A song shared with us to the tune of *Edelweiss*

Bless our friends,
Bless our food,
Come oh Lord and sit with us.
May our talk
Glow with peace,
May your wisdom surround us.
Friendship and love bloom and grow,
Bloom and grow forever.
Bless our friends,
Bless our food,
Come oh Lord and sit with us.
—Barb

The Beginning

So, how did a city girl from south Minneapolis end up paddling the Mississippi to celebrate her fiftieth birthday? I am that girl, that woman. This is the story of how the adventure unfolded. The project began in December of 2003 with my plan to paddle 575 miles of the river with a friend. Soon the plan embraced other paddlers, ceremonial gatherings of grandmothers, and the collection of women's wisdom. With the river as my teacher, I was to learn to show up, pay attention, and to go with the flow.

Nancy, age 8
Taken the year
she first saw the
Headwaters of the
Mississippi

My proposed adventure brought forth a variety of emotions and responses from the many people in my life. Most greeted the idea with excitement and awe. Some even celebrated with cheers of "You Go Girl" which became the slogan of the grand journey. However, that was not the only reaction. *"Who the hell do you think you are?"* wrote one close friend in a letter. While her words were hurtful, I admit I sometimes shared a similar feeling. When another friend called this project an *"expedition,"* I was taken aback. Who was I to plan an expedition? Wasn't that something only very special people did? I wanted only to spend a couple of months paddling. And as my son-in-law Doug put it,

It's not an expedition if you aren't bringing a professional photographer.

My critical friend apologized for her, *"moment of pettiness,"* and I did come to think of the trip as an expedition, photographer or not. This trip would be an opportunity to grow in ways I had not imagined.

While planning the day-to-day details of the trip, I thought about how Auntie Joyce had told me I was courageous. That meant a lot because to me she is one of the most inspirational and tenacious examples of and symbols of what women can do. Auntie Joyce drove the volunteer fire truck in her home town in Texas until she was 80. At 88 she was still involved with the fire department because, as she put it, *"They need me to keep it lively."*

I was reading a book that had great impact on me, *Red Moon Passage; The Power and Wisdom of Menopause* by Bonnie Horrigan. A yearning began to grow within as I thought about the extraordinary women I might meet along the river. Their life experiences and stories could bring light into the world. I wanted to meet those women. What if I invited women to gather with me as I stopped on the riverbank in the evenings? What sort of community gathering of women would I experience? What would I hear?

As I focused on the collection of women's wisdom, the journey began to enrich my life with connections to people around the country. An acquaintance from Chicago told me Native Americans believe *"Now is the time for the feminine to come forward."* Later a friend of mine from Ely, Rebecca, told me that the Daoists share that same philosophy. People became excited about the ways in which the trip would honor women. I watched the venturing spirit in them rise to the surface. It became clear this journey was not just about my fiftieth birthday. My birthday had been the catalyst that got me moving. This trip would impact many people and was bigger than my sphere of the world.

The impact was personal at first. I was married and had two jobs. I worked with youth-at-risk at a local agency and was also putting together a business plan with my husband for a coffee and tea shop and in between, I was sneaking moments for my artwork. Waves of fear rolled into my thoughts. How could I leave home for two months? Did I have enough money set aside to complete the trip? As I delved into plans, the waves of fear changed direction. What if no one came to the gatherings? What if too many came? I was running myself ragged trying to contact everyone who might attend, getting media coverage, organizing paddlers, supplies, campsites, and schedules. At times I wondered if I was as crazy as the look on some people's faces told me I was.

In today's lingo, I was a raging co-dependent, trying to control everything. After a lifetime of believing I had control of things, I was forced to let go of my rampant perfectionism. What purpose did it serve to worry about the gatherings? The people who were meant to be there would show up. I was being invited to practice "going with the flow."

In May I was in the thick of planning and had yet to hit the water in any kind of boat. I looked longingly at the lakes in northeastern Minnesota and wished I had time to enjoy paddling before the trip began. I'd held a vision of how I ought to get in shape but, as usual, life was not proceeding as I planned.

On May 13 I smiled and watched the snowfall. Spring was late. Like the weather, I had held to the familiarity of darkness and cold of the past. I had always been comfortable working invisibly in the background to keep everybody happy and make their dreams come true. This trip was my dream. I realized it was forcing me to step out of the dark and into the sunshine of growth and life.

I had been particularly nervous about how the gatherings would work, whether my concept would flow and engender women to want to share wisdom. Then I realized many women right here in Ely had a great deal of wisdom to share. I invited women to my home for the first gathering of *Grandmothers* on May 18. Women who attended didn't really have to be grandmothers or even mothers. I chose the word from the Native American culture because it is a title of great respect that recognizes wisdom born out of time and experience. I decided only women aged 50 or older would be allowed to speak at the gatherings. In our culture we have done a great deal to empower young women to speak. But many older women are not heard. It is their knowing that has the capacity to bring peace, love, and healing back into the world. Women not yet 50 who attended were respectfully asked not to speak at the gatherings. I was not yet 50 so I would be there to listen.

The focus of each gathering was as unique as the women who attended. With the help of some friends I had written five questions, "conversation starters." Some women chose to stay with the questions. Others chose to ignore them. Each gathering took on a life of its own. The questions I presented were:

1. Describe how your spirituality influenced your life.
2. What direction has the river of life taken you? Did it follow a path you expected? How has the flow shaped who you are and who you are becoming?
3. What wisdom would you like to share with younger women as they travel their river of life?
4. At what points did you choose to navigate the waters of life, as opposed to go with the flow? How did those choices affect your experience?
5. How would you like to be remembered by family and friends after your death?

Eleven women came to the Ely gathering. The women were promised that their words would be shared with others only if they gave permission. I would use only their first names in relating the stories from these nights of personal talk gathered around a fire.

Winnie began her story with a disclaimer I heard time after time.

I do not think of myself as a woman of wisdom.

Invariably after making that statement, each woman would speak with wisdom that brought us to laughter, sometimes tears, and many nods of recognition indicating they had been there, done that, and survived to tell about it, too.

The women told stories of living with a disability, or how they came to a life of love in the wilderness. They talked about the profound meaning of trees, the intentional creation of our lives, the best canoe trip they ever had, and their searches for simplicity and Spirit. One brought a song, another a poem and one quoted Mark Twain, *"Most of the things in my life never really happened."* That quote echoed in my head for days following the gathering.

Paula began.

I guess I will share something that has changed my life in some ways. Four years ago I was diagnosed with breast cancer. I had recently been remarried and started a new life—very different from a painful marriage of 21 years. I was very excited about a whole new chapter of my life. So that diagnosis was just scary. I thought, "Wait a minute!" (I had been feeling so good about where I was headed.)

I want to talk about it in terms of spirituality. The day I went to the appointment, my husband was there. He is not someone who keeps a time and date in his mind. I didn't even ask him to come to the appointment, but he showed up, I said, 'What are you doing here?'

"I don't know. I just felt I should be here today," he said.

I thought that was wonderful. I got called in, and the doctor said, "Is that your husband out there? Why doesn't he come in too?"

As soon as she said that, I thought, "This could be serious." I was glad he was there, because when the doctor said I had cancer I cried. I couldn't even ask questions. But my husband asked lots of questions, and it was very helpful. When we finished we walked outside of the clinic. He held me and we cried together. We were both faced with a difficult struggle when we had just begun our life together. We wondered what this would mean for each of us. I said in my silliness, "I need to go to the post office." He looked at me funny, and said, "I will meet you at home." So he drove home.

I went to my car to get the mail. When I turned around there was a woman from church standing there. She said, "How did your appointment turn out?"

I said, "Well, not good, I have breast cancer." She put her arm around me and said, "I just know it is going to be okay." We talked a minute. I was parked about a half a block from the post office.

Then I was on a mission. I walked so fast, thinking, "I don't know what I am going to do," when I physically ran into a person right by the steps of the post office. I mean bam! Hard! I looked up. It was a friend I hadn't seen for awhile. She grabbed me and said, "You're not okay." I said, "You're right. I'm not." Then I told her I had breast cancer. She held me and she cried with me. That was so touching. At that moment peace came over me. I thought, "I am not alone in this at all. I have faith." An assurance came over me that calmed me and helped me relax. I went and got my nails done, (which sounds silly).

Later I had a chance to reflect. The doctor I happened to get on this day was not my regular doctor. This was a physician from Virginia, Minnesota, who someone had recommended. From the beginning she was absolutely a great doctor for the whole process. She encouraged me to educate myself. She gave me lots of treatment options. I ended up having a lumpectomy and chemo and radiation. Then that doctor moved away. I was cared for so well during a difficult time in life.

It is now four years down the road. Here I am and I feel very well. It has taught me to take more time each day to be quiet. I take time to pray. I keep an active list now for the needs of other people, including people in our city and our government and our world. I think I am much more sensitive now.

I like what you are doing here because we all have a part to play to make peace. I think it is a privilege. We all really need to lift up our voices both in prayer and in support of people.

One more thing: When I lost my hair, my dear husband shaved his head. We shaved our heads together. It was great. I could not have felt more loved.

To close each of the gatherings, I led a ritual. Each woman was given two sticks which I referred to as *aspiration sticks,* along with two pieces of yarn, one white and one purple. The women were instructed to wrap the white yarn around the first stick while they visualized tying their struggles and the pain of life onto the stick. As a ritual of letting-go this first stick was then respectfully placed in the fire and burned. The women were encouraged so say a prayer of gratitude. While wrapping the second stick with purple yarn, the women visualized their hopes, dreams and aspirations for their life. This stick is to be placed in the river so the river can carry one's wishes into the future to be manifested.

Heather Jeske, 27, an avid paddler with extensive wilderness experience and a degree in wilderness management, would be my paddling partner for this expedition. We carefully bundled the Ely gathering's participant's sticks and made a commitment to the women. We would set the sticks free when

Women's Wisdom

Humor & Happiness

Life itself is funny. Look at yourself in the morning. Then you make it through the day and start all over doing the same thing the next day. How dumb is that? —Mary G.

Did we know what happiness was when we were 29 or even 34 years old? Could we answer that question then? *What is happiness?* We were people who were performing what we thought was our job or our duty. —Sandra

I wouldn't have survived without humor. It was my ability to find the silliness in bad situations that saved my sanity. I guess it was a defense mechanism that just came up in childhood. I do have the tendency to find the really silly things. —Shaughn

I have specific ways I get to humor. One is watching *I Love Lucy* videos. I was recovering from surgery and I started every day watching an episode. There is one I could watch over and over and that is the *Chocolate Factory*. I "go find" humor. If it is not there I go find it. It is what gets me through life. Especially if I am dating. [Laughter] —Deborah

I was in a water park in the Wisconsin Dells with my daughters. I floated alongside a little boy who was floating on the inner tube and he said to someone in his group, *"You know, I feel just like a Cheerio in a bowl of milk."* He was the cutest thing. He was a 6 or 7 years old. It was the cutest wisest thing I have ever heard. I just wanted to be that cheerio. —Nancy O.

I think humor is an easier flowing energy. The opposite of it is just too draining. I guess that is why humor has helped me get through life. I had a friend who was coming to visit and I needed to get my house clean and I was planning on doing just that. I came home and the electricity was out. So what did I do? Well I at least needed to clean the bathroom. So I cleaned the bathroom by candle light. Whether or not it really got clean I don't know. And I was thinking: "How was I going to get all this stuff done?" Then I decide to do what was important. Clean the toilet and that was it. —Mary Jo we got on the river. I felt a great sense of responsibility. Carefully we put them with our gear. As I tucked them away I was glad I had found a yarn that was biodegradable. I knew nothing harmful would be added to the river.

That night as the stories of community continued, I realized how deeply I wished to experience more of the inspiring tenacity and wisdom of older women.

After the gathering it was back to work. After two more weeks of hectic trip preparations, my spirits waned. While steadfast in my desire for the adventure, I was also resistant to leaving home. My body ached. I was easily distracted. Although the preparations were not yet complete, I decided to take a week of spiritual respite to unwind and reflect. I packed my camping gear and headed for Cascade Falls, a state park 15 minutes south of Grand Marais, Minnesota.

Driving toward the North Shore of Lake Superior, I spotted a deer whose gentle nature reminded me to be gentle with myself. It seems to me when we are quiet, attentive, and open we see how the Spirit moves through all of nature to direct us or to provide the companionship we need at the moment. We are spiritually connected to everything on earth whether or not we pay attention.

As I continued the drive a glorious moose clambered out of the lake next to the dirt road and trotted a few feet ahead of me. Watching her I connected with the joy that comes from a job well done. Her enormous plodding feet reminded me of the momentous job I had taken on. Just as I realized it was time to let go and watch the rest of the trip unfold, she turned and disappeared into the woods. I could now lean into trusting that all would work out as it was supposed to.

I believe we are all here with a purpose, though we may not know what it is. I believe an idea that won't go away, or a drive to action is connected to a divinely inspired purpose. We might choose to say no to inspiration. If we say yes, be ready! A whirlwind of change begins. Say yes, and the ride is in motion! Keep your eyes open and your hands inside the car!

I sat at the foot of a grand cedar tree whose trunk divided into two and then interwove and branched out overhead. The wide expanse of Lake Superior lay calm and blue before me. I began to write my personal goals for the trip. I realized I had spent much time searching for a life-changing experience that would make me into a different person, *a better person;* one empowered to begin to honor herself. I imagined it might be a great spiritual awaking with a

Women's Wisdom

If you can release your stress you can't help but be happy. Just look at animals, cats particularly. They are happy all the time. They have no stress in their life unless you move your foot too fast when they are walking by. Then they go straight up. So they have, what? ten seconds of stress and then they take a nap. We can learn a lot from cats. —Mary G.

Laughter is essential . . . and being able to say, "My God, here comes another wave." I can joke about it differently than I did when I was younger and know that this wave will pass too. —Deborah

Caring for Yourself

If you paddled all the time you would get exhausted too. You need those times to rest. —Terry B.

Accept where you are and make the most of what you are doing right now, whatever it is. Even if it is something that is bad or difficult and painful, this is where you are. And instead of waiting to get through it, acknowledge this is where you are and this is what you deal with now. —Kathryn

We need to have time to be still. Busyness keeps us from being still. If we give ourselves time to be still this is when we do our spirituality. This is when we do our soul work. This is the value of stillness and why it is very very important. If we keep busy and diverted, we never ever truly get in touch with ourselves. —Sally

Something a lot of women have not learned is how to take care of themselves. They give and they give and they give and they give until there is nothing left. There has to be a time when you have to back off and heal. You have to find a way to fill your cup. —Alice

I look back on those years of poverty and trying to achieve and live according to somebody else's standards. What is right for somebody is not right for you. Find your own way in life. That is what I had to find out. —Barbara bright light or angels, or perhaps a billboard with clear instructions I could not miss. But so far, the experiences that have changed me have often come in other forms. My mother died when I was 11. As a very young adult I survived and left an abusive relationship. Later, I learned my daughters had been sexually abused, and together we began the heartbreaking process of healing. After my father's death when I was 41, I felt like an orphan. Now I am one of the elders of my family. These experiences changed my life. Though on the surface they appear to be tragedies, they each came with beautiful gifts that involved a deeper connection with another person and myself. Each of these experiences made me who I am. With each experience I grew in courage or wisdom. As a result, I created artwork that spoke to other women's hearts and became part of their healing.

In my journal I wrote that I wanted to come back from this trip a different person, to leave the old one behind. But that thought caused me to stop for a moment. It implied something was wrong with that old self, that I was done with her. In reality, I didn't want to leave her at all. I wanted her to come out of the darkness of self-judgment and to step away from the fear of what others might think. I was ready to see her strength and tenacity. I wanted to stand in my power and move forward.

I remembered the words of Lynne Twist, longtime leader of The Hunger Project,

We can't really change our everyday actions, because at their root will always be the dream we have for our future, and we will always act consistently with that dream. However, the dream can change.

My husband Doug joined me for a day so we could have some time away from daily routines and connect before the trip. A porcupine waddled across our path while we hiked. She didn't seem to see us, and strolled within two feet of us. Her behavior spoke of innocence and the power of faith. She reminded me to not be too intellectual and to trust that The Spirit has a plan for me. I was grateful for the time with Doug. For the moment we had quiet refuge without the distractions of planning and home life.

On June 2nd I was back in Ely. With excitement building, the final details fell into place. The next day I would make the last call to firm up a gathering of Grandmothers at the Leech Lake Indian Reservation. That June evening, singer-songwriter Ann Reed, a nationally know folk singer, came to perform in concert as a benefit for the project, now called **Water Women Wisdom**. The theater was packed with energy and exhilaration. We were joined at the concert by other adventurous women, Sarah LaKosky

Women's Wisdom

I can go on empty for a long time, but I don't enjoy life. —Gretchen

Eventually my body will tell me. Anytime I am under any kind of stress my body will tell me really quickly. Things just go to heck, or I get sick. —Alice

I used to feel guilty if I did something for myself or even took a break. Now I just go out on the porch with my coffee and relax. My husband is out there working his butt off and it feels great because that is his choice. —Terry B.

When you take care of yourself you are giving out of the best instead of the bottom. —Nancy R.

Relationship to Self

Pretty much, I am who I am right now. It has taken a lot of years to get where I am. —Sharon W.

My mother's name was Lorraine. Actually her born name was Clara Lorraine. She hated Clara so much she had it legally switched to Lorraine Clara. When she was older she went only as Mrs. Bernard Schuler. That is how she signed her checks and everything. I said, "Mom if you don't start signing your own name I am going to put Mrs. Bernard Schuler on your headstone when you die." She said *"Well that wouldn't be me."* I said, "Then quit saying that." She did. So we put her name on the stone the way it was supposed to be. —Mary G

I am the one that has to take charge of where I go in this life. It doesn't matter if I am alcoholic or not. I have a different concept about what life is about. Life is about healing ourselves. Our skin scabs over. We have tears to keep that pain away. The laughter, too, feels good and lets that stress inside go. It is beneficial in a lot of ways, to go back to that spiritual way of life and spiritual train of thought. —Barbara

It is much easier to steer by yourself than with someone else. —Nancy O.

and Suellen Sack, who had just completed Arctic Quest, a four-woman dog-sled expedition through northern Canada, ending in Churchill, Manitoba. It was thrilling to hear them say they were excited for us.

One of the songs Ann sang was about how power tools are a girl's best friend, in which she mentioned the Knox and Menards home improvement stores. She shared with the audience that she had received a letter from a woman not living in the state of Minnesota who misinterpreted the reference, and thought "Knox-Menards" was a secret code word. Heather and I decided we would yell "Knox-Menards" as a signal whenever one of us ran into trouble. We would use it often, most of the time humorously.

When Ann Reed sang "Every Long Journey" (words to song page 232) for us, I cried. She had written that song for Ann Bancroft, who became the first woman to cross Antarctica's landmass by skis and by sail in February of 2001. As a speaker, teacher, and co-author of *No Horizon Is So Far,* and founder of the Ann Bancroft Foundation, the famed explorer helps girls and women realize their highest dreams and potential. The foundation promotes initiatives that inspire courage, risk-taking, integrity and individuality in girls and women.

It began to really sink in that **Water Women Wisdom** was a big deal. We were touching many lives. I felt such a huge sense of responsibility. Ann Reed and others told us we were courageous and inspiring. While it was wonderful to hear those words, I knew I was just doing what I must. It was hard to see the courage in that.

I felt supported by many women and men, and by Doug, whose work on the project over the past week had been incredible. Without his understanding and willingness for me to do this, it would not have happened. It felt odd knowing he wouldn't be with me. He had been a big part of the other adventures in my life. Now it was time for me to stand on my own.

On June 3rd we panic-packed. It was time to leave. All we wanted to do was to get everything in the Jeep and head out. Doug, friend Pam, and Heather helped cram our gear and supplies into a disorganized, overloaded Jeep and trailer. We left home with two kayaks, a two-person canoe and a solo canoe. Doug joined Heather and me on the five-hour drive through Hibbing, Grand Rapids, and Cass Lake to our put-in point in Itasca State Park.

Heather had paddled the first section of our trip on

Women's Wisdom

I think we all need to look inside. We look out upon that which we feel inside. We need to find a zest for life. Joy and meaning come in recognizing the little picture in the big picture. It's natural and simple to learn to really look and to be present and appreciate. Just learning to love, whatever that means. —Susan

I learned a lot from my mom and some of it in a not so positive way. She had a role of being a housewife and mom even when those roles were not around anymore. The kids were raised and my dad had died. She just kind of gave up. What I have learned is that you have to have your own passion. You have to wake up everyday and say, "This is what I want for myself." There are people you care about and want to be with and do things for, but you have to have something that you are passionate about. —Deborah

None of us truly choose the river we are in. It is a matter of navigating and taking charge. I have my philosophy that I share with anybody. It is "You Go Girl." The choices you make for you are the right ones. And life as it comes is generally as it should be for some reason. Sometimes you need to have something bad happen to make you rethink, to make you wake up. *Wake up!* [She exclaimed loudly] Enjoy, appreciate. This is how it is. You can offer so much. We can loose so much by worrying about things. —Sally

A lot of what I have done in my life has been a big detour. Finally, at 50, I get to return to what I want to do. I guess I still don't know what that is, but at least I know I am on the right path. The detour has been like an information gathering session, like getting off the path while you are berry picking. —Amy

50 was absolutely fabulous. It is freedom. It is a sense that you are a grown up. It doesn't matter how you view yourself or whether you wake up and understand all your warts and know where all your weaknesses are, or your faults and flaws, or that you feel silly in this area or that area. You are a grown up and nobody has any authority over you unless you let them have it. —Mary O.

the Mississippi in 2003 and was glad to be back at the river's headwaters. Heather was not only a good friend; she had been dating my son Wade for the past year. Heather said,

I get the feeling a big part of last year's trip was to take some of the 'scary' out of this one. Without some knowledge of what we were in for, I'd have been a basket case.

As it was she was a little overwhelmed thinking about being away from her dogs for two months. Heather has two dogs, Arrow and Rush who are very special to her. Generally, she takes them everywhere she goes, but that was not possible on this trip. To ease the separation she brought her stuffed horse, Topaz, to ride the bow of her kayak and keep her company. Topaz had been with Heather most of her life. She laughed as  she said, "I'm looking forward to some girl-and-horse-bonding time. The River Rat is back!" Previously when Heather traveled the river, her sister and cousins had named themselves the River Rats.

As we drove and hiked through scenic Itasca State Park, I noticed with growing irritation the roads, buildings, and everything, were named after men. It was as if we women had not contributed anything. When we came upon a sign with a picture of Mary Gibbs on it I was ecstatic. Eagerly I read every word printed about her.

Mary Gibbs, 1903–1983, at age 24 was designated, "Courageous Protector of Itasca's Trees." She was the first woman to manage a state or national park, and her goal here was to protect the trees from logging. She stood up to armed guards at a log dam, and her actions increased awareness for park protection. After leaving Itasca, she moved to Canada, raised four boys, and died at the age of 104.

I realized I needed to search out women who gave meaning to our history. There are many names, most lost due to the quiet nature of their work. Mary was not quiet. She spoke out in what could be identified as a masculine style. She showed courage in front of men when other men could not and therefore earned the right to be noted in history. She was a beautiful symbol of what women will do when they feel the need to protect something dear to them.

Other beautiful things we found in the park included flowers and

Women's Wisdom

Risk-taking has increased a lot because for me. Now I think, "What is the worst thing that could possibly happen? Oh I might meet some nice people; I might have fun and, okay, let's see if I can handle that now." What we focus on expands. There might be a grander adventure on the other side of that hill. If you never go to the top of the hill you will never know. —JoAn

I was listening to these other women and I didn't know what to say. I still don't know so I am thinking, "Where did I learn or pick up some things?" Like some of you, I was raised on a farm out in the garden digging, sneaking the sweet peas when they were fresh. I smelled the wild roses when they were blooming. I bailed hay, at the same time enjoying the smell of the hay. So I think that was the start of it. As I went through life and tried to direct my river, ultimately some points came along and said *"Sorry, you are not going that direction."* Okay. I had this job and that is where I was going to go but that didn't pan out. So I thought, "Okay. I will go back to school and become an architect." But I didn't get accepted for that. But that refusal pushed me into art. If I am in not going the right direction, something comes up and says I have to go a different direction. There are no coincidences. It is synchronicity. It is like flags are raised saying you need to go in a different direction. I know sometimes I struggle but when I can get the perspective it is "Oh yeah I see now where that was leading me." So, just when you think you are going to get into a nice comfortable rut, somebody is going to come along and fill it with water. —Mary Jo

Years ago I was given the formula to avoid burnout. I was fascinated by it. You take your calendar for the year and block out two weeks to do something other than work. And you need two weeks in a row because it takes that second week to really rebuild. You don't wait until you can squeeze it in. Then every month you take a long weekend to do something other than work. Go someplace; take the phone off the hook . . . whatever. And every week take several hours, it could be pizza and a movie, it could be a long lunch with a friend. And every day 20 minutes (the 20 minutes is not to exercise), it is to smell the roses. I wondered what that would total. I sat down and estimated it would be 52.3 days a year. In other words, one full day a week. We are not made to go seven. So all of a sudden it became pretty powerful. —Nancy R.

breathtaking scenic views. As we hiked up the road leading to the fire tower we found several plants of bright yellow lady slippers. At the top of the tower we could see a great distance. What astonished and fascinated me most was looking straight down. The leaves on the oak trees below appeared like a giant fabric of green lace stretched out before me. Subtle changes in the green tones of the leaves and patches of brighter areas where the sun shown clearly on them and a delicate natural masterpiece. As we walked up to see the oldest white pine in Minnesota. We saw marsh marigolds in bloom, scattered on the forest floor. Doug and Heather checked out the tree. I found myself searching for more blooming treasures and was rewarded with a nodding trillium. We had a trillium in our campsite as well.

Lady Slipper

Later that evening my daughter from Colorado, Sara Jo (we call her Jo) arrived. Jo would be paddling the first two weeks of the trip with us. She rode up from the Twin Cities with my friend Barb. Barb would be paddling with us for the first three days. Then Lorrie, Heather's Mom pulled in with strawberry pie from Baker's Square! She came to give us all a good send off. As we sat around the fire enjoying the pie, Heather attempted to fix Jo's bracelet. Her headlamp provided her with the light she needed, but was also a beacon for June bugs. The big, brown, crunchy bugs kept slamming into her face and buzzing past her. As annoying as she found it, we thought it an amusing entertainment to end the evening.

Jo wrote in her journal,

As I arrive with Barb, we pull into the camp to see friendly smiles and a tarp piled with gear. There was so much stuff it looked like we were about to mount an expedition. I have seen mountaineers bring this much to far off countries. It was clear we'd be prepared for anything. . . . I wish my Doug (her husband) was here. I will carry the quartz stone he gave me. He said it would cleanse, bring peace and remove pain. I know this time apart will be a time of growth for us both.

June 5, Saturday, Day 1

We woke to an overcast sky. Anticipation was thick in the air. Doug cooked us a wonderful send-off breakfast and mixed what had become known to us as "moose juice" for the journey. Moose juice is really a drink, similar to Gatorade, that replaces electrolytes. I had found this drink at a health food store. I did not want to drink the other electrolyte replacement prod-

Women's Wisdom

My grandmother Louise responded to one of her daughters when she asked *"This person can play the piano. This person has a beautiful voice. What is the talent that our family has?"* My grandmother replied, *"We have the talent to appreciate it."* She would always say goodbye to us with either, *"Stay as good as you are,"* or, *"Stay as nice as you are."*
—Maureen

Most of the time in my life I couldn't even have thought of being alone. I couldn't stand to be alone. I had to have somebody around all the time. But not anymore. I like being with other people, but I also like very much to be with myself and like my company. What I think wisdom is about is being smart enough to know what is your business and what is your neighbor's business. —Sharon W.

The thing I am always concerned about is women being independent before they are into a committed relationship with a man. Be self sufficient and independent. Find out who you are away from your family, your friends and from high school. Go away. The only way you find yourself is when you don't have those roles to play anymore. Go away, even if it is for just a year. Go to a different place in the world. You will be so amazed at who you are and what you can do. —Kathryn

I was young and reckless, but at 30 I was no longer that way with my children. I would say, "I can't do it, I can't do it." And I had a friend who would say *"Well sure you can."* It was not a lady that said this but Chief Clearwater. His real name was Paul Macky. When I knew him he was 80 years old. He had been a liberty horse trainer and rode with his father on wagons in movies. He used his favorite saying on me because he was convinced I could learn to trick ride. I was a pretty good horse person. I would say, "I can't do it, I can't do it," and he would say, *"Well sure you can, just get up there. You can do anything you think you are big enough to do."* I didn't have the confidence to do it, but if I thought I did, I probably could have. I shared this with my kids when they were feeling down. —Sally

Don't be afraid to be by yourself. There are all those people who can't be alone. They have all this external stuff just so they don't have to spend down time by themselves. I think you learn more about yourself when you are by yourself. —Amy

ucts that are primarily sugar saturated water. It became moose juice because of its color, and (for Doug) its bad taste. To round off our breakfast we finished the heavenly strawberry pie Lorrie had brought the night before.

At the shore of Lake Itasca the women gathered in a circle and I sang a sacred Anishnaabeg song that would be our companion on the trip. I had sung this song every morning for the past month in preparation for the trip. The song was given to me by Dan, a Chicago man I had yet to meet. Dan had heard about the trip from a mutual friend and immediately began sending encouragement. He was deeply integrated into Native American spirituality and we often talked about the spiritual significance of women stepping forward to heal our world. Dan felt it was appropriate I be given the song to guide me and assist me in staying focused on my true mission: bringing women's wisdom forward. I felt honored the words had been shared with me. It was a privilege to sing them. The words call us to stand together and face the light of dawn. They instruct us to make plans and set the course for future generations and to fulfill our obligations to nature, the Spirit world and the creator. They remind us that our work for others is recognized in the Spirit world. Dan also helped me see that I was on was a pilgrimage. He shared with me Joseph Campbell's words.

The whole idea of pilgrimage is translating into a literal, physical act— the pilgrimage of moving into the center of your own heart.

This expedition was indeed a personal pilgrimage coming from and moving to the center of my heart.

At the end of the song the girls scampered into their canoe as Doug rejoined us to say goodbye. I made an offering of Kinnickinnick which Dan had sent me. I will make an offering of Kinnickinnick at the beginning of each day, sprinkling a small amount in the water and ask for safe passage and protection by the Spirits (The Lady of the Lake). At the end of the day I will make another offering, in gratitude for our safe passage, as well as the wonderful things that will have transpired that day. Kinnickinnick is a combination of dried plants including cedar and the Kinnickinnick plant, also known as bearberry. Natives believe Kinnickinnick connects us to the ancient ones, the old ways and the Spirits. Practicing this quiet personal gesture keeps me connected to Spirit and life and brings a sense of peace.

Women's Wisdom

I think my energy level now is in direct proportion to how happy I am with myself. Using it more wisely, choosing where I am going to put my energy and to what I am going to devote it is the key. —JoAn

Relationships with Others

Find affirming people. —Mary Jo

As women, the older women were taught that everybody came before us, our husbands, fathers or whomever. We were always the lowest on the totem pole. Then it dawned on me that it is time to take care of yourself. It is a very hard decision to make. That one very small word "No" is very difficult to say. It gets easier with time. —Shaughn

My husband and I have worked with youth a lot. Other couples would ask us what clues we had for parenting, especially teenagers. We both would say this one; just enjoy them—just enjoy them. We are reaping the benefits of having enjoyed our children. I think people that feel they have been enjoyed have much to offer the world. —Millie

Some things work and some things don't. Sometimes you don't know what works until you have done it. Not only until you have done it but until after have you done it. I will give you an example. We adopted a half Indian boy when he was seven. It was very difficult. He had a hard time and we had a hard time. We ended up having to throw our hands up and say, "You have to go." He went into foster care when he was sixteen. They got him to go through school. We have not had direct contact with him, but a couple of our children have. He has settled down and has had a fairly decent life. It looks as if our life helped him. He has said to the other kids, *"I don't know how mom and dad put up with me."* I can't say it was all his fault. When your own children do things that are wrong you understand their desire to do what they are doing because you have the history; you have the same type of thoughts. Somebody you take on from a different culture thinks differently. A lot of us learn things too late. I don't know if we were good for him or not. —Norma

Heather, Jo, Nancy, and Barb-the first paddle strokes

By canoe Barb and I followed the girls the short distance across the lake to the headwaters of the Mississippi. We carried our canoes over the rocks where the crystal clear water becomes the Mississippi River. Our expedition was officially under way. We paused for a for a "muscle woman" pose in front of the headwaters marker and then proceeded downstream under the watchful eyes of tourists who stood near and in the river at its headwaters. Barb and I lead the way with the girls close behind. Just past the headwaters, the river is barely six feet wide and the reeds and grass towered over our heads. Passing under a footbridge, Barb and I were greeted by a beaver that swam ahead of us like a guide. Three eagles perched on a nest overhead. What a send-off!

Jo, Nancy, and Heather

Rounding a bend we spotted Doug and Lorrie waiting for us. They were standing at what was our first portage. The river ran through a culvert under a road, not large enough to pass through. Doug and Lorrie cheered us on as we lifted the canoes and carried them over the road. We said our final goodbye to Lorrie. She was headed home. We would see Doug at camp that night. We

Women's Wisdom

Nurture your friendships with other women. Sometimes I just need to step back and gather with women. I have had some incredibly life changing experiences by just being with other women. —Terry B.

I will love my friends unconditionally forever. Today I pick and choose my friends. There are some people that maybe I don't want as my friends and that's okay. I do have choices. It is all about relationships to me and that I am honest. That is one thing about me. If you ask a question you will hear it. You'll get it. That is where I am at today and it is so different. —Bonnie

Sometimes you have to be gracious and accept help whether you need it or not. Once when I was going into the hospital, an older man held the door for me and I thanked him. He looked very sad and said, *"This is about the only thing I am any good for anymore."* I thought, that is really a sad situation. But maybe he felt just a little bit better by opening the door for me. I don't know. —Winnie

My husband, Don, and I are both from very large Minnesota families. One of the things I have learned is that in that large family setting there are feelings of abandonment. I felt love but it got lost in the chaos. I am at a point of really learning how to recognize what is chaos and how to be in it and not of it. That is a very wonderful kind of feeling. —Millie

I ask myself, what I could do to show love more in my life. If I am walking through my neighborhood on my daily walk I can choose to greet the people I meet or not. What would be a loving thing? Maybe that greeting would help somebody's day and I wouldn't even know it. Maybe there would be this ripple effect. Maybe stopping to tie someone's shoe in school and while I was doing it ask them something about their baby sister, instead of just being in a hurry to tie their shoe would make a difference. You know, little acts of love . . . that is what I mean. What didn't I do today or in the last hour that really could have made the world a different and better place for people? Not asking as a guilt thing, but rather being reflective. What different way could I do something to share that love and be open about my own spiritually? —Jan paddled on and saw an osprey, a snapping turtle, birds, frogs and butter-flies. Big redhorse fish swirled under the boats. One nearly flopped into Jo and Heather's canoe in one of the rapids downstream.

Everything we saw was exciting. Heather exclaimed that the first three-mile stretch of rapids on the trip was a blast, if a little long. She said.

Jo and I started out really well. I yelled, "paddle!" and she paddled imme-diately—a dream come true. Our communication was on! Towards the end of that set of rapids, though, we got pretty tired. We reached a point where I completely forgot how to steer. Left and right meant nothing. "Where do we go?" I asked forlornly, "I don't know," she said. Then we both cracked up laughing as the river heaved our canoe over a rock field.

The roots of a downed tree stretched out high above the water. The dirt had long since been lost to time and weather. Jo, who is an avid climber, stopped to investigate. Soon she was climbing over, around and behind it. She had earned the title of "monkey" as a child on our first family rock climbing trip. Back then she went up a rock wall as if it had stairs.

Between rapids we glided gen-tly through a forest of pine, birch, maple and oak. Downed trees created obstacles to maneuver around or crawl over. The bright green and brown reeds danced on the bottom of the river. The air was fresh. In the distance the sound of ravens echoed in the air. Occasionally a beaver dam chal-lenged us. Each time we crossed one I looked down into the water and was awestruck by the creative ingenuity and shear physical effort required to construct one. Beavers are remarkable creatures.

The river narrowed into a maze of switchbacks and disappearing chan-nels. Soon we found ourselves in a thicket of willow and alder. The river seemed to disappear before our very eyes. We followed the current and found ourselves dragging the boats through mud, brush, and trees. At one point I had to reach into the "brownie mud"—so named for its texture of raw, dark brown dough—up to my elbow to free my shoe from the glop. We feared we were lost, but we could see the current, so we kept moving forward. I saw places where others had cut away trees and shrubs to get through and found it reassuring. As Jo slogged waist-deep in water and

Women's Wisdom

My sister and I and a lot of friends get together once a month. The few years we have been doing that have been the best years of my life. I have come out of myself and have learned to share more. I think that is what women need these days is to learn to share. You can share only when you are with women and comfortable. —Roxana

I think it is real important to be yourself with your children. Not necessarily avoiding the subject of religion, but it can't be the only thing you share. I truly believe that. We have four children. We have two daughters. One is 20 and is going to college and trying to get into medical school. After all these years she has gone in a complete circle. The second daughter and our son who is 22 have always struggled in school and in the family. My son is very brave, but an independent thinker. I never thought he was prepared for huge responsibilities, but this winter he told us that he and his girlfriend are expecting a child. I was very worried, but our youngest son was born out of wedlock and adopted, so I couldn't go there. I felt a lot better paying attention to him and not necessarily the responsibilities he was facing, because he was finding those along the way. I found it best to not be judgmental which helped me be there for him. That is why I think we don't want situations to control our relationships with our children. —Maureen

I think choices are part of life. We choose to be where we are; if we are down and out and everything is a problem and "woe is me" you chose that path. You can choose to get out of it. Just choose. I have someone in my life I call the "Turd of misery." Since I have known her it has always been *"Poor me."* Every time I see her it is a great big old pity party. I want to bring balloons and candy and stuff for the pity party next time. —Mary G.

When you get to be 80 your mind travels ahead of you. I didn't do what everybody else did. At age 64 I started a new business. It was just like starting over. It was great. It was something I really loved to do and I didn't have to boss those kids around. (She was a physical education teacher for 25 years.) I went from teaching to guiding. I still love canoeing. I am not planning on any other changes, but you never know. —Barb

Cultivate healthy relationships with healthy people. The ones we call family may not necessarily be the ones we grew up with. —JoAn mud, dragging a canoe around a tree, Barb said she thought she could hear traffic in the distance. She began walking through the thicket toward it. We convinced her that we were not lost and should stay together. (I was not convinced we had not gone the wrong way.) Finally we broke through to open water and rejoiced! Then, totally exhausted and suffering from the heat of the day, we rested, floating on the easily discernable river wondering how we had missed it.

We pushed on for another six miles. A cold was draining my energy. I had been struggling with a low fever, runny nose and headache that started just before we left home. We pushed on looking for the campsite marker. Each of the canoe campsites along the Minnesota section of the Mississippi are marked with a dark brown wooden marker displaying a bright yellow canoe in the background with a teepee in the center.

Endurance was the word for the day. At 7 pm we pulled into Coffee Pot campsite, proud of our nine-hour, 17.5-mile day. Doug was waiting for us and had our tents already set up. Heather said she learned that

> No matter which way you choose, there will always be challenges, but if you trust your intuition and keep moving forward, you will end up where you need to be. This comment would be deeper (more reflective) if I wasn't so tired.

After a beautiful sunset, everyone slept the sleep of the tired voyageur.

June 6, Sunday, Day 2

I woke early and quietly left the tent to sing at the shore of the river. The mist rose off the surface of the river and the dew gently rested on a spider web transforming it into glistening lace. I lingered on the shore of the effortlessly moving river allowing the quiet and peace to penetrate my skin with the cool mist. I felt in perfect harmony with life as I headed back to camp to assist in preparing for the day.

As the sun rose the day grew clear and the wind remained calm. It was an easy day of paddling. Easy paddling was good. I was still feverish and Heather had begun to feel ill as well. The rapids were few. Each we considered a delightful challenge.

When we reached the first of the floating bogs we would encounter, we floated while we debated which way to go. Our debate was interrupted by three otters that playfully popped out of the tall grass at shore. Upon seeing us they dove into the water, trailing bubbles. We decided they were

Women's Wisdom

I have one thing that I think of as one major mistake I made with my children. I tried to give them too much. Even during those tough times when I was just divorced and we didn't have any money, I would find a way to get things done. It is still difficult today. I want to treat the grandchildren all the time. It just it takes such a major effort to say, *"Hey, the simpler the life the better it will be in the end for sure."* There is so little any of us need. Kids will often pick up an empty box and play with that versus an expensive toy. I really think my kids are blessed right now. They don't have much money. They can't get into that situation. It is going to be better for their children for sure. Something else too. I know it is tough to parent. I know. I see a lot of parents today who, for some reason, think they need to be friends with their kids. It just kills me. I still believe in values. I don't believe in accepting what the world says is okay—like people coming to my house and sleeping together if they are not married. It is my house. I hear everybody does it. I say, "I don't care." Quit being so accepting. —Bonnie

I would do things for people and then expect something back. I had expectations of everybody. But I let go of that because it doesn't work. Now I get up every day and say "FUN!" Whatever I have to do today is great, because I like everything I do. I have made my life like that; everything I do I like to do. If today it's to stay home and clean and iron, I turn on my favorite music and I love the day.

Sometimes I have felt guilty if I am busy for days because I have been having fun doing all the things that I like. I have not talked to all my friends to see if they are fine or if there is a need. Then suddenly it just hits me like brick. Oh my gosh, I haven't called Heather, or Arlene. I hope they are okay. Then I spend a half a day or a day writing cards or making phone calls because that is a need I have. I come off this high of doing everything for Sandra that makes me feel good and my world hits me in the forehead. I think, "There are other people in the world besides you that need you." Well, they don't need me; I need them worse than they need me. I need to touch these people and to hear them and to know that they are happy and well and content. —Sandra

Marriage puts you into a situation to get to know yourself better.
—Nancy R.

our messengers and paddled in their direction. We were rewarded by easy passage downstream.

Because of the heat of the day and the fatigue from yesterday, we searched for a spot to take a break. The river meandered through a marsh. Off in the distance we could see the shore, or what we believed was shore. Just as we would get close, anticipating a much needed a break, the river turned towards the middle of the marsh. Frustrated we surrendered our hope of taking a break out of the sun. Then we came upon a dry, shady bank and were grateful to be able to use our legs again. We stretched out in the grass with logs for pillows and napped. When we woke, we leisurely enjoyed cheese and crackers, dried fruit and warm water. We were not eager to get back out in the sun but we made our way to the canoes. Back on the river, we had an eagle for a guide. It flew ahead of us most of the rest of the day. Ducks noisily quacked around us.

The river widened to about 40 feet where we passed under County Road 5. Under the bridge lived a colony of swallows; their mud nests lined the trusses and beams of the bridge. We disturbed them and they flew out in swarms encompassing the sky and darting in every direction. Their aerial dance mesmerized me. We moved from forest to marsh and back again. The air was filled with the sound of birds. The red-winged black bird call became a familiar and comforting sound.

Nodding Trillium

Doug greeted us in his solo canoe about a quarter mile from the Bear Den campsite where he had already set up camp. We pulled into shore at 3 pm. It was an 8.5-hour paddle, and we'd made 16.5 miles. Doug cooked for us. As the wind came up, we spent a lazy late afternoon exploring the area. Bear Den is on a peninsula that is predominantly a mound of sand. Our tents were nestled in a grove of old pines. As we contemplated turning in for the night a pair of trumpeter swans graced the evening sky. Heather said, "If there is a right place for me to be, I am here now."

June 7, Monday, Day 3

On Day Three the wind spirits were at our back. When they paused, we paddled harder to make good time. My muscles ached. The training I did before the trip had focused on getting ready for kayaking which uses different muscles than canoe padding. We navigated switchbacks

Women's Wisdom

Being the oldest (at the gathering) is such a responsibility because I feel like I should say something really wise and I don't think I will. One thing I have developed over the years is a great respect for women's ability to share things with each other. I think that is tremendously important because I grew up in a time when women didn't share. We hid behind our high heels and our pompadour. It wasn't a sharing thing between women. —Vi

One of the nice things about being married for over 50 years is that we totally accept each other for who we are. We don't need to ask permission from each other. When I decided to come on this trip I arranged it and told him I was going to go. He can go anywhere he wants to go with my blessing. Many times we have real separate lives, but we have a very close relationship. We have let each other go. Like Kahil Gibran says, *"You let it go and it comes back to you."* That is what has happened to our relationship. It wasn't always that way. The interesting thing to me is where we started out when we were first married. The things we thought marriage was and where we are now, well it is not the same cat. There is a lot of growth that has taken place and a lot of big rocks in this river we traveled together. I am glad I stayed with him. —Alice

I know it is tough to parent. If I have done what I feel is the best for my children, even if it wasn't so popular, it will come around to be a blessing when they do grow up. That is what I have seen. It is hard to be a tough parent. Tough love and saying no is hard. Fighting the norm of today's world is really hard, but it is still the best way. It will still bring the biggest rewards and blessings in life later on for everyone. —Bonnie

My son's girlfriend was sad the other day because he is not reliable. She was crying in her youthfulness. *"Do you think he will ever change?"* I said, "Oh yes I can guarantee he will change. It might not be for the good but he will change. We all change. You need to love him first for who he is and not for who you want him to be." —Jan and floating bogs. We often determined which way to go by reading the direction of the reeds and plant life growing from the bottom of the river. We could not trust our eyes. Often what appeared to be an opening in the tall marsh grass was a dead end. The analogy that kept running through my mind as we passed through the bog was how this was so much like life. What we see on the outside is often so deceptive. But if we trust what comes from within, we most often make the best decisions. We did an excellent job of navigating except for once.

It was difficult to read the direction of the reeds on the bottom. We guessed on the best direction and met a dead end and stopped surrounded by lofty marsh grass.

Next to us scattered in the tall grass and reeds were the nests of several yellow-headed blackbirds. Soon we were surrounded by the males who screamed at us from the reed tops while the females called to us from inside their enclosed nests. The males sounded their alarm and flashed their colors with as much bravado as they could muster. I studied the oblong shaped nest with the small hole at the top, attempting to catch a glimpse of the females, but could only hear them. Beautiful flashes of bright yellow engulfed us.

Not wanting to disturb them anymore than we already had we backed out of the dead end and found the right channel. As we moved through the marsh we occasionally lost sight of each other as we took slightly different routes through the grass, but we were always able to find one another around the next bend.

A thunderstorm threatened. On the afternoon horizon lightning blasted down into the trees. We counted the seconds between lightning and thunder, and guessed the storm was about five miles away. With the storm too close for comfort, we got as close to shore as the channel of water would allow and waited it out. Like yesterday we could not get near solid ground. Jo wasted no time in relaxing and taking advantage of a chance to rest. She found a way to adjust the gear in the canoe so she could lie back. Jo and Heather were jovial and began to joke around. Traveling with them was a deep joy. They have light hearts, see Spirit everywhere, and create raucous laughter whenever possible. What treasures! Just as quickly as the storm moved in it moved out. We marveled at the billowing clouds as we paddled on.

Grandmother Stories

Mary G.'s Story

I got married young and in those days marriage was forever. I lived 25 years, for better or worse, with a very intimidating and bully of a man. I raised three wonderful children, but lost self-confidence. I was not happy. The flow of life changed June of '95 when he had a massive stroke and could not care for himself or live at home. He had severe brain damage and was completely disabled.

After I came home from spending several days at the hospital with my husband, I sat my kids down. My youngest being 14 at the time. I said, "Look, we are all going to go through different things. Go through what ever you have to go through in what ever way you need to do it, if you want to go see him or if you don't. There will be no guilt. All I require now is that you are all working and when you are a little bit older we need to get together and talk once a week and discuss how we are feeling." My son, bless his heart, looked at me and said, *"Do you suppose God made Dad so ornery so we wouldn't miss him quite so much when he is gone?"* I said yes maybe that is it. I always say the same thing about teenagers. That God makes them kind of ornery so you don't miss them when they move out.

That was the first indication that my kids had been intimidated by their father as well. It was sad. He tried but I think it was some type of a personality disorder or something. We never did figure it out. He could turn on a dime. I loved this man dearly, but I didn't feel I could do anything good enough for him because he would shoot me down all the time. My kids had never indicated their opinions so I thought that was an interesting way for my son to put it.

It seems like that was God's way of helping me out without damaging our children through a divorce at their young ages. However, divorce isn't always damaging. It was like a big weight had lifted.

I had two girlfriends whose husbands died. One jumped right into dating and went to singles clubs and was dating several men. The other one moved in with her mother, which she should have never done. She ended up not able to tolerate living there so she moved in with the first guy that came around. I took five years. I didn't think I had the right to look at a man. My husband was never coming back, but he was still there. So I just started doing things for me and found out that I am a pretty nice person and I had a lot of fun.

For the next five years I spent time learning to like myself again and accepting all my imperfections. I don't mind that I am overweight, too

We took a break at Pine Point Landing. It had a log shelter where we could get out of the sun and enjoy the luxury of a picnic table. We snacked on dried fruit. We talked about how much fun it would be to name a Lesson or Motto-of-the-Day. Two were rather profound: First—Short cuts may be faster, but they sometimes are more difficult in the long run. Second—Trust the simple things that offer you direction, like the reeds in the river.

It was not long before we arrived at the boat landing where we were to say goodbye to Barb. Doug met us at the landing and helped Barb load her canoe and gear. As she said goodbye she made a point of reminding us that she was headed for a hot shower, food, and a bed for the night. We countered her kidding with our own by reminding her she would soon be home at her job in Minnetonka. Though she was exhausted from the trip, Barb wrote in our journal.

Paddling team: Jo, Nancy, Barb, and Healther

Grandmother Stories

short and all those things, or talk too much and this and that. I have learned to really like myself, to make myself happy again. This made me who I am today, a strong, capable, loving, self-assured woman who is totally happy with who I am. I continued caring for my husband to make sure his needs were met. But I went on with my life and made a very good life. I am still in my home. I have a successful job and I make good money. I have wonderful children and I have met the love of my life. When I eventually met Ted, I knew what I wanted out of life, and no one was going to intimidate me again.

My husband has since died and I have learned if you don't bring happiness to yourself through who you are, others can't make you happy. I think too many people do that. I think in my own way I did that at times too.

For so many years you are somebody's mom or somebody's wife. For years I was just known as Kevin's mom. I don't think half the people at school knew my name. I was just Kevin's mom. I thought how sad that was. I was really proud to be his mom and I still am. But it was kind of nice to get back to who I am. I am kind of nice to hang around with, so if you ever want a good time give me a call.

Sandra's Story

I think I have had a good life. I have gone through many stages of my life. I think growing up in northern Idaho with nature and green and water made me appreciate the outdoors and that the world that has been created for us to enjoy. Then I married somebody who took me traveling all over the world because that was his job. I was exposed to different cultures, different religious practices, and all these varieties of ethnicity. That broadened me so much. I was born in a very small town in Idaho, so to travel to Puerto Rico and all over Europe and to live there was an eye-opening experience for me.

I was so busy then raising four children and being a wife that I didn't take the time for me. I thought that my biggest role and concern all those years was to take care of those four children and my husband. I did what I had to do that involved them, Scouts and being the social wife, and entertaining. I never never in my wildest dreams thought about myself or what really makes me happy. I felt fulfilled. I felt happy doing this. I felt like I did a good job and I think I did.

But sometimes your world comes crashing down on you and you

Though I am leaving, the experience of wilderness has been expansive, inspiring and filled with adventure, fun, exhaustion and laughter. I wish for you wind at your backs, soft rain, and the guidance of Spirits.

After the usual long Minnesota goodbye Barb drove off and Doug helped us with our gear. With Barb gone and because we were past the worst of bogs, switchbacks and downed trees, I switched from the canoe to a kayak because it would be easier to paddle. Jo and Heather continued to share their canoe. I had been anticipating getting into the kayak since we started this adventure and excited to get it into the water. In the process of moving the gear we all learned a hard lesson. Doug hurt his back moving my kayak from the vehicle into the water. Next time we will wait until the kayak is floating in the river before packing it.

Saying good night to Doug, who was staying in a motel, we made our way a half-mile back up river to Iron Bridge campsite. Sitting at the picnic table I looked over the day's totals: 14.5 miles in five hours. I looked out at the water and realized the river was now about 40 feet across. It had widened rather quickly in three days; it no longer resembled that creek spilling out of Lake Itasca.

We enjoyed each other's company, savoring the river view on a perfect evening. The sun set and filled the western sky with many shades of orange and yellow. Across the water, a huge flock of American white pelicans landed and bedded down for the night in the tall grass. Frogs were singing a chorus that echoed across the water creating a stereo effect. The only thing that disturbed our serenity was a miscommunication. Neen and her daughter Linda from Bemidji were schedule to paddle with us the next day, but they had arrived a day early. Luckily they happened to meet Doug and Barb when they were shuffling cars and realized their problem. Neen and Linda decided to paddle on without us. I felt disappointed. I hoped we would see them at the gathering on Thursday. As we said good night a bat swooped just above our heads snatching bugs from the night air.

June 8, Tuesday, Day 4

The morning blew in cloudy and windy. The pelicans seemed to glow in the early light. They were majestic, soaring in the sky with their nine-foot wingspans. My cold was better, but Jo and Heather were sick. The motto for the day was, *Nyquil and paddle like hell.* For the second day in a row, a great blue heron led us as we navigated easily through marshland and past farms and woods. At one point we took a shortcut and ended up in a lake

Grandmother Stories

have to find out what makes you happy. Things happen to us in life that change the way we live and the choices we have to make. That happened to me. Suddenly I was alone. I thought I was always going to be married all my life and just be an extension of this other person. Or, we were going to be a whole together. Well that didn't' happen. I had to figure out: "Okay Sandra what makes you happy? How can you live a fulfilled life now without those children and that husband?" I read. I went to counseling. I went to church. I joined discussion groups and all of a sudden it dawned on me that I was responsible. I was the only one responsible for my happiness. I had to find it. I had to look for it. I had been exposed to lots of other women in my life, friends in the Air Force. But now I was in a smaller town in a small church. I became friends with lots of women. I reached out to these women and I started figuring out what made me happy. I started doing all the things that made me happy.

One of the things that made me happy was doing things for other people—being a helpmate, a friend and a confidant. Helping people move. Doing whatever. But I also found time to do the things that had always been important to me, like reading, crafts and hand work. I became very involved in the church, which opened up a whole new world for me. I got in touch with my inner heart, my inner soul and I became so peaceful that I was able to sleep at night. I was able to start a day even if I was tired. I did what I had to do and was thankful for that day and the people in it. If eight years ago you would have asked me what makes me fulfilled I could not have answered that question. Now I know the answer. I am 70 years old and I finally figured out what life is all about. I have friends who say to me *"You do too much for other people. You are never home; you can never go to lunch with me, never, never."* Well I am busy making Sandra happy. I am busy doing the things that I want to do for other people, and for other organizations, and it is wonderful!

Terry O.'s Story

For years and years I worried about myself. I wasn't comfortable with myself. I am a loner who will gladly dance all night in a party of people if given the chance. But I am a loner. It wasn't until I turned 50 that I made any peace with being a loner, or understood what it meant to be that kind of person.

we hadn't planned to visit. We had not checked the reeds at the bottom of the river and relied instead on what we could see.

We grew cold, and soon stopped for lunch. With sickness and exhaustion overcoming us, we napped at a rest area. That afternoon we paddled into a beautiful patch of river where the trees leaned in over the water creating a luscious canopy of green. Some trees had fallen in and across the water. I fine-tuned my ruddering skills among the downed trees. Up to this point I had not practiced enough, so using the rudder at the rear of the kayak was not automatic. To move the rudder and turn I used my feet on pedals in the kayak. It was a challenge for me because after years of canoeing it seemed counter intuitive. I instinctively wanted to push the opposite pedal and had to concentrate. Unlike a car, the steering is slightly delayed. I had to pay attention to what was ahead of me to have time to adjust my course.

Before long I found myself pinned in the branches of a tree that traversed the entire river. I nearly went over in the kayak. I struggled to say upright and get under and through the maze of branches. Compared to a canoe paddle, the kayak paddle is much longer. This extra length of paddle was a deterrent. Each time I thought I was going to glide forward and be free of the tree, one end of the paddle would catch on the tree and

Nancy victorious

Grandmother Stories

Sally's Story

I experienced my first "speed bump" was when I lost my husband. At the ripe old age of 50 I was a widow. At that point I didn't really know quite what to do but I had to do something. There is this force within us and you just do and you don't even realize that you do. The realization came to me that nobody is going to do it for me. People give me support and caring and concern, but the actual doing was up to me. This was the lesson I used, pulled myself forward, made some life changes, and reinvented myself. So at 50 I had an opportunity to reinvent myself. I read this book that said *When I am old I will wear purple* and spit. It showed that you give yourself permission to be who you are. That was a good discovery to make. I had the feeling of being an independent unit. I think it helped me to make better choices as I went along in relationships. I got married 8 years later to a very wonderful man.

Vi's Story

I have been on lots of creeks that flow into the river. I was married when I was 18 and I did everything after that. Fortunately, and probably through nothing of my own except good luck, I did marry a man who was able to help me make my own path. I must have been a real pain for him at times. But when he died (after we had been married for 27 years), I realized the things he had done for me. He made no objection when I wanted to go to college. And when I finished college he said, *"Gee maybe you should get your Masters."* It was almost as if he knew I was going to be going on by myself for awhile. So at least I had some economic security when he died. But I also had two children.

Kathryn's Story

Jane's and my mother died of cancer when we were young. Jane was ten and I was fourteen. There were nine children in our family when she died—the youngest was 6 months old. Three years later my dad married a widow who had four children. My dad and stepmother then had a child of their own. So there were fourteen children in this family. I was seventeen when my Dad remarried. Because I was seventeen—

stop me. Repeating *Knox-Menards* to myself, I was determined to be successful. Already having easily navigated around this tree in the canoe, Jo and Heather floated and watched me with anticipation. Jo was ready with her camera hoping to document the moment I went over. I was delighted to disappoint them. Later Jo shared her version of the event with me from her journal.

Mom almost went over several times as we tried to negotiate a downed tree. Both Heather and I almost jumped overboard to rescue her, but she managed to get balanced on a piece of tree and remained upright.

After five hours and 11 miles of paddling, we called it a day and camped in the rain at Silver Maple campsite. We set up camp and took another nap. Then Doug picked us up in the Jeep and took us to his campsite at Royal Oak campground. We showered and pared down our gear. Heidi and Winnie joined us. They would paddle with us the next day. Doug's back was very painful and he was moving pretty gingerly. Each step was taken with care and deliberation. Sitting was a process of carefully lowering himself down and then shifting until he found a position that did not hurt. He had called the doctor back home to get medication to ease the pain. I felt bad that he would not be paddling with us the next two days as planned. At the end of the evening Doug brought us back to Silver Maple campsite.

June 9, Wednesday, Day 5

We left camp at 8 am and dodged downed trees for two plus miles. The river opened into Lake Irving. The lake felt expansive compared to the intimacy of the river with its overhanging trees. The big homes along the shore were a stark contrast to the wilderness we had traveled the past four days. After crossing the open water we took a quick break at a boat launch adjacent to the three bridges over the water leading to Lake Bemidji. *Bemidji* is an Ojibwa word meaning "lake with cross waters" referring to how the Mississippi River crosses Lake Bemidji. Passing under the bridges, we spotted Doug who directed us to Nymore Beach Park on the south shore of the lake. Heidi and Winnie joined us for the stretch across Lake Bemidji. The lake felt boundless to me as I looked across to the trees on the other side, which appeared small and very distant.

On the other side of the lake we once again entered the river where homes lined the shoreline. Then we were back into the woods. Before long we arrived at the Ottertail Power County Dam and Bemidji Fish Hatchery.

Grandmother Stories

and because 17-year-old girls are the way they are, (but also because of the confusion of the *"merged"* family and still stinging from the loss of my mother at a tender age), I was a very difficult young woman. My stepmother and I had a lot of problems for many, many years.

I never would have imagined I would ever feel any differently. I don't believe I ever wanted to feel any other way—that's how bitter I was. Then, over a period of a year or so, something happened for me that I was unaware of. All of those horrible feelings were seemingly flushed from my system. My stepmother hung in there for me and now she has become a very good and important friend of mine. I have learned so much from her in the last few years because I have opened up. I am listening now. This beautiful woman knows so much and she doesn't even know it. If she were sitting here right now she would say, *"I don't know anything."* But she is very wise.

JoAn's Story

I want to share a story about having love in your heart. As a baby I was adopted into a family that was emotionally cold, untouching and uncaring. Dad was a man who had been hurt very badly as a child. He took it out on us kids and the animals. After I had studied Buddhism for a while and he was getting towards the end of his life. How I saw him shifted because one of the Buddhist tenants says there is basic goodness in everyone. A human being is born with basic goodness. So for me my journey was seeing the basic goodness in him in spite of what I saw on the surface and what came out of him.

It was Christmas. Mom had passed away about five years prior. I decided I would buy a turkey and go home to cook him Christmas dinner. People around me said, *"You know how he is and you know what he will say."* I replied, "Yes but I still need to do this and I still want to do this. What I need to do is hold on to my intention of what I want to do no matter what he does or what happens."

I went home and one of the first things that happened to me was a huge appreciation for what my mom had gone through living with this person. I just kept going back to why I was there and what I was doing. He was loosing his sight. At one point he asked me if I would trim his fingernails. The thought that went through my head was, "Yes I can do that, but I draw the line at the toenails." I did his fingernails and when I went to bed that night I thought, "I can do his toenails."

Paddling team: Heather, Nancy, Heidi, Winnie, and Jo

We portaged the hot dry 201 yards around the structures where the power dam drops the level of the river about 30 feet. Below the dam the water was shallow and there were several people fishing. A rusty-headed merganser floated near the opposite shore with her brood of fuzzy little ducklings and didn't seem to mind all the commotion caused by us and those fishing.

Not too far from the dam the water grew shallow. At one point we had to get out of the boats and walk the pebbly bottom. That stretch reminded me of streams I had seen in Colorado.

Along our route we were gifted by visits from a variety of feathered friends. The heron saw us off, and eagles abounded. At one time we saw two eagles in a tree and three flying. We believe we saw an oriole, but it flitted off so quickly we could not be sure. There were a variety of ducks, grackles, and many songbirds which were new to me. The redhorse fish were spawning in this part of the river. Hundreds of incredibly huge fish with bright red fins and tails performed a free-flowing dance around and under our boats. It was difficult to focus on the river and watch for the rocks in the rapids because the fish fascinated us.

We faced some headwind, which inspired Jo's motto for the day: *We are bringing the wind with us because change sometimes requires turmoil.*

Winnie inspired me all day. She could be found

Grandmother Stories

So the next morning he asked me and I thought to myself, "He took a bath last night so they can't be that bad." I went back to my heart and the reason I was there. Then I sat and trimmed his toe nails and for the first time in his life this man said thank you to me.

We had a wonderful Christmas dinner. The next day I realized he was alone because of the way he had lived his life. He had ended up alone. I was aware of the sadness in his heart. But there wasn't anything I could do about that sadness. So the next day I packed up to drive back to the cities. (This is a man who I never saw hug my mom, never saw him hold her hand, and never saw him touch or be close to anybody. There was a couple of times in my life when I was really brave and I was gonna give Dad a hug no matter what. And out came his arm and literally barricaded me so I could not get close to him.) That Sunday as I was leaving the house, I walked through the kitchen into a little walkway attached to the garage where the washer and dryer are. He was standing by the washer. As I reached for the door knob and turned around to look at him, he had his arms outstretched and came over and gave me a hug. This is a man who would never ever have done that. He gave me a hug! I didn't initiate it. He did it all on his own. That was the only hug I ever got from him. For me what it meant was that I hold in my heart the vibration of loving this man and it physically, (via quantum physics,) changed the vibration in his heart. For him it was something he had never done in his life and probably never had intention of ever doing. So the power of love is amazing. The power of love. I was in shock all the way back to the cities. He never did it again. Even when I tried to initiate it, there was no response. It didn't matter. What mattered was how I felt towards him. It was a very amazing moment. That is my story and witness to the power of love.

Ronnie's Story

An experience which directed the flow of my life was at the age of 31, I found myself pregnant and engaged to a man I was planning to marry. Not necessarily in that order. I was mortified that as a nurse I hadn't managed to keep myself out of a predicament I expected youth to be able to handle. His response to the whole situation was to have an abortion. I said, "This is not the way it is going to be, even if it is at the expense of losing the relationship." For a while it looked like that might be the case. There is a long history there in terms of his health and so forth.

smiling no matter what was happening and seemed to find good in everything. Even though she walked with two canes, she was incredibly resil-
ient and challenged people's ideas that her handicap should limit her. It
may have taken her a little longer to climb up the bank from the canoe at
lunch, but next thing I knew, she was sitting next to us laughing. I found
her very matter of fact; a very genuine and very gentle spirit.

We talked about a wider variety of things with Winnie and Heidi than
we had while Barb was along. While Barb was with us, our conversation
focused on the river, and what was coming next. Our view of the world had
narrowed to what was before us; the weather, our paddling, the beauty of
the wilderness and how to maintain our bodies. With Winnie and Heidi we
talked about nature and what is being done to protect it. We took time to
really appreciate what was around us.

After a paddle of 14.5 miles in 8.5 hours we were ready for rest and
glad to arrive at the Beltrami County Road 25 boat access. Doug, who
was feeling much better, met us there with fish he had caught for dinner.
Although we enjoyed the clear, cool evening air, the boat access left a lot
to be desired as a campsite. There was no level ground, lots of poison ivy,
no outhouse, no drinking water and relatively no shade.

Sitting in the grass enjoying Doug's cooking Winnie told us how she
paid for half of her three years of nurses training with an unusual form
of tender.

*I had a little cocker spaniel or part cocker spaniel anyway. I had made
a little two-wheel cart out of a wooden cranberry box. I carried all my*

Grandmother Stories

He became more ill over a period of time. I made a decision to join the military. It was a conscious decision on my part to toughen me up for what I knew was sure to come: he was going to die and I was going to end up raising this child by myself and provide for her. I thought the military would do a good job of making me responsible. It has actually been kind of an irony in that I have met wonderful people in the military who are not all that rough and tough.

Making that choice was something I had contemplated when I was twenty during the Viet Nam era. I thought I was in love. So I decided to go with love, (which of course it wasn't). We learn these things in hindsight. Having made the decision to keep my child, I now have a wonderful twenty year old that drives me crazy. I thank God every day that I am alive for her. I think my life would have been so much different had I made a different decision. The decision to join the military has evolved along with other facets of my life to bring me to where I am now. I am very happy with where I have been and what I have done.

Bonnie's Story

I have always been a strong personality, but after the divorce my children looked at me as a workaholic. I had always felt I had been the provider, but I really took that role on. I have some regrets that I wasn't a more fun mother and that I didn't play with my children more. I worked very hard to raise three children after the divorce and I was alone for ten years.

Then I met someone and I remarried. I married a second alcoholic and there was no where to go but forward with it. I had many regrets about it, but I had already made the decision.

Then I discovered when my children walked out of my life that I too was an alcoholic. It took only a week for me to die inside knowing my kids had said, *"We trusted you and now we are walking away."* So I put myself into treatment. That is when my life really started turning around and I started gaining wisdom.

Today I am very proud to I wear four children on my necklace because I almost gave that all away. These are my grandchildren. I am slowly learning that I just have to stay out of the way.

I believe there is a real purpose for my life. I always wanted to be a counselor. It didn't happen. But God is helping me to do that in his own way. Today, I believe it is every trial, every crisis I have gone

Winnie

traps in it and the dog would pull the cart with the traps. I caught gophers in my traps and then I hit them on the head with a ball-peen hammer. I got a dollar a gopher. Later I made a box on a sled so my dog could be pulled in the wintertime. She had asthma and she'd start to wheeze real bad if she ran too much so she got to ride. She thought she was the queen.

Jo scrunched up her face when Winnie mentioned the ball-peen hammer, but we were all fascinated by her stories.

Tomorrow would be our first gathering on the river, and I was a nervous. We changed our plans so it would be a shorter paddling day. I didn't want to be tired at the gathering. Shortening the route also meant we could better enjoy our remaining paddling time with Heidi and Winnie.

June 10. Thursday, Day 6

With three of us not feeling well, we slept later in the morning than we usually do. Jo was feeling pretty bad so she decided not to paddle, and went with Doug for coffee. Heather, Heidi, Winnie and I headed into a strong wind that increased as we crossed the north end of Wolf Lake and even more so as we crossed the south end of Lake Andrusia. We paddled into big waves on the last stretch. Reaching our destination for the day, we landed. Envy rose in the group as we found Doug and Jo napping in the shade. We rested, and enjoyed lunch.

Doug drove us to the Knutson Dam Recreation Area. The campground is well maintained with ash, oak and pine. The camp host, a humorous Native American man greeted us. When camp was set up, I began to get ready for the gathering. My daughter, Naomi, joined us. She would be taking over car support when Doug headed home and back to work.

I felt particularly nervous and less than confident preparing for the gathering. I walked to the river, made an offering of Kinnickinnick, and said a prayer. Then I walked a circle around our site dropping tobacco and continuing my prayer. I prayed for words and guidance to make this gathering a positive experience for all participants and for those who would be touched by the women's sharing. As I prayed I felt at peace. I would create this same circle with tobacco and prayer before each gathering.

I started a sacred peace fire in the traditional manner, using flint and steel and placed the ashes from the Ely gathering in the fire. In the fire at the Ely gathering I had placed a Peace Fire Coal Bundle. Dan had

Grandmother Stories

through that has given me the knowledge I need. The divorce, now I can relate to those who get divorced. The alcoholic, I can relate to other alcoholics and recovering people. Now in my own way I can reach out and be that counselor because of my own experiences.

Terry B.'s Story

I have always had someone behind me. I am surrounded by men that are wonderful: men who support me and argue with me, of course. I am able to argue. I am able to do what I want and they respect that. I wanted a daughter very badly. I had two sons and I love them to pieces. We decided to adopt. We asked for a girl and got a boy. Go figure.

When we finally got our daughter she was nine years old and had been through some really troubling things in life. She is now 39. I think the things that I have learned being with her have been incredibly painful, but have been the things I can use in my whole life. The wisdom I gained watching her struggle to find herself, and my trying to help her and support her have helped me in my work. It helped me with my outlook towards life and other women. It has just been so incredible for me.

Sharon F.'s Story

I grew up on the Red Lake Reservation the first 5 or 6 years of my life. I remember a different kind of life. It was easy going. There wasn't any rush. When I started school in first grade all of us children spoke Ojibwa. They taught us how to speak English. Then my father decided to move up to the Iron Range with nothing but white society around us. At the time we moved I hadn't quite mastered the English language. I spoke broken English when I started second grade there. I remember the teacher always calling on me. I didn't like to answer. I tried to shrink down in my seat, because kids would laugh at me because I spoke broken English. For a long time I was really shy. I did not like to answer.

Another thing that really would get me upset is when the teacher would call on me. When she made me stand up. It was always in history class when we were talking about Native Americans. She would say *"Well we have one of the first Americans here in our class, Sharon* introduced me to the Peace Fire Coal Bundle which would be a part of each gathering. Students at Northeastern Illinois University tie 2,000 bundles a year and send them all over the world. They explain:

Each bundle contains a piece of white cedar, a piece of birch bark, a seed from a paper birch tree, bark from a tree struck by the Thunders, and a coal from The Fire.

The coal came from The Peace Fire started in 1995 by Bruce Hardwick, a fire keeper in his home area of Rapid River, Michigan. Bruce started the fire at an international conference at Lake Geneva, Wisconsin. The bundles represent a physical and spiritual connection to the fires that have burned for thousands of years and to those who have gathered around those fires. The purpose of the fire is to awaken our consciousness about peace, love, sisterhood and brotherhood. Coals from the original fire have been distributed around the world, where people are gathered with peace in their hearts. The stories of Peace Fire Coal Bundles used in rituals for peace and healing are rich with contributors, including Jane Goodall and the Dalai Lama. They are linked to places in China, Australia, Ireland and around the United States.

At the end of each gathering women were given coals from the fire to take with them, and I carefully collected ashes to carry to the next gathering. Participants heard the following message from those who care for the bundles:

It is our hope that you will carry this coal bundle with a sense of purpose and an understanding that our thoughts, intentions, and actions, at this moment, do influence the next seven generations.

As I finished with the fire, the women began to arrive. Six women including five Native American women made up the circle, plus Heidi, Winnie, Jo, Heather, Naomi and me. Doug again made himself scarce. These beautiful women brought food with them to share with us, as is their way. The girls were particularly excited about the fresh fruit and the wild rice salad. The Native American women seemed a bit cautious, and watched us closely.

I did not blame them. Recently the *Minneapolis Star and Tribune* had spotlighted the Leech Lake Reservation in a number of articles, which highlighted issues that held them in a bad light. The articles focused on problems with drugs and other common social issues not limited to any reservation or town in our country. Their side of the story had not been heard.

Barbara began,

Grandmother Stories

would you stand up?" I would stand up and she would have everybody look at me. The kids had this concept I lived in a teepee.

It seems like I was in the Native American world and still in the white society. My mother was full-blooded Leech Lake Indian. She was third degree Mide [Short for Midewewin, meaning the person belongs to the Midewewin sacred medicine society, a healing society] in the Indian religion. She really believed in the Indian religion. However, my father was a half-breed. Mide women would call him, sak a da winini (half-breed). He went to boarding schools and was raised as a practicing Catholic. When we were on the reservations I remember a lot of ceremonies there. Then when we moved to the Iron Range, there was my father sending us to church school where we had to study catechism. It was okay. Whatever. To this day I guess when you talk spirituality I can accept anybody's concept of what spirituality is. I believe a lot. I have learned a lot from both. In my life it has helped. My mother is buried in the Mide section of the Native American cemetery and my father is buried in the Catholic section of the town cemetery. So even in death there is that separation.

There are certain things that identify me as being a Native American. Then you have to *"cross over"* sometimes because of your professional dealings. I have to put that behind me and now act like I am white. I guess it serves its purpose.

I have had a lot of professions in my life. I have been a seamstress, and worked in a factory with Mexicans in Los Angeles. We first moved out there when we were newly married. I worked as a government clerical worker for social security in Los Angeles. I came back here and worked as a file clerk, stumbled into a planning division as an assistant planner, helped with surveys, and did research for grant writers. Then I became the housing authority director for the reservation for 14 years and got fired there. I don't know what I did. What ever it was, I managed to get away with it for 14 years before they figured it out. I was unemployed for about a year. Then I was hired by Beltrami County as a financial worker for the welfare program. I was assigned to the Red Lake Reservation, back to where I grew up. Then back to the Leech Lake Reservation as a planner/grant writer and on to my current job, which is a domestic abuse program coordinator. I think I have enjoyed all of it. I like working with people. I have good people skills.

A lot of us as native women have experienced violence in our lives. Intimate partner violence. We have seen our mothers abused, but it

I told Nancy I was very uncomfortable and I had to be very cautious. People on Leech Lake have gone through a lot of media and a lot of negativity towards our people. I told Nancy that I didn't want our people exploited. But I talked with her. I had to trust my instincts and go with that because, (as I talked with Elaine) we have to think globally—we have to connect with people from the outside. Because of things that have happened we have to start reaching out and connecting with other people. It's the spider web making the connections. This is just one of those pieces. This is doing the work, fastening those boundaries and connecting.

Nancy and I talked about the ceremonies and the medicines from a gentleman that had influenced her life. The peace fire going on internationally. Spreading peace and love. I really believe that things like this have to happen. You talk about the water and traveling on the water. The women are the caretakers of that water. That is what Mother Earth really needs for survival. That's why I am here.

I would have been surprised if they had not been cautious in deciding to trust a non-native, non-reservation member who was asking for their personal stories (knowing I was planning to print them).

As I began, I gave them each tobacco I had carefully wrapped in red cloth and tied with white yarn. I told them my intentions and goals for this trip. I told them I wanted to hold women's wisdom sacred and bring it out into the light. I felt their wisdom was an important piece of the information to be shared. They seemed to relax. I could see they were eager to be part of the evening.

As I turned the speaking over to them they followed native tradition and deferred to their elder, Josie (age 72), to set the tone for the evening. Josie had come to the gathering even though she was not well. She shared with me later she had questioned whether she should come, but decided to because it felt important. As the evening progressed Josie became wrapped in blankets and sleeping bags to help her stay warm in the cool evening air. Soon all we could see was her sweet face attentively peering out of the fabric. She listened to everything that was shared. After Josie openly shared her story, each of the other women told their stories. It was personal information. Heartbreaking. I was impressed by their ability to laugh at themselves. I felt honored to be part of this circle and was moved by the depth of the role of spirituality in their daily lives.

Native American people come from an oral background which share information through stories. Native people speak in complete stories because for them everything is connected. No event stands alone. Some of

Grandmother Stories

was not an everyday thing. More than likely alcohol was involved. As a coordinator for a battered women's program we held a focus group about it two weeks ago and we had women of all ages. Two elder women were at the focus group. These women recalled their great grandmothers said that there was no violence like that when they were growing up. It was when Native Americans were allowed to go into bars. The men would go and they couldn't handle alcohol. It was something they could now get legally after years of having to sneak to drink.

I remember my father being half-breed and being quite light (skinned). He would go off the reservation and purchase bottles and bring it home because it wasn't allowed on the reservation. On Red Lake it was outlawed, but he got it anyway. That is one thing about the Native American culture, it didn't turn to violence until alcohol was introduced. Now alcohol has affected all of us. All of our lives, our selves personally, and now our children. Our children have more than alcohol to deal with. Our children have cocaine and marijuana and everything else, as well as the gang culture to deal with.

We are starting to see a lot of violence. Before, I think it was maybe 20 years ago, you didn't have to lock your doors. Now a days, even if you do lock up you are still not safe. The bullets come right through your walls. We try to get our youth back to their spirituality, their Native American spirituality because a lot of them have been raised in the Christian religion. Christianity just doesn't work. I had the benefit of both. I feel I was doubly blessed so I could believe whatever I wanted.

I came from a family of 12 children. My mother and father both had to work. We had a dilapidated shelter over our heads. They both worked at low paying jobs. My father was a proud man. He would not go and get welfare. I remember him getting up at 5 o'clock in the morning and walking to work when his car wouldn't start. He was a lumberjack and worked outside. The older children had to look after the younger ones. It was all family; each one had a job to do to keep the family going. I think that is gone today. In today's society both parents have to work to keep the house going. Now days cable TV and cell phones are considered basic.

the non-native women on this trip spoke of events in their lives as if they were disconnected. However, it seems with time and retrospection they too saw the connection of everything. Therein lies the access to wisdom.

Josie

Josie told us about her life as a young woman.

I started out in life being the only Indian in town. I went to an all white school. I had to fight most of the way. I realized even then how important education is. In the eighth grade I dropped out, got married and had a baby. We went to Minneapolis. I told my mother I was still going to become a nurse and get my education. She said, "How are you going to do that now?" and I said, 'I will find a way.' So when my husband and I got to Minneapolis, we were lucky enough to get jobs. I was saving up money because it cost $700 to go to West High to get your high school diploma. As we went along with life in a new community, he got in trouble and was sent away. I got help and found these places that help you with the program you want. Mine was the WIN program. That is how I got my GED. I also got scores high enough to go to college at St. Mary's Jr. College. I graduated as an RN. That is what I try to explain to all the younger people, the younger ladies. All that is important is getting an education because you can never go anyplace without it.

Gloria spoke about her background.

My parents came from boarding school. They really lived under a fear all the time, since they were taken away, afraid they were gonna' loose something more. So I grew up with developmental chaos. I was aware of a lot of chaos, a lot of fear, fear of white people, and misconceptions that white people had no pain. Nervousness came over me. I thought they were one up. I thought they were all perfect. They all had money. They had what we didn't have—basic things like food and shelter. And you know, it didn't matter we were poor and living in poverty, what mattered was we were together.

Elaine described how she became silent in a white culture.

When I started to go to grade school I started reading their stories and it got where I couldn't tell my stories anymore. It was like those happy endings just went away. The stories I would tell myself, that I would tell nobody else; they were horrible stories. I know what it had to do with; it had to do with going to school and going into where you are not respected and you are looked down on. It is about being called names and having no voice. When we went to school we had no voices. A teacher would ask us a question and we would know the answer, but we wouldn't say anything. We would just sit there and be quiet. A lot of that behavior is generational learning from the boarding schools. My mother went to one and so did my Dad. I think about what happens when you leave an oral background, which our people had. Your history, your teachings, are all passed down by storytellers. When your language is taken from you, touch is taken from you. When you are touched they hurt you. You are introduced to a kind of silence.

Each woman spoke of spirituality as the uppermost aspect in her heal-ing and life. Each had a message for the younger women in their lives. *Be true to your story, to yourself!* All were concerned for the future of all children. This powerful group of women believed the spirit of a feminine community is healing. They said women are the motivating force for change and they need the men to protect them while they do their work. They believe women can and will make a difference. Not only did they believe women will make a positive difference in our world, but now is the time for the grandmothers and women in general to speak the truth they have learned from quiet participation for so many years.

So much was shared with words and deep emotion that after the women left, I was at a loss for words. I busied myself putting things away listening to Winnie and Elaine who talked further. I felt gifted to have the opportunity to be witness to this special moment between them.

Winnie asked Elaine,

You're the mayor of Cass Lake. You were voted in. So, is the influence to break out of the barriers?

Elaine responded,

With me, in this community I am at that age where I realized I had to invest myself in the community because it will come back around to help my family. A lot of men don't believe that. They go to work. They think that work is enough and the off time is their time. But there are more women willing to give of their time to make sacrifices. The men, we keep asking them to walk with us.

Men are the leaders. Women are in the community doing the work. That whole thing about government setting the priorities, well my priorities are different. So much is based on attitude. Attitude about self has to be changed. We are right where we are at. It is beautiful. There is no reason why we can't be successful. We have to start talking a different talk before things will change.

After everyone had gone, and everything was put away, I crawled into the tent and had a meltdown. I cried in Doug's arms, overwhelmed by the project and wondering whether I was up to the challenge I had felt called to do. I didn't want Doug to go home. His presence had been a stabilizer for me. I wondered if he know how deeply I love him. I realized that without him on the trip I would have an opportunity to really get in touch with my personal power and independence. But, the child in me felt frightened of the responsibilities I had assumed. As I went to sleep, I thought about the many ways in which the day had been a blessing.

June 11, Friday, Day 7

Even though Doug, Jo, Heather, Naomi and I got up early, Heidi and Winnie were already packed up and ready to head home. After a quick breakfast they journaled their thoughts about the trip and the gathering before leaving.

Heidi confided,

When I was growing up, I knew the Mississippi as the river under the big bridge we crossed on the way to Great Grandma Elleson's house in Burlington, Iowa. We tried to hold our breath all the way across the bridge. Family legend said if you made a wish and held your breath the whole way, your wish would come true. The only time I said I made it, I had actually cheated and sneaked a breath.

I love the Boundary Waters for the peacefulness and total removal from all the hustle and bustle. But even in all that wilderness, I've never seen so many birds in a single day as we did padding this gorgeous, winding river.

It's hard to believe we could have damaged the Mississippi so much with chemicals and control. Maybe it's like the women at last night's gathering— filled with an amazing strong sprit and life that will overcome whatever gets in their way. Giving thanks, speaking our truth, bonding together, and believing—we can make change.

Winnie found the river thrilling and was delighted by baby ducks, loons, herons, songbirds and eagles.

The gathering last night was a once-in-a-lifetime experience. The honesty and eloquence of the women was really moving and thought provoking... more than my brain can handle. The women had so much courage, and obviously great trust in Nancy as they shared their experiences.

The wind seemed to have abated and the lake appeared to be calm, so Jo, Heather and I decided to take off from the boat landing at Lake Andrusia with one canoe. We chose one canoe for three people because it provided us with more safety and an opportunity to take turns paddling so none of us would get too tired. We paddled a quarter mile of river into the west end of Cass Lake where we discovered the wind kicking up whitecaps and sending waves over the bow. After only a couple of waves crossed the bow we commented that we were grateful we did not take the solo canoe. The wind would have certainly capsized it. Working hard we made it to the first of the two Potato Islands. Then we bounced our way to the second. The waves rolled in higher. We began to joke, with some sincerity, that we should find a fisherman to tow us to the opposite shore.

Between each island we rotated paddlers. Rain poured down. We headed to Star Island. Not even halfway across the lake, we were tired and aware that our situation was very perilous. We kept our spirits up, paddling hard, joking (mostly about our situation), and having fun. At the far end of Star Island it became clear that trying to canoe the rest of the way was too dangerous. We were now wet, cold, and exhausted—a perfect scenario for hypothermia. We had paddled five hours and traveled four of the nine miles we had planned for the day. We were also three miles south of our originally planned route across the lake.

While resting on the southeast point of Star Island we could see two marinas on the southern shore of Cass Lake. Again we pushed east into the big waves leaving the protection of the island. It wasn't long before Heather and I were out of steam, and the wind was getting the best of us. We had to paddle into the waves, past the town of Cass Lake, so that when we turned our backs would be to the wind and waves letting them carry us back to the shelter of the town. If we had tried to go straight across, the waves would have hit us broadside and we could have capsized. We turned the canoe as quickly as possible taking on a some water and headed to a marina. (The girls told me later they were terrified I was going to make them keep going. I am a little stubborn. My desire to paddle the entire river is strong, but I'm not crazy.)

We stumbled into a marina where the man behind the counter hesitantly let us use the phone. He was unwilling to give us any other assistance and seemed irritated that we were dripping puddles on his floor. Unable to reach Naomi, we got back in the canoe and aimed for the highway wayside rest which we had seen when paddling into the marina. Intuitively I sensed we would get help there. I was not sure how getting to the wayside rest for cars was going to help three women in a canoe, but it was clear we were not welcome at the marina.

The wayside rest was further down shore, near Highway 2 and the channel that connects Cass Lake to Pike Bay. Heading back into the waves to get to the rest stop was a defeating proposition. Our muscles argued with pain as we forced ourselves into the oncoming wind. Arriving at the wayside rest, we pulled the canoe up and dragged it across the lawn. We dropped it, dumped our stuff into it and went inside. We took turns ringing out our cloths and attempting to dry them with the hand dryer in the restroom.

Our continued attempts to call Doug and Naomi went unanswered. Ironically they were in town (just a couple of blocks from us) but, without Naomi's cell phone or our two-way radios. We arranged a ride to our camp at Knutson Dam for Heather with the friend of the manager of the wayside rest. These men were very helpful and interested in our trip. They thought we were a bit crazy, especially being out on the lake with the weather the way it was. Jo and I were a bit nervous about letting Heather go with a stranger, but Heather reassured us that her intuition said it would work out fine. Jo joked, *I think I need to move out of the city.*

Heather arrived at camp just as Doug and Naomi returned from town. They came for Jo, me, and the gear. We were relieved to dry off, eat and nap. We sorted our gear, sending extra stuff home. Then we went out to dinner at the Canal House Restaurant at Stony Point Resort to celebrate surviving Cass Lake.

The mottos for the day: *Challenge your limits. Know when you're done and call it quits.* Heather said the water spirits told her we would have a safe crossing, but we would have to earn their respect.

Heather said,

Today I learned that just because the spirits grant you permission to do something doesn't mean they're going to make it easy for you. Also, perhaps as we prove ourselves worthy of the name "people of the water" we've learned not to pit ourselves against the water to conquer it, but rather to accept we are weaker, smaller, and need to be humble.

Jo wrote in her journal,

It comes easy in this life of such beauty and simplicity to be grateful for each day. The world's pace is slowed in the natural world of the river. The mind is cleared of unimportant clutter and we are able to see beauty and growth deeper within if we dare. We find ourselves and reconnect with what is important in this short but powerful physical life.

June 12, Saturday, Day 8

I quickly finished writing an update on our trip. Doug would distribute it via e-mail to our supporters when he got home. It would be the first of periodic updates. Doug had agreed to be our communications person back home.

We would now travel with two kayaks and Doug's solo canoe. To Jo's delight, she was reunited with the canoe she had used the previous summer to explore the Boundary Waters Canoe Area Wilderness. Jo, Heather and I prepared to leave Knutson Dam. Lily pads dotted the river entry point. I found it difficult to say goodbye to Doug that morning. Doug took my written update, the trailer with all the extra gear, and ceremoniously turned the support function for the trip over to Naomi.

Doug's parting words where,

You are all inspirations. I like telling people I'm with a bunch of women paddling down the Mississippi. They give me looks of awe and envy. Keep up the good work and keep heading downstream. I'll miss you.

He told me he was amazed at what I had done. I had trouble hearing that. I still held it in my mind it was one big camping trip. I continued to hold the importance of what we were doing at bay. I paddled away looking back several times to wave but did not see him. I cried quietly and focused on the beauty of the nature around me. Soon it was back to tall reeds on either side of us.

Heather and I were surprised at what different muscles kayaking used. After adjusting to canoeing we now endured new aches and pains as our bodies used different muscles. I had begun this adjustment earlier when I paddled my kayak. But at that point I was so involved with staying upright that I had not noticed my muscles speaking to me.

Early in the day we passed under a bridge and noticed an inner tube floating in the water caught in some trees. It was as if we all had the same idea at the same time. *Let's take it with us.* Jo paddled over and put it in the

back of her canoe. We decided to present it to Naomi as a special treasure to show our appreciation for the work she was doing for us. As the day progressed we got more excited about giving it to her. It was no treasure at all. It was dirty, stinky and had no real use on this trip, but we were adamantly tied to the intention.

Once we entered a wide, grassy channel leading to the lake, the wind started tossing Jo in the solo canoe. She was working much harder than Heather or I and was tiring fast. The inner tube in the back of the canoe did not help the situation. It acted as a sail, catching the wind. We tried towing it behind the canoe and behind one of the kayaks, but that was worse. Dumping it was never considered as a viable option. Letting the air out of it did not occur to us until later when we were trying to put it in the car. Eventually we managed to squish it down into the canoe so it would not catch the wind.

For lunch we stopped on a point that was home to 100-year-old trees. As we landed, I noticed a frog at the water's edge. She sat motionless on the reeds watching me with her big black eyes. She was green with black spots and yellow strips. She appeared to be wet from the way her skin glistened in the sun. We gazed at each other for a while before I moved. She

Leopard Frog

leapt into the water. Whenever I saw a frog on the trip, I thought of how they represent ritual cleansing to some Native American tribes. This trip was itself, a cleansing ceremony for me.

The point felt sacred. None of us could explain the feeling we had as we enjoyed our time on the peninsula. The grand trees provided us with much needed shade from the day's relentless sun. We munched our lunch of peanut butter and jam on crackers, dried fruit, and granola bars. We washed it down with moose juice. Before we left the girls gave the trees a hug.

Jo wrote about how this place in the woods touched her.

I could hear the trees speak to me—almost instantly calling me to paddle in. Upon hugging the trees I felt nourishing, warm energy. As guardians of this forest the great trees welcomed us. The energy of one touch awakened the whole forest family. Every tree chattered with excitement and delight. I felt a welcoming home as if I had been here before. I felt honored that the forest knew me. We could not stay. There were important lessons to learn further

downriver. I left the arms of these trees having hugged two and felt them all. I was inspired and refueled.

In the quiet of paddling, the words I heard at the Leech Lake gathering drifted into my mind. I was struck by how the women strung the events of their lives together, highlighting the meaning of the painful events. Meaning appeared to give them peace. The Great Spirit was woven into the very fabric of their stories. I was deeply touched by their caring for their children. Perhaps the drive to help children is born out of the discrimination and struggle they have experienced and still experience. I was awed by their wisdom and dedication to a vision of a peaceful place for all. Their willingness to reach out beyond their own people and work to help everyone, even those who had at one time persecuted them, was inspiring beyond words. The similarity they shared was finding their voice. So many women have been silenced; some remain unaware of it. These women not only realized it but were doing something about it.

In the afternoon, the wind continued to blow Jo's canoe around. There was nothing we could do to help her. The scenery was stunning, but Jo was working so hard she couldn't enjoy it. We decided the solo canoe would not be used to cross Lake Winnibigoshish; it would be too dangerous.

The channel of the river leading to Lake Winnibigoshish had a sprinkling of houses on the south shore. As we entered the lake and turned north, we were grateful the wind was no longer in our faces. Paddling past minnow seining nets set up just off shore, we spotted Naomi waving at us. She had news and was eager to share. First, that Doug had bought us a new stove. The old one wasn't working consistently. She also informed us that the back door of the Jeep would no longer open. That was going to make packing it more challenging. We decided we would deal with the Jeep door when we reached Grand Rapids.

Naomi was a little puzzled as to how to respond to our inner tube gift. She was afraid to touch it at first because of what might be on it. Then she received it as if she were being given an award of high honor. She said, "Thank you, thank you, thank you. This is really too much." She paused for a moment and then said, "Do I really have to keep it?"

Of course we said *yes* and later when she tried to ditch it we caught her and pretended to be hurt. Finding this inner tube began a pattern that would last to the end of the trip. We found all kinds of things along the shore and brought them to her. For example: a yellow baby air mattress, a happy face balloon (which later escaped from the car and floated away, bringing much sorrow to Naomi. It was the only thing we brought her that

she became attached to),
a screw driver (she said
she needed that one), a
nasty beach ball, and more.
There were many things we
passed up: a lawn chair, a
bar-b-que grill. We made a
point of telling her about
each item so she knew we
were thinking about her
while we were paddling. It

was amusing to spot something and imagine bringing it to her. The fact
that she did not want most of these things made it all the more enjoyable.

Naomi had set up camp at West Winnie Campground on the west end
of Lake Winnibigoshish. Winnibigoshish in Ojibwa means miserable,
wretched, dirty water. It was named that because of the way the high
winds churned mud up from the bottom. Today the winds had not been
high enough to churn up the bottom. The water was clear. Naomi showed
us our site and we unloaded gear. Then we walked to the shore and played,
as best we could in the freezing water. I delighted in how the sand on the
bottom cradled my feet and toes. Between shivers, it felt luxurious to wash
off a layer of sweat and get my scalp to stop itching for a while.

After dinner we walked to the shore to catch the sunset. The water
was as still as a mirror. After being among trees so much of the time, the
sky appeared to be infinite over the lake. The far shore was a thin sliver
of greenish gray dividing the deep blue of the water from the pale blue
sky. As I looked at that thin sliver of greenish gray shore, I pondered the
importance of paddling the entire distance. This lake demands even more
respect than Cass Lake. The weather can change quickly turning calm
water into a churning tossing nightmare for a small boat. I took to heart
what the attendant at the park said, "If you are dumb enough to try it you
won't be the first bodies I helped fish out of the water."

The fact that we did not paddle all of Cass Lake continued to tug at me.
What would this lake hand us in the morning? The colors of the sky began
to change and the surface reflected and magnified them. Wispy clouds
reflected the yellows, pinks and purples while the heavier higher clouds
held their white and silver shades.

Nothing brings a person into the present faster than a wood tick. Up to
this point we'd seen virtually no mosquitoes, which was delightful beyond

my wildest dreams. However the number of wood ticks made up for them. After enjoying our time on shore we got back to camp and found them crawling on us, sometimes as many as 20 at a time among us. At County Road 25 boat launch, Doug won the prize for the Oddest Wood Tick Bedding Location when he discovered one snuggled comfortably in his belly button. Naomi was particularly disturbed by them crawling on her. She has hated them since she was a small child.

Wood ticks removed, we settled in for the night. I realized a week had gone by more quickly than I had expected. I'd not taken time for reflection. Every day had been occupied with details, maintaining our bodies, and just plain endurance.

Thinking back over the days of paddling and the gathering, I noticed I couldn't seem to help taking care of people. I'm always making sure others are welcomed, warm, fed and feel good. Sometimes I tend to go to an extreme and forget to take care of myself. I could see how that role gets in the way of being present and fully enjoying my life. Traveling with my two twenty-something daughters and paddling partner naturally increased my mothering instincts. I noticed that sometimes my role seemed to separate me from them when I really wanted to feel an equal member of the group. I decided to pay attention and see how that might change as the trip unfolded.

June 13, Sunday, Day 9

It rained during the night, but we woke to a calm, cloudless morning. I walked to the shore, gave thanks, made my offering of Kinnickinnick, and asked the Spirits for permission to cross. I sang the Anishnaabeg song, and watched a pelican land a few yards away on the water. I watched her for a time as she moved closer. Her calm presence seemed to tell me it would be a good day to be on the lake.

I looked out over the water and soaked in the sense of serenity I always get when near big water. I took the long way back to camp so I could explore this "out of the way" park. Everything was still wet from the evening's rain. A mist rose out of nowhere and hung in the air giving it a mystical feeling. I expected to see a fairy come from behind these old red pines. The pines comforted me, standing tall enough to kiss the clouds and protecting all who passed under them.

We said goodbye to the tall pines. Heather and I packed our kayaks as Naomi and Jo sat watching. Jo looked out over the vast water of Lake

Winnibigoshish and she felt good about her decision not to take the solo canoe out. Heather and I headed out, finding paddling to be relaxing and enjoyable, even with our weary muscles. We followed the south shore and did not cut across the big water. Where the Mississippi flows into Lake Winnibigoshish we passed a flock of pelicans bobbing about in a little group. Heather said they reminded her of a gathering of little old men meeting for coffee and a game of cards, all sitting in their usual spots. As we watched, one flew in just above the water with the grace and power of a well-piloted 747. He landed a little apart from the group. We laughed as he eased into his place among the others.

With the wind at our backs we paddled to Richard's Townsite boat landing to meet Naomi and Jo for a break. When in sight, we found them kicked back in lawn chairs cross-stitching and swatting black flies. I could see from a distance that Naomi's patience with the flies had grown thin. Once we were on shore, the girls were quite excited about a giant, tarpaper fish tourist attraction who's open mouth had double doors. They had seen it on Highway 2. In their words, "It was so hideous it was really cool." They really wanted to take us there to see it, but that would have to wait. Naomi assured us she took a good picture of it.

Naomi and Jo found great joy in visiting odd statues and figures along the road. Some of their road trips were for the sole purpose of seeking out these marvels of human creation. There was always a story accompanying these roadside creations. If the objects they discovered lacked corresponding stories, the two of them were quite skilled at imagining something. The story they created for this particular fish is that it was just about to clamp its might jaws down and swallow Jo whole if Naomi had not blinded it with her camera's flash, which provided Jo with an opportunity to escape!

The wind picked up while we sat with them. It wouldn't be safe to paddle the next ten miles to Tamarack Point Campground on the west side of the lake. Instead we would paddle two miles to the town of Bena while the girls went to Tamarack and dropped our gear so we could fit in the Jeep. As we paddled, the wind picked up even more. Waves piled up behind us. At times, the waves picked up our kayaks like surf boards and carried us forward with an exhilarating surge. Even though I knew the water was growing more dangerous, I wanted to stay out and play in it. Common sense prevailed and I was glad to pull into Denny's Resort at Bena. Heather entered the channel leading to the resort first. I watched as the waves pushed her around. She was getting wet. When I turned my kayak to enter the channel, an ice cold wave caught me broadside and filled the cockpit. I squealed as I kept paddling to safety.

While waiting for Naomi and Jo to pick us up, Heather befriended an 11-year-old girl who had watched us with great interest. Her name was Lindsey. This bubbly little girl was intrigued by our kayaks. Soon we had her in one while we held it steady. Her eyes sparkled as she struggled to maintain her balance. We held on to the rope attached to the front of the kayak and she paddled a short distance from shore. The whole time she talked endlessly about her dreams of wanting to have her own kayak.

The girls picked us up and soon we were in camp helping set things up. I silently struggled with disappointment because we didn't make our distance that day. Eventually I succumbed to a nap in the tent, out of the wind. Awake and feeling better after three hours of sleep, I heard the wind still roaring and the waves thrashing on shore. Naomi and I walked the road to check out the put-in spot for the next day and wondered what the weather would allow.

We had time to ponder the oddities of nature we'd encountered on the trip. For example, the driver (support person) had been the most plagued by woodticks. It was Doug who first attracted herds of ticks, and constantly pulled them off. Now it was Naomi. While on our walk to the put-in spot we also walked into a field to get a better look at some grazing deer. When we came out of the field Naomi had two ticks on her pants. I picked them off. After we settled in by the camp fire, we discovered many more. We picked more than two dozen of the little suckers off Naomi in less than fifteen minutes. Ticks were crawling out of her jeans and her shoes. She would not touch them so we picked them off while she anxiously waved her hands in the air. Sadly, Heather noted, Naomi was never the same again. She was, however given a tee-shirt with the slogan, *Tick Free and Fart Free is the Way to Be.* The second reference was about being in close quarters while camping and the unfortunate ability of gas to escape a sleeping bag.

Another oddity was the leach episode. Doug bought leaches for bait and put them in the food cooler to protect them from the heat. Naturally, the container broke, and the bloodsuckers dispersed in the ice-melt. The girls tried to keep this detail from me, scooping leaches out on the sly so I wouldn't freak out. Back at Denny's Resort, I caught on when I tried to drain the excess water from the cooler, and the water wouldn't flow. I found one little leach stuck half way out of the cooler drain spout and calmly pulled him out and held him up to the girls with a quizzical look. Looking both guilty and greatly entertained they clued me in. The girls thought they had already found and tossed all the leaches. Later, when I looked for the ketchup and mustard, I found another one tucked in the corner of the cooler. By then all we could do was laugh.

June 14, Monday, Day 10

I woke to the sound of waves beating against the rocks on the shore. I felt defeated and discouraged. The wind on the last two big lakes blew away my enthusiasm. I had been clinging to the thought I would paddle the entire route. Now it had become clear that I had to let go of that goal. Compromising my vision led to a feeling of failure.

Perhaps learning to go easy on myself and compromise was one of the lessons for me to learn out here. When it comes to what others want I will compromise so they can have it. But for me it is a different story. I knew I always set my standards too high and judged myself severely when I couldn't meet them. I had slept well and felt rested, but hard paddling and disappointment had taken a big toll. I wasn't excited to get out on the water.

Jo told me she felt sad. She felt a little left out since Heather and I had planned the trip together. Heather often took the lead in decision-making. Usually when Jo and I canoed or camped together she was an equal partner with me in every

Nancy and Jo

aspect of the trip. As we talked about it, we realized the difference on this trip was a result of Jo living so far away and arriving just a couple of days before we launched. Besides, Heather had paddled this first stretch of river the year before and was in the best position to make some decisions. As we talked it out, Jo seemed to feel better.

For safety, we decided not to paddle any more of Lake Winnibigoshish. Naomi drove us east to Winnie Dam Recreation Area. After clowning around on shore for a while we set off under a cloudy sky with a breeze at our backs. Soon the clouds cleared and the breeze kept us cool, making for a very pleasant paddling day. My mood began to brighten along with the sky.

As we passed through Little Winnie Lake we drifted quietly into a flock of eight pelicans. When they took off and flew over our heads, I felt uplifted to be among such magnificent creatures. Their take off was quite awkward, but once they were airborne they were transformed into graceful gliders, skilled at riding the currents.

As I watched the pelicans my mind wandered to thoughts of native people using this river as a main source of travel and food. It had sounded romantic to me, but I had become aware of the amount of work that lifestyle required. I thought about their connection to the land and their belief that Spirit is in everything. What I have learned about them and their spirituality has attracted me and speaks to my heart. In their beliefs, we are all connected, plants, animals, earth and humans. That just feels right.

Heather and Jo have shared a similar draw to native ways. Heather is extremely sensitive to plants and animals. A few miles downriver she caught her first fish, a northern pike. She was so happy she almost cried. She had not been sure she could catch a fish in a kayak and stay upright. We took pictures and released the fish as fast as possible

so it would not be traumatized. Eating it occurred to us but no one was willing to kill it.

We stopped for lunch at spectacular Crazy James Point campsite. After paddling at water level, it felt exhilarating to sit high up on a cliff and take in a curving length of river. Heather caught a bass from shore. After a photo (so she could show Wade) she released it. Crazy James was where we had planned to camp if we had kept to our schedule. We had already traveled six miles by 1 pm. So we headed on to the next camping opportunity on our map, the Leech Lake River Access.

Along the river I spotted a heron perched in a dead tree. It looked surreal, like some kind of abstract painting. I ran aground looking at it. The river here was all switchbacks. It bounced off the banks, changing direction only to bounce off the opposite bank. Inside the curves, tall grass grew in deep soft mud.

After setting up camp and fixing a cook-in-a-pouch teriyaki chicken dinner, I wandered off by myself and gazed into the water where Leech Lake River and the Mississippi River come together. In this peaceful place I said a prayer and sang "Oh Great Spirit." Soon I became aware of activity. Water flowed around the rocks and sand, creating swirling patterns at the river bottom. It carved delicate grooves in the sand and around each rock causing the weeds to dance.

A little bullhead swam up and played in the calm water, then flashed back out into the flow. Little fish jumped in the rippling current where the two rivers converged. Birds ran along the edge of the opposite shore. A gray bird flitted close in the nearby tree and didn't seem to notice me. As the sun set, bugs began to dart in unison in the air. They appeared to be a dancing cloud. I watched a dragonfly catch a big mosquito and hoped she was really hungry.

We had paddled 16.5 miles in seven hours, and had completed a total of 117 miles of the trip. By not paddling all of Cass Lake and Winnibigosh-ish Lake we cut 13 miles from what we had anticipated we would travel. At the end of day, I sensed a calm both outside the tent and within me. The water, sky and animals had filled me with awe. How could I be anything but inspired and grateful?

June 15, Tuesday, Day 11

We were a day ahead of our paddling schedule and planned to lay up the next day to rest. We awoke to a majestic sky full of puffy orange-tinted clouds floating overhead. Storm clouds were stacking up on the horizon, so we quickly packed and hit the river. At this point, the river is about 40 feet wide in most spots; it has long since lost the intimacy of arching trees.

The clouds rolled in, but it did not rain. The highlight of this day was watching a deer swim across the river in front of us. It reached the other side, turned to snort at us, ran a few feet, snorted again, and then bounded off, snorting all the way.

Around the next bend, in the distance I could see the billowing stacks of the cement-colored Minnesota Power Plant in Cohasset. Up to this point, the trip had felt like a wilderness voyage. The contrast between the towering power plant and our recent experience with wild water, birdsong, and swimming deer struck me hard. While we had passed houses, dams and bridges, they were few and far between. I knew as we moved further downriver the scene would continue to change. Human influence would be more evident. We would soon see more buildings, docks and places where the forest had been stripped away from this pristine shore.

We traveled many curves in the river. Jutting out from the river were many oxbows. They were named oxbows because from above they resembled the u-shaped part of an oxen's yoke. As we rounded the next curve we watched a flock of pelicans in synchronized flight high in the sky. The sun peeked through gray clouds and gave the pelicans' white feathers a luminous glow. We spent sweet moments drifting on the water admiring things. When the wind was down, we floated, enjoying the peace and calm.

It was fun to watch the girls play and joke around. Jo and Heather were like sisters from the moment they met. The three girls were always laughing or singing, and I was grateful they could be part of this. It wouldn't have been right without them.

Schoolcraft had been a long awaited stop. It held a special place in Heather's heart. With an almost daydream expression she described the amazing "Mother Pine" that guarded the riverside entrance. We knew this would be a powerful and fun place to rest our weary muscles and hear tales of Naomi's road trip adventures. As we neared the boat access, Heather pointed out her special gigantic old white pine. Jo and Heather stopped on the river's edge across from the tree to absorb its entirety and beauty. I paddled to shore and walked up to it. Then I touched it and looked up into its branches, feeling small and awed. It's shape and scars held tribute to the long history it represents—the history of the woods as well as the history of people in the area.

As we expected from Heather's descriptions, Schoolcraft State Park was lovely. We had it all to ourselves that afternoon. Naomi had camped here the night before. As usual, she had arranged things with such care we felt welcomed upon our arrival. Naomi's big heart shows in how she assists others and adds special touches to an ordinary situation. This time, we could not help but notice our lawn chairs around the fire pit. In each chair was a water jug with a face drawn on it. When we asked Naomi about it she said that she had missed us so she turned the water jugs into us by putting our faces on them. She added that we had a great time by the fire last night, even though we were a little quiet!

Looking around we were dumbfounded by the fact she put up the tarp over the picnic table by herself. This is a job generally requiring three people. She was quite proud of her accomplishment and told us it was her evening project—and she did mean all evening.

Later it rained, and our view from under the tarp was green and soft. When the clouds and rain cleared we took a bath with water from the spigot. Then the girls provided some comic relief by playing with the rainpants they were wearing. First, Jo pulled hers by the waistband as high as she could. Naomi and Heather copied and they tried to see just how far up they could pull them, giggling at how silly they looked with their waist up to their armpits.

I thought about how I was doing things, like cooking, washing dishes and managing little details. (I internally whine at home—sometimes not so internally.) Here I'm less fussy about food and eat most anything. At home, our routines are set. I could picture exactly what Doug was doing each day that I was away. I wondered how we could change that and

Heather, Jo, and Naomi in rainpants

Mother Pine

add more spontaneity to our lives. I hoped the trip would initiate a shift in our relationship.

Sitting in her tent and journaling, Heather discovered a leak. "What's this? You're leaking? How could you?" followed by mumbling that included something about the tent being tried and true and having traveled everywhere with her. Her sense of betrayal from a long time friend became clear when we heard her threatening "You just better knock it off or I am buying a new tent and you're history." As we helped her cover it with a tarp, she went about plotting, in the presence of her tent, the purchase of the new one.

June 16, Wednesday, Day 12

This was our layover day, and did we need it! Our campsite was an impressive lush area surrounded by oak and pine overlooking a grassy wide spot in the river. Frogs croaked and a heron hung out. A few clouds and a cool breeze completed perfect conditions for us to relax. We napped, read, wrote and enjoyed serenity. Jo started her day with a short jog. Her leg muscles were feeling neglected from so many days of sitting. She returned invigorated, thankful for the change in activity.

We found entertainment in watching a turtle meander across our campsite and into the woods. On a hike, we found blooming bunchberry carpeting the forest floor. In the distance we heard what we thought sounded like a rookery. The bird noises were loud and plentiful. Most of the bracken fern had reached its mature height, but occasionally Jo or Heather would squeal with delight as they spotted a fiddlehead pushing its way up through the earth's surface.

Naomi tried kayaking for the first time. Her face reflected her discomfort as she struggled to get into the cockpit without rolling it. Each stoke of the paddle caused her to hold her breath, waiting for the inevitable plunge. We paddled the boats to our camp from the boat launch. The short paddle was not enough for Naomi to get comfortable, but the discomfort on her face evolved to pride. We cheered as her smile grew wider. I was delighted to see her rise above her fear.

While Naomi tried kayaking Jo was lying on the dock investigating bugs on and under the surface of the water. Like a small child she was totally enthralled. Soon she was pulling up little pieces of muddy green goop from the river bottom to examine closer. Each subtle change in color or texture delighted her. She talked about the ecology of it all and how amazing it is that everything works together. To me it was still goop and bugs.

I had an opportunity to spend time with the big old white pine. Trying to get a feel for how big she was, I went three arms lengths around and still did not get back to where I started. The tree divided into four main trunks. Two of those enormous trunks had curved back and grew together for a short length, making the tree seem all the more mystical. This tree represents a long timeline in human history. I am glad the loggers who came through here at the end of the 19th century missed this one.

The girls also took time to visit the tree. Heather refrained from climbing it because that was her way of paying respect to such a "great one." Jo, however, was called into the tree. She pulled off her shoes so she would not hurt the bark and so she could feel the tree's energy. With a few short steps she was in the arms of the great tree. Naomi chose to watch. She is often found observing and smiling at those she loves.

Fatigue seemed to have affected my brain. Twice when Naomi was headed to the post office I gave her things to mail with either no address or a significant part of it missing.

In the evening Bea, Barb and Paula arrived from Ely, bringing a new wave of feminine adventurous courage and excitement. They were obvious voyageurs with great stories to tell. I was delighted to get to know each of them. The three of them had attended the Ely gathering, where we learned how Bea and Barb had become friends in their 60s and ran a canoe outfitting company in Ely.

At the Ely gathering Bea had shared,

I was leading a group of women on a canoe trip and Barb's daughter, Donna, happened to hear conversations between myself and others in the group. She asked,

"Can anyone go on that trip?"

I said yes and asked if she was interested. She replied,

"No, but I know someone else who would be very much interested. Does she have to live here?"

"No, that doesn't matter. We'll take anybody."

Donna called her mother and told her there was group going on a canoe trip out of Big Fork River and asked her if she would be interested in going. Barb said,

"It sounds like fun. When are they going?"

"In just two days."

"Oh, I guess I can do that," Barb replied. So she came from Omaha to Minneapolis and went on the canoe trip which I was leading.

On the trip, the person in the front of the canoe did not alert her to the

fact a branch was coming right across her neck. She spotted the branch, jumped out of the canoe into the water and came up with both her glasses and her hat on. I said,
"Anyone that can do that is for me."
I asked her if she would like to come next year and told her she could come at half price. She said she would. The following year she joined me full time. That is how we started the B's Wilderness Paddlers when we were in our 60s.

While we made dinner, a kayaker from Georgia visited us. Reverend Dale was kayaking to Louisiana, doing a ministry along the way. He stayed for dinner. Some of our group were bothered that his ideas reeked of fire and brimstone. His stereotypical remarks about Native Americans bothered all of us, especially my girls who are part Chickasaw. He seemed to have no compassion for the ways in which Native people have been oppressed, and had limited perspectives on women. I wanted to tell him he needed to learn about the distorted perspective brought on by white male privilege, but I chose to keep my mouth shut. His religious righteousness kept us from caring about his mission. Then Bea said she was an ordained minister and had attended the Colgate Rochester Divinity School in Rochester, New York. He stopped preaching and left a short time later. Bea believed his quick departure may have been because of the divinity school she attended, which is well known, but not appreciated amongst the conservative end.

Later he came back through our campsite to tell me he'd had an "epiphany." After talking with me about the mission and purpose of our trip, he realized it was women from his church who financed his trip and who were tracking him to be sure he was safe. He seemed profoundly moved by his new perspective that these women were making a difference, sharing his vision, and were willing to sacrifice to make his trip happen. The men in his church were not. I hoped that realization would stay with him and expand his view of women and their roles. I was grateful I had kept my mouth shut.

June 17, Thursday, Day 13

I was up early in the morning watching the mist swirl over the water. Tiny droplets of water were perched on the tips of each blade of grass making the ground glisten. Just as I turned back to the tent I notice an otter swimming past me. Our eyes connected briefly and she arched her back, disappearing under the surface. I packed my gear and headed to the dock where I found Paula. As the cool breeze ruffled our hair and the morning sun warmed our skin, I sang the Anishnaabeg song while Paula hummed along with me.

That morning Janice and Wanda from Marcell, Minnesota, and Vickie from Deer River, Minnesota, joined us. We shuffled cars, took photos, and hit the water about 9:30 am. The first thing I noticed was the waves of laughter that echoed across the water. Everyone was enjoying each other's company. Jo connected with Janice, who raises perennials. Jo has a great interest in plants. She had been working on a research project while at the University of Colorado, in Boulder. Her focus is on non-native plant species and how they are invading the wilderness and killing off native plants. Her research project was limited to a number of portages in the Boundary Waters Canoe Area Wilderness.

Paddling team: Wanda, Janice, Barb, Vickie, Nancy, Paula, Jo, Bea, and Heather

Jo was also starting her own gardening business and felt some fear about making this change in her life. On this trip she received many messages telling her to make the move and trust herself. Janice was one of the messengers.

We stopped early in the day for a break at a campsite, and interrupted a dispute over a fish between a weasel and an otter. The weasel repeatedly ran through the grass charging us, while the otter disappeared into the tall grass. I was closest to the charging weasel and was sure she was going to bite my leg. It was more comical than scary. She didn't calm down until we left.

After four miles, Bea, Barb and Paula pulled off the river to head home. Bea was not feeling well. Going just this far had been a stretch for her. Paula had paddled my kayak the last mile and enjoyed herself so much it was hard for her to return it to me.

As we continued I became better acquainted with the other women. Wanda was particularly interesting. She had just turned 80. The day before

Wanda

she had put in 20 fence posts. She mentioned she had undergone three back surgeries, but said, "You can't let that stop you." At the end of the day, after 16 miles and six hours of paddling she headed home to work in the garden.

Janice was outspoken and had an infectious laugh. No matter how far away, her laugh reached me across the water and made me smile.

Vicki was an unemployed pastor who was married just six weeks ago. Pastors seemed to be the theme for the day. Rev. Dale had waved goodbye to us. Bea had been in our company. Each came from a denomination different from the others and all found themselves drawn to journey down this mighty river.

Soon we passed the Minnesota Power generating plant towering above the trees and water. I could see it as a marvel of human ingenuity and as an eyesore marring the natural beauty of the area. Steam rolled out of the chimneys, and I felt grateful the contents of that steam were monitored for pollutants. A deep hum emanated from the plant. I could feel it in my body. I was glad not to live near it. I could hear Heather and Jo were contemplating these same thoughts as they discussed this new scenery.

Entering Blackwater Lake we were graced with the presence of a loon who stretched her wings wide and played in the water as we glided by. We paddled through shallows, with reeds growing heavily across the top of the water. Fish, startled by our paddles, jumped and splashed the water, surprising me so that I laughed out loud. My amusement was overshadowed by the challenge of navigation. It was difficult to read the shoreline. I doubted my navigational skills and felt a deep sense of responsibility for the women relying on my guidance. I conferred with Heather who was experiencing the same challenge. Anxiously I scanned the shore for an opening. I took a chance on a dark area in what I thought was about the

right place and paddled towards it followed by the four other boats. Luckily I was correct and felt a sense of relief. We entered the river where it flows through Cohasset. They didn't know how unsure of myself I was and I didn't tell them.

Passing through Cohasset we saw, secured along shore, the first of many houseboats. We passed two young girls fishing, one was on a dock and the other on a large bolder just off shore. Her Siamese cat, Sophie, was with her. The cat did not look happy on the rock. Sophie moved from one side of the rock to the other, stopping briefly to poke its paw hesitantly at the surface of the water, unsuccessfully searching for a place to escape. The girl dressed in coveralls, with her long blond curly hair that glowed in the sun, was unconcerned about her cat's dilemma.

Nearing Pokegema Dam we came around a corner where there was a steep cliff of black and gray jagged rock. It reminded me of places in the Boundary Waters Canoe Area Wilderness. Rounding the last bend we saw Naomi standing on shore, holding a sign in her hands like an airport limousine driver. Naomi's sign was colorful and read "Are you a fairy queen princess?" Because this was Jo's last day on the water, Naomi wanted to give us a special welcome. She had made and hung many clever signs for us along the way. Usually we moved faster than she expected and we passed before she got the sign out.

Pokegema is a well groomed and landscaped campground but not tent friendly. Our campsite was nestled between the outhouse (with its own special aroma) and the woodpile where chainsaws were used. Although some grass grew nearby, tents were allowed only on the gravel-covered area which tent stakes refused to penetrate. The picnic table sat on a concrete pad. Then I noticed the light. A large overhead beam that could illuminate a parking lot would shine on us all night. Just 40 feet from our tents a train rumbled past. This would be a regular occurrence during the night. RVs with their humming air conditioners filled the rest of the sites.

We headed into Grand Rapids for dinner, where I enjoyed a wonderful Greek salad. Grand Rapids is proud to be the birthplace of Judy Garland. There is a yellow brick road (walkway) leading to the Judy Garland Museum and a mural on the side of a building depicting scenes from *The Wizard of Oz*.

Back at camp for fun we all polished our toenails. Naomi and I chose purple, Heather and Jo ,green. Heather also painted her finger nails red. Heather would later be sorry she chose green for her toes. With her feet in and out of the water so often it transformed the once attractive shade of green into something that looked more like gangrene. To make matters worse, this particular nail polish would not come off.

After nail painting the experiment in leg waxing began. This was Jo's first time to try it. Heather had agreed to coach her through the process. Jo and Heather sat near the fire in the cold and dark, drinking wine for warmth and courage. With head lamps on to see the details, they struggled to get the wax strips warm enough to work properly. Having placed her first strip on her leg, carefully following Heather's instructions, Jo quickly pealed it off and squealed in pain. Both girls emitted painful little noises each time they pulled a strip off their legs. After she had finished, one leg Jo had had enough and stopped. Heather continued until she had ripped the wax and hair off both of her legs. With some badgering they talked me into trying it. One strip was all I needed to determine it was not for me! Ripping my hair from its follicles was too barbaric.

Naomi, Jo, and Heather seemed to connect with one another effortlessly. Watching them I felt sad at times. I was isolated when I was a young woman and had missed those types of friendships. Because of our age difference the girls often didn't understand what I was saying and corrected me as if my view was flawed. It reminded me of how teenagers perceive their parents as no longer being in touch with the real world and feel they must bring their parents up to speed. It was clear the girls perspective and

Heather and Jo waxing by campfire

mine were different, and I didn't feel heard. I felt grateful for my phone connection to Doug.

While planning this trip I knew, in part, that this could be a solitary adventure. I knew I would have a great deal of time to delve into my thoughts and feelings with so many hours of paddling. What surprised me as I communicated with the girls and felt unheard was a feeling of being an outsider on my own expedition.

One of the ways the girls connected was cross stitching. Jo and Naomi taught Heather how to do it at camp that night, having purchased an "easy" kit in town. They sat around the fire with headlamps on and cross stitched. Cross stitching by headlamp was to become the scene most every night.

June 18, Friday, Day 14

My sense of isolation seeped over into the next morning. I had a hard time rolling out of the sleeping bag. In the wind and cold I went to the water and sang. Three loons floated by, but my heart still felt heavy. My prayers failed to lift my spirits.

Most of the day was spent running around town. I was disappointed to discover that the photos I had taken didn't turn out. One of the settings on the camera had been changed by its constant in and out of the camera case. This was not the last time that would happen.

We got the Jeep door fixed. (It cost more and took longer than expected). Then we hauled our dirty clothes to the laundromat. It was a beehive of anxious and irritable people. They swarmed the aisles, hovering near machines at the end of their cycles, waiting their turn. I walked up to a washer with five minutes left on the indicator, and a woman yelled, "That's my machine!" "Okay." I responded.

Lugging our smelly bundle of clothes, we searched out another laundromat. It was a King Koin, the same name as my Dad's old business. With only two other people occupying the building, we peacefully washed our laundry, read books, and cross-stitched. Pleasant memories of my Dad's laundromat returned with the scent of soap and the hum of dryers.

At 5 pm we were back in the car that smelled of the lube on the repaired door latch and fresh laundry We headed for camp to set up for the evening's gathering.

Earlier in the day we met and spoke with Jackie, who had recognized the logo on our car from the local paper's news release. She came to Pokegema occasionally to walk. She was thrilled to find us in the campground. Because she was so inspired by the story, Jackie asked what she could do to assist us. We told her that her excitement was an inspiration for us and we invited her to the gathering. However, she was unable to attend because of a commitment she could not change. I had already headed to the shelter to arrange things for the gathering when she came back to give us a rhubarb cake, still warm from the oven.

I felt anxious as I walked to the dark brown log shelter with its gray, wooden shake roof. A large gopher ran across the sidewalk in front of me and paused for a moment as if to greet me. She seemed to be suggesting I could calm down and trust that the gathering would go well. It took me a while to absorb that.

The wind gusted and blew our "You Go Girl" tee shirts and bandanas from the table and across the grass. I had trouble getting the fire going. I found it hard to think about the sacredness of the gathering or the fire.

As the fire lit with the flint, I finally let go of needing the fire, the night, or the gathering to be perfect. The women began to arrive. Some were not sure why they had come. Others came because someone said they should. Some arrived full of excitement, others hesitant.

We began just after 6:30 pm. Naomi told me that as we started a loon rose up and danced on the water behind us. The group was made up of 18 women, besides the four of us. Most were over age 50. The Grandmothers jumped right into conversation. Soon they were enthralled listening to each other. Some of the women had just come from a storytelling workshop, which may have contributed to the immediate flow of words. I saw the younger women watch, smile, nod, and soak up every word of the elders. The last of my heart's agitation melted away, and was replaced with gratitude.

As we started, I gave tobacco pouches to the two Native women in the group. They had just met.

Sharon W. put it this way,

A moment ago an amazing thing happened over here with my new young friend. It is as though a daughter arrived. We were signing up and that is when I recognized Anishanabeg right away and I said Boozhoo to her and she said Boozhoo back. That is how we greet one another in the Ojibwa language. We talked with one another. I asked her where she was from. She said Cass Lake. I said I was born there and you know how conversations just take off when a couple of girls get together. Her husband, was a playmate of mine. On occasions when we had a chance to go back and visit, he had a horse. He was the only kid I knew that ever had a horse. I never forgot his name, Harry. Here we meet. She wasn't even sure she was going to come. They presented us both with tobacco when we got here. We have a commitment now for the rest of our lives and into the next world because we put down tobacco together. Our commitment came out of this group. Something you could not have planned Nancy, certainly neither one of us. We did not really know each other until just a matter of an hour ago. Neither one of us could have planned this either.

Peg added,

There is a lot of wisdom here. I am feeling it. I said a prayer before I came tonight. I put out tobacco and asked for this gathering to be wonderful. It has already been beyond my expectations. I do healing circles. We put the women who come on opposite sides of a circle: north, south, east, west, to take the power and spread it around. Right now I am sitting between an old friend, and a new friend and I can feel that power. I remember my grandmother, who raised me and my two aunts, when they were standing beside me. I can feel that now. It is a power kind of thing. It is not in my imagination I can feel it. I am feeling I just want to sit here and not say a word and just enjoy this.

The energy in the circle intensified as each woman spoke.
Susan W. shared,

Going through a lot of loss and a lot pain I discovered that the meaning of life isn't necessarily about the really big things. I think we all need to look inside. We need to find a zest for life. Joy and meaning comes in recognizing the little picture in the big picture. Learning means to really look and learning to be present and appreciate all that is. Just learn to love! Whatever that might mean.

Nature, art and spirituality have always been the core of my life, even as a teenager. Nature was the umbilical cord that kept me connected to beauty and truth. Marrying and having children taught me patience and love. Loss taught me acceptance. My spirituality strengthened. Now I am not afraid of life or death. In these ways, life influences my spirituality and spirituality my life.

I think I made some poor decisions when I was young. I regretted them for a very long time. That made me restless and feel unfulfilled. Now, I feel that there really are no 'mistakes.' All the experiences helped me recognize that we do make choices. Those choices have consequences. I now appreciate having some balance in my life and the ability to choose to be happy and fulfill dreams.

I would like younger women to be gentle with themselves. Don't lose touch with your own center. Tune into other people and give of yourself. Also, tune in and give to your own heart's desire. You can't love till you love who you are.

Terry O. began her story by saying,

I never really thought I was a spiritual person until somebody told me I was. I was raised Catholic, so I thought spirituality was the Father the Son and the Holy Ghost. There wasn't really anything beyond that. It wasn't until I heard a song on the radio about glory in the meetinghouse, glory in the fields that I said "Oh yeah that would be me out in the fields."

I'd like to be remembered as a person who sometimes followed her heart, even to the alarm of the rest of her family. Advice to younger women? Don't be afraid of criticism. Don't be afraid of being nudged out of the rest of the group. No matter what is going on in the rest of your life be true to your dreams. If you have an idea of how things could be better in your family or among your group of friends or what ever organization you belong to—even if they drive you out for your good idea or speaking your truth. You never know, the others might just end up following you.

Terry B. joined in,

I grew up in a wonderful family that encouraged me to follow my dreams. I have always had someone behind me. I am surrounded by wonderful men who support me and argue with me, of course!

I think one of the things I would have told my daughter is to nurture your friendships with other women. I find sometimes I get so busy in life that I forget to nurture those friendships. Sometimes I just need to step back and gather with women. I have had some incredibly life changing experiences by just being with other women.

Sandy added,

When I look back at the years when I was working, my vision was always to the day I could quit, to the day I could move on and could go somewhere else. When I think back on it, I never really sat back and enjoyed where I was at the time. I was always looking ahead. We spent a lot of time traveling, looking for where we were going to go and we didn't stay where we were, hiking and walking.

As soon as I moved here, I was diagnosed with breast cancer. My whole life fell apart. I lost a breast and I thought I was loosing my life. As Terry knows, every time I had an ache or a pain I would call up Mayo (Clinic) and I would say I am on my way down. I figured I was dying. And I died for five years. Now I am still alive!

It (life) is not always over the next hill. It's right now. It's right in your own back yard, at your own kitchen table.

Kathryn addressed the question about spirituality.

The word is obscure for me—not something that can be explained easily. However, when I realized religion and spirituality were two different things, it was an important turning point. I began to be more appreciative of the world and people. I was able to see the big picture, relaxed and peaceful, more adventurous, happier. My heart and soul have never stirred in a church or through some religious ritual as they have while I was walking through the woods, sitting by the water, collecting rocks, building a fire, or having a good laugh. Today, I feel closer to God than I ever have. I thank Her constantly.

I really want to urge young women to live away from family and friends for at least a year before making a commitment to a partner. We all serve in so many roles as we are growing. We are someone's daughter, sister, high school friend, student. All the roles carry certain expectations. We're so busy meeting those expectations that we don't find out who we really are.

We closed the gathering with the aspiration stick ritual and the women walked to the river bank and tossed their sticks into the water.

Jo, Heather, and Naomi listened to the women with interest. Later it was enlightening to me to hear which pieces of wisdom the girls held important. Naomi had been going through rough water after a relationship break up. It was hard for her to hear some of the stories without crying. She still had so much to learn. All of the gatherings were taped. The girls said they wanted to listen to the recordings.

After everyone said warm goodbyes and left, I walked over to where some of the women were camping. My friend Deborah offered me a massage for my sore shoulder. I sat at the women's fire, and we talked while Deborah rubbed my shoulder with tea tree oil. It was a pleasure to savor the conversation of women my own age as the ache in my shoulder began to ease.

Back at camp, the girls lit a farewell fire for Jo. None of us were happy to see her go. She had been with us from the first day and added many moments of laughter and wisdom.

June 19, Saturday, Day 15

Last night I asked the girls what they thought of the gathering. Jo said she felt validated and empowered. In her journal, Heather wrote,

> *Wisdom from the gathering is this: Make your own path. Only you know what is right for you. Don't be afraid of criticism. Spirituality is not the same as religion. It often takes a difficult event to get your life going in a different, and perhaps better, direction. Learn to make where you are the best place in the world to be. Focus on living today.*
>
> *So wait a minute. I sit and nod when these women talk. I recognize much of what they say to be true. They are all at least (or close to) twice my age. Now I know the wisdom they have learned over time. Ponder that a bit. Let that sink in. Remember these lessons when I feel helpless, lost, confused.*

Naomi said it was still hard to hear the women's wisdom without making comparisons to herself and coming up short. She said she knew she was being too hard on herself but was hopeful she could change. I hoped that by the last gathering she would not be judging herself so harshly.

Saying good-bye to Naomi and Jo wasn't easy. Naomi would rejoin us on Wednesday, but I didn't know when I would next see Jo. Wanting to continue to feel part of the trip, Jo gave her hat to Heather to wear. Embroidered on it was a picture of a cup of coffee and the words "Cup of Jo."

In her good-byes, Jo wrote,

> *For me, this journey started with few expectations. I knew time in the woods with you women (and Doug and Naomi as support) would lead to spiritual growth and emotional bonding. Intuition told me it was the right time for such a gathering. The spirits of nature would welcome us. Every day we were blessed with, not just one animal guide and the wisdom of the reeds, but many guides: bald eagles, herons, loons, and playful otters caught off guard. While the winds challenged us a few days, they also brought aid, growth, knowledge of our own physical limits, and respect for nature's power. The waters have carried us graciously. The trees have called us to our night's home.*

In the silence of paddle strokes on windless days, I have learned to calm myself and to listen to my inner voice. In the dancing branches of the trees I have learned to celebrate the beauty of the moment and of our bodies in rhythm with nature. In the breathtaking encounters with Mother Nature's splendid creatures I have learned to hand over the worries and cares of the unknown and embrace a feeling of trust. In the words of the women who gather, I find confirmation of a path known deep inside. In the laughter, song and words of my friend I have found inspiration to follow my intuition and make my dreams come true.

I am forever blessed by these past few days.

Love, joy and health.

Light as a feather

Free with the breeze.

We packed our gear. After another muscle woman shot with Jo, we headed to the water. As we passed the campsite of the gathering women we stopped for a few moments. They gave us a bunch of grapes, and were all a-buzz about what they had heard the night before.

Sharon, a Native American, and Deborah, an African American, came down to the water to see us off. Deborah played a moving native song on her wooden flute. Sharon wrapped blueberries in a red cloth and placed the small food bundle into the water as an offering for the River Spirits.

Jo, Heather, and Nancy, Pokegema muscles

Sharon and Deborah

She respectfully asked them in a quiet prayer to give us safe passage. With the sounds of the wind gently singing in the background, my heart and soul felt full. Paddling away I felt excited about the trip. My accomplishment had begun to sink in and feel real.

After an unhurried hour on the water we came to Sylvan Municipal Park and waited for a Minnesota Power courtesy shuttle to portage us around the Blanchard Dam. The park was no more than a turnaround and the water had the rather unpleasant smell of decay and rot. We expected a taxi with a standard trailer but were surprised when a man pulled up in his car with a canoe trailer. Brad was a jolly man who enjoyed helping us. He had received three calls for shuttles so far that year, but not from women. As he helped us lift our loaded kayaks onto the trailer he struggled. He was surprised at what Heather and I could lift. We smiled at each other and felt a sense of pride in our strength.

South of the dam, the river widened and moved quickly. The banks were steep and heavily wooded. At times we paddled past people's back yards. A transient man startled us both as we passed under a bridge. I didn't see him until he yelled, "Roll." He wanted to see us roll the kayaks. I don't know how to roll, and neither Heather nor I would intentionally want to roll in the water of the Mississippi. It is so dark that it is difficult to determine what lurks beneath the surface.

As we paddled on, stretching no longer relieved my sore mid-back. I kept adjusting my position in the kayak, but it didn't seem to help. I accepted that this discomfort would stay with me for the rest of the trip.

In places along the river, erosion had caused large chunks of the bank to drop horizontally into the water. Entire trees had slid down the bank, landed right side up and continued to grow, even though a third or more was submerged in the river. Others ended up horizontal as if levitating just above the river. Those trees sent new leafy branches skyward from the trunk. I wondered why some survived and others didn't. Large older trees poised on the edge of the river which had exposed their strong root systems. The way the roots curved back into the bank anchored them and kept from being swept away. Now there was a metaphor for life. No matter what erodes the ground of our daily life if we anchor our roots and bend as needed, we can withstand whatever life throws at us. We could become a stronger expression of power and beauty.

Along the way we spotted large snapping turtles sunning themselves on mud banks and downed trees. With their large awkward bodies, we wondered how they managed to get up on the tree branches. I attempted to get a close look at one high in a tree, but got caught in a current and made some rather panicked moves to keep from running into the tree. I frightened the turtle and she dropped into the water. Once I was safe again I looked over at Heather and received the usual compassionate yet taunting laughter.

At lunch we sat in tall fragrant grass. Teresa and Krista, two of the women from the gathering last night, paddled up in a canoe to visit for a while. They were canoe racers who competed most weekends. They said one of the best parts of racing was showing up the college boys who race. They assume women are not good at it. We watched as they headed up stream stroking fast and hard in unison. The woman in the stern yelled out and they switched with precise timing. Their paddling was inspiring, and more work than I am interested in. I prefer to enjoy my paddling and focus on my surroundings. For me it was not so much about pushing, or for that matter, focusing on a win. However, it was clear they enjoyed it and were very good.

On the water in the heat of the sun I felt extremely tired. I could have easily fallen asleep in the kayak. I knew my sense of balance is diminished with my eyes closed, and even worse when I am unconscious. I would be in danger of rolling the kayak if I fell asleep. This potential danger kept me awake.

The terrain is ever-changing on this section of the river. Although we were still predominantly in the woods, it was clear we had entered farm country evidenced by the periodic pastures, fences, barns and cows. It is odd to know that just beyond our sight is a whole other world—a world of fields, barns, farm animals, highways, cars, houses and other "civilized" elements.

Some of the farms have fences along the river to keep the cows away from the water. I appreciated that. Those farms stood in contrast to the ones where there were cow-paths to the water. In some places we saw cows standing in the water along the banks. They made me wonder about the contamination level. I know there is concern for pollution in the river. I wanted to know if the farmers who had fenced off the river were doing it to protect the water or for other reasons. We never saw a farmer that we could ask, so the question still stands.

At Blackberry campsite, the landing was almost nonexistent. It consisted of goopy mud. After some struggling to unload the gear, Heather and I were in camp. With my sore back, I was unable to find a comfortable position at the table.

It was 8 pm when we finished dinner. I crawled into the tent and discovered the ground under the tent was anything but level. In an attempt to ease the discomfort in my back, I stretched and found myself rolling all over and doing unintentional summersaults. My efforts were very entertaining and I laughed out loud. Heather was curious about what I was doing, but I had a hard time explaining why it was so humorous to me. It occurred to me I'd only gotten five hours of sleep the night before, paddled 18.5 miles, (5 miles as the crow flys), and portaged with a sore back that day—I had done pretty darn good, all things considered. Mustering up some ingenuity, I stuffed clothes into the holes and dips in the ground under my mat, crawled into my sleeping bag and drifted off to sleep.

June 20, Sunday, Day 16

The day started with an adrenalin rush. We packed our gear. I carried my clothes and put the pack sack down on the riverbank on what I thought was solid ground. Because of the shoreline's tall grass I misjudge the edge of the bank. The pack sack teetered precariously for a few seconds and fell a few feet down the bank. It caught half way down and dangled at the edge of the water.

I jumped from the top of the bank to a narrow strip of solid ground yelling "Knox-Menards." I did not move quickly enough. Just as I landed on that sliver of earth, the pack sack rolled into the water beyond my reach. I felt a wave of panic as I anticipated it sinking. To my delight, it floated. I hopped into my kayak, keeping my eye on the pack sack, and was again delighted when the bag got tangled in a tree that had fallen into the water. I knew I would not have to race to catch it. I was easily able to retrieve it from the trees and put it safely into my cockpit. Heather found the entire incident quite entertaining.

With all of our gear safely stowed away we paddled under an open sky streaked with wispy clouds. The wind gusted, and was rarely at our backs. Sheltered by hardwood forest, we seldom paddled directly into

the wind. Instead we were able to enjoy the wind from a friendly perspective. This day it was keeping us cool and provided a opportunity for
birds to play. Hawks soared in the wind currents, and a mottled immature eagle flew near us. I delighted in imagining she was trying out her
wings for the first time.

As I paddled, I considered the wisdom of the gathering. The women
had spoken of nurturing friendships. I am one of those people who finds
herself so busy little time is left for friends and important things in life
such as nurturing my spirituality. I forget what my priorities really are and
what really feeds me. Yet when I make time I have experience deeply moving moments with other women that I have not had with men or in mixed
groups. Women are indeed lucky to have each other.

The women at the gathering also spoke of trusting yourself. Over time
I have come to trust my intuition, even though I don't always follow what
it suggests for my life. I know this trip is profoundly strengthening my
trust in my self and my intuition. I used to hide the wisdom my intuition
provided. I hid it because when ever I was asked how I knew something,
I could never come up with a satisfying answer. All I could say was *"I just
know."* My response was often followed by a question that requested refer-
ences on where I acquired my information. Because I could not name a
book or newspaper or any other source that would legitimize my information, I learned to dismiss my intuition. Now I trust my intuition, I value
it greatly. I now embrace what I once held at bay and in doing so have
reclaimed part of who I am.

Heather is good at claiming who she is and what she wants. She
considers all animals valuable beings on this planet. She wanted to photograph the turtles we have been seeing along the shore. So we stayed
alert searching for them. We spotted several, but like yesterday, they
wouldn't let us get close. They were gigantic—about two feet wide with

chunky legs and tails. I did photograph two sitting on a tree just before they scrambled into the water. One of them ended up in a large pile of branches. We watched as it frantically scrambled back over the log it had just left and awkwardly dove into the water. For being so large and clumsy they were able to move rather gracefully in the water.

The turtles reminded Heather of Douglas Wood's book, *Old Turtle*, and set her wondering about her passion for rivers. She wrote in her journal,

> *It's not without reason that I love rivers. Their steadfast determination to get where they are going and their unwavering confidence in where they have been gives me comfort.*

Heather described the river as gentle and winding like the St. Croix River where she grew up. Yet it was powerful with grass-lined banks and shores thick with mud. At one point she felt so overwhelmed with pleasure she yelled out for the world to hear, *"I am SO HAPPY!!"* I think I saw a couple of chipmunks on the bank cheering for her.

As we paddled past the hardwoods, I started to wonder if we were traveling with the same water every day. This is one of the many odd questions that passed through my mind. We were moving faster than the water, but we stopped each night. The water kept moving. So did it catch up to us? Did we start each day with the same water? Or did it silently flow past us while we slept? I'm afraid the latter is true but it's more fun to believe the same water is our daily companion. The water in this part of the river is murky brown from the muddy banks and bottom.

Continuous hours spent in a kayak encourage the mind to wander. Questions form about all kinds of things. Heather wrote down our questions at the end of each day: How long have the campsites been there? How often do they check them? How often do they update the map? What is Saint Peter the saint of? How did wood ticks and oxbows get their names? How do osprey and eagles land in trees while carrying fish in their talons?

Around a bend, we caught our first view of Swimming Bear campsite. The landing at this campsite was even more challenging than the last. We each chose a spot along shore that looked accessible to us. What we found was deep slippery mud. Snuggling my kayak up against shore and hanging on to some grass to keep from being swept away by the current, I scraped down enough mud from the bank to stand on with one foot. Then, grabbing the grass to keep me stable, I managed to eject myself from the kayak after several tries.

The next challenge was to unload the gear without sliding into the river

Swimming Bear Campsite

or letting the current take the kayak. I tied the kayak to a twig and prayed it would be strong enough. I was able to unpacked one of the storage compartments. Because of the curve in the bank I could not reach the other one. So I had to pull the kayak up the bank still bearing half its load. While I struggled with my mucky problem Heather was facing an identical challenge out of sight downstream. Occasionally I could hear her muttering.

Using all my strength I wrestled the kayak half way up the embankment. I was spent and stopped to rest for a moment. This was bad idea because the kayak slid back towards the river. Quickly grabbing it, I mustered the last of my energy and pulled it to solid level ground. My feet were caked with mud and I was done in. I laid in the grass for a moment thinking this still beats the midnight trains and other serenity disturbing elements of the Pokegema campsite.

Arriving at the top of the cliff I unloaded gear and set my things on the picnic table, which sat atop a mud bank. Heather and I were by the campsite's superb view of the river, and level ground for sleeping as well!. A busy little kingfisher chattered at us, flitting from one tree to another. She objected to our presence.

After dinner, a canoe approached, and we invited a father-daughter paddling team to join us. We assisted them in landing their canoe and unloading it. The daughter, Katie, wore a tie dyed tee shirt and a blue camouflage hat. She was 11. She and her family lived outside Chicago. Katie seemed

Katie

quiet, but her dark eyes watched Heather and me closely. I could see she had many questions, but was too shy or perhaps to exhausted to speak up. She gave us short answers to our questions. We learned that she played soccer and was going into the sixth grade. Her father, Pat, said they started their trip in Grand Rapids and planned to travel until Friday, when Katie's grandma would pick them up.

We cleared our things from half the table and they ate dinner. Katie just sat gazing at her food or stared off into the woods. Pat kept encouraging her to eat; she would take a couple more bites and drift off again. It was hard to tell if this was normal behavior for her or if fatigue was getting the better of her. Pat put up their tent while he continued to encourage Katie to eat.

Soon we were all in our tents looking forward to a night's rest. I could not sleep. I kept thinking about our food sitting out on the table and grew concerned that bears or raccoons would find it. Heather stirred so I knew she was awake. She told me she had a bad feeling about us not having hung our food safely in a tree as well. Attempting to be quiet so as to not disturb our camp mates, we hung it in a tree near our tent using Heather's mug as a weight to toss the rope. Miraculously though the handle stayed on. Her mug had traveled with her many times and has seen much better days; she had already reattached the handle three times.

June 21, Monday, Day 17

I woke up remembering how, as a child, I was afraid of the woods. The forest scared me because it was full of the unknown and I did not understand the creatures that lived in it. While living in Ely I took college courses that included hands-on learning and a great deal of fieldwork in the forest. As a result of that time, trees, flowers and animals became friends to me.

Since then summer solstice has also held more meaning. This year's solstice would be in four days. I see solstice as a celebration of the magic of nature. Is a time to stop and really take notice of how the earth supports us in so many ways.

We said good-bye to our campmates at 9:30 am. Pat and Katie planned to cover at least 30 miles that day. That pace would be challenging to keep on a daily basis. I felt it was too much for Katie. It appeared Pat could not see how tired Katie was or that she was not enjoying herself. The upside was that it is heart-warming to see a father and daughter doing something together.

Getting back in the kayaks was easier than getting out. Working together, we loaded them on shore and pushed them down the hill on the slick mud into the river. We climbed in and were on our way. We made better time than usual because the wind wasn't blowing us around. By 11:30 am we were at Jacobson campground, needing water and a nap. We quickly put up the tent and were fast asleep. I awoke to the sound of laughter as three maintenance women pounded a post into the ground nearby. I was tickled they were having such a good time.

From our picnic table I watched swallows dart and swoop in large numbers. They lived in hundreds of holes lining the top of the sandy cliff on which the campground sat. They were constant companions while we stayed at Jacobson campground. They offered a steady stream of entertainment and their chatter filled the air.

On a hike through the lush green woods I found four trees that looked as though they had been hula dancing, when Mother Nature yelled, "Freeze." They stood in a row and from every angle they all had the same twisty shape. I could not begin to imagine what could have caused their uniform contortions.

Back from my hike, I found Heather tucked under the tent vestibule out of the sudden drizzle cross-stitching. I went back to reading a delicious book, *The Secret Life of Bees*, by Sue Monk Kidd. It was a rich and sometimes mysterious story in which women supported each other through lives beset by personal trials. In an interview at the end of the book, the author said.

> *When women bond together in a community in such a way that "sisterhood" is created, it gives them an accepting and intimate forum to tell their stories and have them heard and validated by others. The community not only helps to heal their circumstance, but encourages them to grow into their larger destiny.*

Her words reminded me of the relationships and connections we were forging on this river journey.

June 22, Tuesday, Day 18

Each morning we listened to our weather radio. The voice delivering the information was nearly always the same woman. She had an odd way of saying "cloudy." The accent was placed on the first part of the word while the rest was drawn out and nasal. We had begun to mimic it in jest for our own entertainment. Today she indicated we would enjoy perfect weather. After another cold night we looked forward to summer's warmth—although not the blazing heat that will come with it. Summer wasn't all I was wishing for. Doug was on my mind.

I found myself staying busy around camp and wondered if busyness was how I avoided a familiar yet unidentified yearning nudging me subconsciously. That question reoccurred throughout the day.

On the water, we paddled past trees sticking out of the water like a scene in a creepy movie. They made me think of sea monsters or dragons trying to break free, reaching for air before they went down for the last time. The silvery gray branches of some of those trees seemed to be reaching for us. We stayed clear. If we ended up tangled in them there would be no escape. The roots of one large basswood were stripped clean of dirt and wrapped back around into the bank under the trunk. Though over half of the roots were exposed, the branches flourished. Clearly this tree had been dealing with the river for many generations.

There were random stairways on the bank that from our perspective seemed to go nowhere. We could only assume there was a house or a cabin on top of the bank. Most of the stairs appeared to be levitating, not quite reaching the top of the bank, and well above the water level. We did not see how they were anchored to the slope.

Ten eagles graced the sky, two of them immature. It was a day for birds: hawks, orioles, robins, ravens, and a host of others. Sandpipers perched on the outermost branches of trees down in the water. They danced when we approached and flew away squawking, skimming the river's surface. Wispy clouds raced high then evolved to billowing white mountainous clouds reaching upwards thousands of feet. Over lunch we watched as the sun's blaze turned the clouds a brilliant white in a vivid blue sky.

The headwind we had experienced since we started our day became challenging. We hit patches of rain and stretches of river choppy with white caps. We felt exhausted but exhilarated by the chance to kayak in challenging conditions. Around each corner, we'd find a bit of refuge out of the wind. Exhilaration soon began to turn to defeat and I had a choice

Women's Wisdom

Thoughts on Men

I think it is real important to value men as well as women and to have that balance and sharing back and forth. Neither one is more powerful than the other. We each have our own strengths. —Peggy

My grandma Ruth used to say, *"Well honey, those men they just don't know how to think. They try and they do a lot of things really well. They are really good at what they do. But the thinking thing is just confusing. They ask you a lot and you just have to help them."* —Gretchen

The only other person who can understand a woman is a woman. That other side, 'them" guys, they can't get it, they don't get it. We are strong and we have had to go through a lot. —Sharon W.

The men need to organize. They need to start walking beside us or a step ahead of us and start protecting us. Men are the leaders while we are in the community doing the work. We are right where we are. It is beautiful. There is no reason why we can't be successful. It is about attitude about self. We have to start talking a different talk before things will change. There are more women willing to give of their time to make the sacrifices. As for the men, we will keep asking them to walk with us. —Elaine

It is a whole different kind of living when we share with each other. I don't like the *"which side is better"* competition thing at all. I sure would not want to get rid of one or the other. Not just one sex can prevail. —Gretchen

The BaHi faith says that men and women are two wings of a bird. You can't fly with one wing. It has to be balanced. —Amy to make. I could let defeat become the driving force of my experience or I could consciously choose a different frame of mind. I choose to see the oncoming waves as an adventure. As we rounded a bend and headed into them I psyched myself up and yelled, *"YES! Here we go!"*

I grinned, hearing Heather sing, almost yelling, when the waves grew high, but I couldn't make out the words because of the wind in my ears. She sang softly as she bounded along in the quieter water. Once, she stopped, cocked her head to one side and then started again with a new song. Heather's singing was one of the ways I was able to determine what her mood was. When she was frustrated she got particularly loud. Keeping an accurate melodic line was no longer a priority.

Paddling parallel to each other, Heather told me she created fantasy stories when she was on a trip like this. Her stories included important people in her life and were generally some kind of adventure. I asked her if I could be in one of her fantasy adventure stories and she said, "Not with that hat on." I was wearing a light blue cloth hat with a wide floppy brim, and it had a wide band of black mesh. I agreed it was not flattering or fun but it served my purpose of keeping the sun out of my face and my head cool. Without another word she laughed and paddled on ahead of me.

We came to a spot in the river called a "riffle." At first I thought the map said "rifle" and wondered if it was a warning and thought of the movie *Deliverance.* A riffle is a section of the river where a man made walls are constructed out of large rocks to form a V. The V directs the water into a narrow chute designed to control erosion. We sped down the V and the water swirled around us, much like in a rapids. Being so close to the water in a kayak I saw for the first time that there are places in the river where the water dips below the water level. This astonished me. I thought the water level was basically the same, except perhaps where it goes over rocks and logs. The dips in the water were nothing new to Heather. She looked at me as if to way, "What did you expect? That is how water works."

At MS Keto campsite we were thrilled when we found easy access and a lush forest of mixed hard and softwoods. Tall ferns rimmed the site, lined the path to the latrine and covered the forest floor for as far as we could see. Sprinkled among the ferns were columbine blooming in bright red and yellow. The colors were vivid, and the woods full of life. We were surrounded by hundreds of tiny birds, each with a bright chirp or gentle twitter. Walking the path to the "outhouse" was magical.

Down the path was one particular tree stump which Heather and I found intriguing. It was large; time and weather had hollowed it out. There

Women's Wisdom

Survivors

I was diagnosed with breast cancer and my whole life fell apart. I lost a breast and I thought I was losing my life. Every time I had an ache or a pain I would call Mayo (Clinic) and I say, "I am on my way down." I figured I was dying . . . and I died for five years. Now I am still alive! One thing I have discovered is that today is the most precious commodity you could have. It is not always over the next hill. It is right now. It is right in your own back yard, or at your own kitchen table. You don't have to go anywhere. —Sandy

When you face your mortality and realize you are transient on this earth, that you are only here for a split second and that split second is staring you in the face, it is quite a realization. There are no guarantees in this life. That is what the cancer experience does. —Sally

You eliminate real quick what is not important. And my life was littered with things that were not important. —Terry B.

I am 59, almost 60, and a cancer survivor. Getting through cancer makes you realize and appreciate every single day you have on this earth. That is why I enjoy things like the greenery. I enjoy life even though it is raining. In the winter I just love to cross country ski, while my husband is complaining about the cold. I don't care because it is nice to be alive. It is nice to have the chance to see things. I just appreciate life. Everyday is special. —Melanie

I worked in hospice for a while. The people I saw who had floated through life unfocused were the ones with the most regrets. The ones who had been out there doing things were the ones with the most memories and seemed to be at peace with the end. —Nancy S.

The first week in November I was told I had gastric cancer. I am so eternally grateful I had those challenging experiences behind me that gave me strong faith through all the crises. To face this one stronger than I had ever been before was awesome. So today when something tough comes up I always say, "There I grow again." I don't look at tough times or crisis as a bad thing. I just don't! I just look at it as I am going to learn. I am going to be a better person. I am going to be able to help others. —Bonnie

MS Keto Campsite

was a hole at the bottom where once critters had made a home. A pink and yellow blooming columbine graced the entrance. Soft green ferns and moss grew in and around it. It was a perfect fairy or gnome house, and I knew it would end up in one of Heather's stories.

Remembering what Heather had said about my hat on the river I picked some bright green ostrich fern and carefully wove a hat, placed it on my head and emerged from the woods and asked, "Can I be in your stories now?" She burst into laughter.

As I drifted off to sleep that night I realized I had not come any closer to the answer to my yearning.

June 23, Wednesday, Day 19

We crawled out of our sleeping bags early to beat the wind and we succeeded. We were on the water before 7 am. It was a quiet day, which provided us with an opportunity to talk. Heather was reluctant at first, but opened up. We talked about relationships and commitment. We talked about how many people avoid commitment because of fear of the loss of freedom or loss of self. For women commitment has meant, *"How much of me do I have to give up to be with you?"* Although the focus was a theo-

Women's Wisdom

I am 52, I think. The biggest piece of wisdom I have, and have actually said to people is this: "You have survived everything that has happened to you to get where you are, so there is nothing that can happen that you are not going to get through." Some days it doesn't seem that way. Sometimes those days are all strung together in a row. Basically my strength comes from within. The truer I have been to that, the more I have been able to be of good to other people. —Ronnie

Parenting

I have a plaque on my kitchen wall that my day care kids made me 18 years ago. It is a piece of cardboard that says, *"I promise to be a kid and just have fun."* They wanted to do the pledge every day, so that is the way we start our day. I still live by that. —Mary G.

I want to share the only advice my mother gave me when I had children. She said, *"It is your job to raise them to be independent and accountable for what they do. Nothing else. So if they grow up and move on and do their thing, you have done your job."* But I keep telling my kids they owe me nine months carrying charge. My mother said we shouldn't expect a lot back from our children. If they give it, great. If they are happy with who they are and successful with their family, then you have done your job. Look at animals; they keep their babies a year and then, Bye! Sometimes that would be nice. —Mary G.

I hear this from so many of my contemporaries. Most of my friends are in their late 70s or 80s. When I hear these people say *"I spent all those years raising my children and now look what they give me. Not enough."* Nobody is happy with what their children do or give them. I am sick of hearing it. I guess that is mean of me to say because we all have to share our feelings about our families and our children. But I think too many parents put expectations on their children. When they are 18 they say *"I want you to go to college and become a dentist or I want you to go to trade school and become a mechanic."* And the children don't want to do that.

When we get older and our children are grown up and independent of us we still shouldn't put any expectations on them. I know that hurts a lot of people who are alone. Ultimately many of us women are alone retical discussion, I knew it was very personal for Heather. Because her boyfriend is my son, Wade, I let her take the lead and stayed neutral. Our family had already decided we liked Heather and wanted her to become a permanent member. But the ultimate decision was up to her and Wade. It was important to not to meddle in any way, so I chose my words carefully. When the conversation ended I was not sure I had been any help. She paddled off ahead of me, a very thoughtful look on her face.

That stretch of river was peaceful and easy to maneuver. We had plenty of time to get to our day's destination. Idly I stroked my paddle. Suddenly to my left up popped an otter just a few inches from my paddle! I was startled and so was she. She began snarling at me and chattering in a way I did not know otters could chatter. I felt threatened being close to her and wondered if she would attack. Heather, a few yards away, looked on with a mixture of amusement and concern. Just ahead of her were two more otters bob-bing in the water watching the spectacle. I was prepared to use my paddle to defend myself when the otter arched her back and quickly disappeared under the surface of the water. Both Heather and I floated until we saw all three otters together. They watched us for a few moments more and disappeared into the water. I breathed a sigh of relief.

Five hours after we started, we turned left into the channel from the Mississippi river to the Sandy Lake Recreation Area. We arrived at the boat launch just as a storm rolled in producing several hours of cold rain.

We could not get to the showers fast enough to wash off the stench we knew we carried but could no longer smell. Arriving at the shower building we discovered it was called the *Comfort Station*. We found the name quite humorous. Naomi arrived, vigilant in her duty as support crew. She tracked us down at the comfort station to see if we were okay. Apparently we had been gone an exceptionally long time. While we finished washing up we had a great time telling her about the day's wildlife count: ten bald eagles, a mink/weasel, muskrat, deer, kingfisher, raccoons, crows and giant turtles. As we shared our wildlife count we watched as a snapping turtle laboriously dug a hole next to the parking lot and then laid eggs near our campsite.

Naomi brought a stack of fun mail, a CD and a newspaper article about us for Heather. I got nothing. I felt pangs of jealousy and envy. Even though Jo sent special candy for both of us, I felt left out. Naomi and Heather fell into their usual comfortable conversation and my sense of or have been alone at one time. Once we reached our senior years it would be nice if all those kids lived down the street in a little house with a white picket fence, but they don't. I have a child I don't hear from for months. But I have let go of that because that is where he is. I know he would be there for me if I needed him. I have other children that can't go by a day without emailing and talking to me. Sometimes I think, "Can't you just leave me alone for one day?" —Sandra

Finding Your Voice

What I saw and experienced was all I had to direct my life. It was my reality. It was a very limited perception of what life is, so I walked into a life of abuse. I thought to be strong I shouldn't talk. I didn't have a voice. I thought to be a strong woman I had to keep my mouth shut, take the beating and go on with life the next day. Then I found my voice and it stopped. —Barbara

Women speaking up is what we need to get the balance back in this world. —Mary O.

I was shy when I was in school and I ended up in an abusive marriage for 20 years. I have five boys. I remember when someone would ask me what I wanted or what I thought, I felt like I did not have anything to say. Because for 20 years I was never allowed to say what I thought, I basically stopped thinking and kept it all inside. Then when I found my voice I was a chatterbox. —Peggy

In groups I was so full of fear because it was going to be my turn to talk. When I finally got to talk it was about crying. So I went to that group, I worked at talking and I did my crying. Then I knew I needed to listen. I knew I needed to really listen to everybody. So every time I made myself sit so I would have to listen and wait to talk. That was a hard thing to do because now I wanted to talk. —Elaine

I am an immigrant and have come from a long line of male dominated women. My journey has been finding my own voice. It has taken a long time. I encourage young women to not be afraid, to be who they are and speak their truth. —Ana isolation rose up again like a fog. What I was meant to learn from this feeling? I may understand it intellectually, but that did not help.

I chose to do what I often do when challenged—something practical. I crawled atop the Jeep where we had strapped the kayaks and began to clean the mud from my kayak. It made sense to me. I was wearing my rain gear and the rain was providing me with a constant flow of water for cleaning. Heather and Naomi were laughing openly at me, but praying I would not slip on the wet Jeep.

Later the rain stopped and I went for a short hike on one of the trails at the campground. The trail was well groomed, as was much of the forest here. On my hike I thought about the hours I have spent watching TV. A wave of sadness washed over me. Television sucks up so much time and energy with no real value in return. Maybe I could justify an educational channel, but that is not generally what I watched. Watching TV is an addiction. I watch even when the show does not interest me. I know going to change that behavior I will really have to put effort into it.

When I got back to camp I found the girls sharing a peach pit with a resident chipmunk. The woman camped next to us came over to visit. After a while I told her what we were doing and asked if I could interview her.

Norma was 70 and had worked hard most of her life. She struggled with severe arthritis. Jack, her husband of 48 years, had a neurological condition that left him crippled as well. She said they relied a great deal on each other. When I asked her how spirituality had influenced her life she responded,

Norma

Very much! I am a committed Christian. With all of the crazy things my husband and I have done I said, "Okay God, is this what you want me to do? If it is you got to help me through it." If you have faith the help is there. It's not about hearing voices. Sometimes, if I am supposed to do this, it works. If not, then I am not supposed to do it. Usually there is a clear answer.

She expressed concern for our river adventure and that the book I was to write would be just for women. She challenged me to keep the book balanced and not get into "man bashing." I could tell she felt quite strongly about it. I thanked her for her thought and assured her that if it were not for my husband, I wouldn't be making this trip. Her words reflect what I have heard from others. It seems that some people believe that to hold someone up or to empower them, (in this case women,) means you have

Women's Wisdom

When your spirit is dull from abuse or discrimination it is hard to speak. So you can't say "No" if a man is going to do something to you. You can't say "No" if someone is going to do something to your kids. You don't have those kinds of skills. Now my spirit is full. I feed it all of the time in different ways. But I have to acknowledge everything around me. I have to listen to other people and have those relationships with their spirits, to be inspired by them and everything else in creation. —Elaine

Women's Intuition

Praying and following the Native way for me has been nothing short of a miracle. I worked in Cass Lake and there were just so many things to do. I was trying to organize a family service center and there was a million things to do. I never knew which thing to do first. But if I stopped in the morning and put down my tobacco into the lake and said a prayer and followed my intuition, that day more miracles happened. I was at the right place at the right time with the right things happening. Maybe that is "going with the flow." For many years I was ruling the universe, pushing the universe. Now I say, "Just don't push the universe. Just let the universe push you around a little bit." That is where I am. —Peg

In thinking about spirituality and how it has affected my life, I think I have always been a deeply spiritual person. I have not necessarily linked that with any formalized religion because organized religion left me with some bad experiences and impressions of people. One of the things I have always done appears to be connected to the lives of my grandmothers. I have always known in my gut what needed to happen next. That is the path I have followed. I used to say the path with heart, but over the years I have realized it is my gut that knows if something is right or wrong. I don't necessarily know where the path is going to wind up, but I can intuit when it is time to make a change. I may not necessarily be comfortable with where that change is going to wind up. I have followed my gut and with few exceptions have been able to travel and flow with that kind of direction to my life. —Ronnie to knock someone down, (in this case men). But that is not how it works. When we empower each other and honor our differences, we all win and are stronger for it. I chose not to get into my theory on that subject with Norma, but assured her I would be respectful to both men and women.

June 24, Thursday, Day 20

We attempted to break camp early, but didn't get on the water until 8:30 am. We were protected from the wind, but paddled in the cold through patches of misty rain. At one point we stopped for a break. Heather got wedged half way out of her kayak and was stuck. She had so many layers of clothing, rain gear in addition to the life vest that inches were added to her size and she could not move. I decided turn about was fair play. I openly snickered for a while before assisting her. Not too much later the day turned sunny and we were reunited with our old friend, the wind. We made 20 miles in six hours, bringing our total mileage to 248.

On a break we stopped at Wold's Ferry Crossing. A marker at the site read,

Ed Wold Family operated a Ferry Boat at this site from 1910 to 1934. The charge was 50 cents for a team and 10 cents for passengers.

I looked across the river at that point and I found it odd to think they had to have a ferry. We now have many bridges crossing the river. A ferry seems cumbersome.

By 1:30 pm we were setting up camp at Berglund County Park. That peculiar campground dumbfounded us. It was flat, nearly bare of trees but was rich in posts. The posts outlined each campsite and its parking area. It looked like a telephone post graveyard. On one side of the park was the river and across the street were homes. Once camp was set up, I wrote letters and waited for my friends, the nuns, Sister Dorcas, Sister Letitia and Postulant Donna to arrive.

I had met Dorcas on an Outward Bound kayak trip in the Apostle Islands three years earlier. I met Sister Letitia and Donna when I went to visit Dorcas. These women were part of an Episcopalian religious order. They lived and worked in Mukwanago, Wisconsin at Mary's Margin, a small house of prayer, hospitality and retreat center overlooking the Fox River Valley outside Milwaukee, Wisconsin. The three of them had been excited to join us on our trip ever since they first heard about it, and were altering a trip to Canada to connect with us.

Looking up from my writing I spotted Heather tearing through every-

Women's Wisdom

Earlier in life I would have wanted to know I had more empowerment. To know the things women know *are* important! They may not be scientific or be able to be proved, but we have intuitive knowledge. Intuitive knowledge gets devalued in today's society. I don't think it was always like that. We can get back to our intuitive knowing. —Peggy

Following my intuition made a difference. Regrets I have heard from people are always about what they didn't do. Not for things they did do. There is something to learn from every experience. Always do the best you can and 99 percent of the time you are right. The other one percent of the time we don't know what we are doing.

I needed to trade in my car so I went with a friend to a car show. She said, *"I think you should get a purple pick-up truck."* I got a magazine that had all the truck accessories in it and I wrote down exactly what I wanted. I listed my accessories based on what I wanted—the essential down to "this would be really nice to have." I had my list complete and was meeting some friends to go bowling one night. At the stop light where Snelling and University cross there is a Chevrolet dealer about three blocks down. I decide to just drive by. I drove by and there was my truck sitting right on the end up on a platform. I thought, "Oh my God, what do I do now? I am sure it won't have everything I want." It had all fifteen items on my list! My first reaction was that I wanted to meet whoever put this package together. Then, "How am I ever going to pay for it?" But it all worked out. I wrote down what I wanted and followed my intuition and there it was. —JoAn

Women's intuition. Is it just intuition? Or is it our spirituality? Are getting messages? I call it intuition, but I think it is more than that. It is a greater spirituality in our life. Intuition seems quite simplistic. But when I review the things in my life that were born out of intuition and things that were just thought, the things based on intuition were much more adventurous and successful. The things that took a lot of deep thought became too complicated. —Debbie

Pay attention to that wee voice and that intuitive stuff. As a woman I think one of the biggest struggles for me has been self-trust because there are a lot of systems and people that make it difficult. They say, *"You don't feel that way."* We as women can help support each other by at least paying attention to others words and intuition. —Bonnie thing like a raging tornado to find lost her sunglasses. Naomi and I just watched. Our previous attempts to help her were fruitless and we had started to see these moments as entertaining.

Two guys from Chicago paddled up. They had heard about us from Reverend Dale. They planned to canoe the entire Mississippi in two weeks total. They had only two weeks of vacation and were determined they were going to make it. They ate lunch in town (Palisade), and headed out again. Their schedule demanded they push on without any rest or breaks. There was tension between and from them. The pace they had set for themselves was taking a toll. Already they had disagreed about when they would complete their trip. It was as if they were in a race they had to win. They were stunned when we told them we had planned 43 days for our trip—but then, ours was not about a conquest.

Naomi and Heather retrieved the mail. We had been using general delivery in Atkin, which was just a few miles away. I received a wonderful letter from Auntie Joyce, whose adventurous life helped inspire this trip. She wrote,

Dear Nancy and Water Women,

I like to refer to you all as Wonder Women! Enjoyed your newsletter and what gallant women you are. The wind and water can be daunting adversaries!

If nothing else, at my young age of almost 88, I've really learned not to sweat the small stuff. Really thankful for a good clean bed (as you must be) heat in the winter and air conditioning in the summer and plenty of food, good friends, wonderful family and a happy outlook! I'm thrilled every morning to see the daylight and it's got to be a great day! That has been a powerful force in my life—seen me through difficult times. I'm known to my fabulous doctors as "the comeback kid."

Enjoy each other and each day. Don't forget to tell your family and friends how much they mean to you and love them as I love you!

Happy Paddling, Auntie Joyce

I tucked her letter into my journal and carried it with me for the rest of the trip.

After the nuns arrived at 4 pm, we chatted for a while. Heather and Naomi headed to Aitkin for pizza. The rest of us took off for McGregor where the nuns would treat me to dinner and a bed in a motel. Riding in the car with these three was like being with three giddy schoolgirls. They talked non-stop and asked so many questions so quickly it was hard to keep up with them. They told me all about their traveling adventures. We

Women's Wisdom

I just turned 55 on the Fourth of July. I guess I didn't realize that 55 was going to be that big a deal. Fifty seemed okay. Fifty and free. Now I am free to do what I really want to do. But 55 has made me stop and think about what I really want to do in life. A year ago I quit my job. There was some land in our family. The land was sold so I had some money. I said, "I am going to take a year off." Up until that point I had spent over 30 years in an office doing accounting. So the year was up in May and I had to decide. I looked back. What did I do over that year and where am I going now? What am I going to do now?

Spirituality has always been a big part of my life. There are times when I have gone away from it, and then gone back to it. I was raised as a Lutheran and grew up on a farm. One of the things that I knew is that I didn't especially care for having to be a certain way and having to do certain things. The doctrine of it. So I was introduced to Buddhism and have been studying and following that path.

I am here this evening because I don't believe in coincidence. My friend Karen and I walk her dogs here all of the time. We normally walk them from 3 to 4 o'clock. Today we got done much later with the walk. Karen said she had to use the bathroom and that never happens. So I came over here with her and my greyhound, Kizzy. Heather was just walking by. She has worked with greyhounds. Heather invited me here tonight. Put all that together and that for me is part of my spirituality. There aren't any coincidences.

I am not comfortable going into new situations where I don't know anybody. But that is something I have become very aware of that I need to do. When things like Heather's invitation happen I need to go there. I need to be there for some reason. What spirituality means to me is being aware of what is going on around me in my surroundings and being willing to participate in it. That for me is a really big deal —participation. —JoAn

Choices

I was independent and I did as I damn well pleased. I set my course and I followed it. But it was the "speed bumps" that occurred in my life that created the challenges and the growth. That development made me a solid individual. You give yourself permission to be who you are. —Sally settled into our room at the Country Meadows Motel and went to dinner at the Fireside Lounge. The food tasted phenomenal. I savored the shrimp and honey almond chicken. Up to that point we had been eating pretty well, but nothing this good. The nun's questions continued, as did their stories about their travels.

Back at the room, I asked if I could interview them. Hesitantly they agreed. The looks on their faces told me they did not think they had anything worth sharing. When I asked them about spirituality they had some difficulty answering the question. Spirituality and religion were so integrated into their lives they couldn't get outside of it to describe its meaning. For them the experience was so personal; it didn't come from their intellects, it came from their hearts, from their very being.

Sisters Dorcas and Letitia had served the church together for many years. I saw them as living symbols of God's joy. They looked for the good in everything. I found their presence delightful and their faith inspiring. Donna, as a postulant in this order, eagerly awaited the time she would become a full-fledged nun.

Sr. Dorcas began,

I fell in love with God when I saw the movie, The Robe, at the age of 12. I knew then I wanted to do something for God. It set the direction of my life. I dreamt of becoming an itinerant missionary, carrying nothing but a knapsack and preaching from town to town like the Apostles. But the summer after I graduated from high school, my sister took me to see the movie, The Nun's Story. That did it. I wanted to be a nun. I wrote to six communities in the Episcopal Church and visited the 20 in the Chicago area where I lived, plus a convent in Kenosha, WI. I had had one quarter of college at the time, and the Mother Superior of the Kenosha convent told me to, "Finish college, dear." I stuck it out and knocked again. I was received as a postulant in Kenosha in April 1962 at the ripe old age of 21. The novitiate was easy for me—TOO easy. I wanted and expected it to be much tougher and I was disappointed. I heard no voices and saw no visions. But I said to God, "If this is where you want me, I'll stay. If not, let them not elect me to the profession." But I was elected and that two-way choice has shaped the rest of my life in ways I could never have dreamed.

The community has given me time and opportunity to grow in knowledge of myself and of God. Some of the learning has been very painful, some like a glorious sunrise after a night of storms.

Donna responded to the question of how she would advise young women,

Women's Wisdom

I have seen the benefits of taking risks. Now I consciously, once a week, I say I have to do something that is fearful for me. A couple of years ago I jumped out of a plane, which was major. I wouldn't do that one again. But for me something that can be just as fearful can be making a hard phone call or taking a step to do something that I have always wanted to do. I have learned over the years the benefit of taking risks so I consciously put it into my life to do weekly. —Deborah

I think a lot of people don't always know when they need help or are able to accept it. —Winnie

(Standing in a crowded mall) *"Of all these people in this whole area you are the only one like you,"* my sister said. I was feeling so insignificant and with one sentence she made me feel so special. I was at the right place at the right time with the right things happening. Now I say go with the flow. —Peg

Life doesn't get any easier you just keep getting better at it. —Gretchen's Grandmother

Spirituality & Religion

Spoken or unspoken, spirituality is important in our lives. For many people it eventually ends up being their quest—that thing that they are searching for. Unexpected things take us there. Often the worst things in our life completely change our lives. It is then we really reflect on what life is, what value we give it and *how we choose to live it*. That search for spirituality, wanting it to be the core of life is what I thought was supposed to happen. I got out in the world and found out not everybody starts out with that idea, or believes in that concept. I got a rude awakening. People treat each other with kindness—right? Not everybody has learned that. I have always felt I should do that. It is a good idea. —Rebecca

Spirituality, I decided it is intertwined with life. Our spirituality is always growing and changing. The more information, and the more differing information or diversity we gather the more it improves our own spirituality. Make it a habit to be more spiritual. —Debbie

Listen to your heart. But that is so difficult because of all the chatter. I want them to know there is no right or wrong. You can't screw it up. So go ahead and just do it. In the great scheme of things it will all work out.

Not only did I get to sleep in a real double-sized bed that night, it was a treat to talk with spiritual women my own age. I was renewed.

June 25, Friday, Day 21

On Friday morning, the nuns and I breakfasted together at the School House Cafe. As we arrived at camp we saw Heather, (who had lost her sunglasses again) parading around with the tent on her head. She refused to finish packing the tent in its bag until she was sure her sunglasses were not in it. When she heard us arrive she stood looking at us through the screen window of the tent. As Heather finished her fruitless search for her glasses, the girls told us they had had an exciting evening which included; a loud party down the street from camp, a big storm that had blown through, and laying with their heads sticking out of the tent eating left over pizza to gaze into the sky full of all the colors of the rainbow which often appear after a storm.

Heather also referred to *the biker guy* across the street who let her play with his yellow lab puppy while he worked on his car. The dog wasn't supposed to be in the campground, but Heather said she thought he could

Dorcas, Letitia, and Heather

Women's Wisdom

I believe the most important lesson in life is to *do unto others as you would have them do unto you.* In other words always be kind to yourself and to others. Our world would be at peace if we all practiced respect. I think the word *"respect"* is the most important word in any language. Respect and love starts with accepting who we are inside; who God created us to be as individuals. When we accept, respect and love ourselves, our inner light shines and lights the hearts of others. Love creates. Hate destroys. I believe God put us here because he loves us and he wants his love to manifest itself through us by taking care of one another with dignity and respect. —Lorrie

The night before my son left for the Marines we went over to a friend's house. They had fry bread, a traditional Indian dinner for him. They presented him with a feather and John said a prayer in Ojibwa. My son had no clue what he was saying because he did not understand the language. But it was a powerful feeling. I just never felt it in a church. It is just a good feeling. —Peg

I pray for my children because none of them are practicing the Catholic faith. To me and my husband it is important. Our one daughter, who has two children, goes to a different church. But I am happy that they are going somewhere every Sunday and getting some training. What I am disappointed in is our son, who goes sometimes, and our other daughter who thinks she can find God in nature. I can find God in nature too. I pray that they come to have some spiritual influence in their life. I pray for that rather than that they come to know the Lord Jesus Christ and have Him come to be a personal part of their life. They say this is such a Christian country. We are fighting for all those rights and freedom of religion. It is a shame people are tossing it aside and that it is not important. So many young people and their families do not go to any church or have any rules. It is more important to them to sleep in, or go to the lake, or mall-shopping, rather than focus on spirituality. And yet our whole country was founded on this premise. That is why people came over here—to have freedom of speech and religion. —Melanie

I don't understand the word stress. I don't understand where it comes from and why it has to exist, because when you have faith and you turn things over and you let them go there is no reason to have any stress. And that is how I lived every day of my life. —Agnes, Bonnie's Mother see how happy she was playing with the dog. She was missing her two dogs, Arrow and Rush, immensely. A dose of that yellow lab really helped.

The nuns helped us bring the gear to the river and gave us a send off. Dorcas and Letitia took turns helping Heather carry her kayak. Every time Letitia picked it up and started walking she took quick tiny steps accompanied by a long *"O-o-o-o-o-o-oh"* until she set it down again. She was determined to help, but the kayak was much heavier than she had expected. The nuns wanted to hear the song, so I sang it for them after we were set to leave. They were grateful to have shared a piece of this trip with us and waved to us as we pulled away. We looked for Naomi when we said goodbye but she was nowhere to be seen. Then we spotted her perched high up on a rusty railroad trellis that had been converted into a bike and walking trail. Grinning ear to ear, she waited with her camera to take an aerial picture of us as we passed under the bridge. The river had widened now to 170 feet across and was the color of a latte.

It was windy again on the water. Heather was particularly quiet—no singing. When I asked if she was okay she snapped at me, but tried to do it with humor. When we took a break I could feel tension in her. Once

Naomi on railroad trellis

we were back in our kayaks she took off down the river—fast. I tried to keep up at first, and then just let her go. Later she told me she realized she was angry at the wind and needed to blow off steam. I was tired of it, too. It wasn't only the waves the wind created that we had to deal with; we had begun to feel physically "beat up." The wind was constantly hitting us in the face and tugged at our hats. It pushed against the paddle blade that

Women's Wisdom

My spirituality stirs within me. It causes me to strive to pay attention to the movement within me, to recognize *consolation* and *desolation* as part of life, part of the onion peeling process. It connects me with all of creation. I love the saying, *"The better I get to know God, the better I get to know myself. The better I know myself the better I know God."* I think that takes a lifetime. If you live a long time that means you needed it. —Millie

I am 65 and my spirituality has been a very strong influence in my life. I was raised Episcopalian. However I kept thinking there had to be more to it than books and people telling me how to believe. I was a farm girl and I knew there were cycles to life. I put that in the back of my head. Then some where after my teen age years I became interested in astrology. The science of cycles and the planets. I am a practicing astrologer along with being a nurse. I have gone more to the earth-based spirituality because that fits my needs and has for the past 25 or 30 years. —Shaughn

Spirituality—The word is obscure for me—not something that can be explained easily. However, when I realized that religion and spirituality were two different things—it was an important turning point for me. I began to be more appreciative of the world and people, able to see the big picture, relaxed and peaceful, more adventurous, happier. My heart and soul have never stirred in a church or through some religious ritual as they have while walking through the woods, sitting by the water, collecting rocks, building a fire, or with a good laugh. Today, I feel closer to God than I ever have and I thank her constantly. —Kathryn

When you reach a point when you don't really know what tomorrow will bring, or life as you knew it is no longer, it is quite an astounding thing. What it does is to draw on your spirituality to again ask for strength to continue to be who you are, the best you can be, for the time that you have. —Sally

The bigger piece is to have that inner strength that you get when you have a sense of something greater than yourself. I truly don't think it has to be Christian. I think it can be Buddhist or whatever, I just think it has to be something. If you have that relationship with God you can do it. There will be things that are so big in life that you need that relationship in order to get through. —Jan was above the water and created resistance. The endless wind had taken a toll, mentally and physically.

My mind drifted back to a news update Naomi had given us about the beheadings happening in Iraq. I couldn't seem to wrap my brain around the fact that I was surrounded day after day with peace and serenity. Yet in another part of the world there was such violence. I was deeply disheartened by what we humans do to each other and could not find the words to express it. I wondered what had happened in those people's lives that they became so violent. That violence had to be born out of a deep pain I cannot relate to. I cannot begin to imagine, even in my worst hours, living in a war zone as so many people do. I felt hollow and helpless. Guilt rose to the surface as I considered the trifle issues Americans become so indignant over.

I thought about the similarities between Norma who I had interviewed back at Big Sandy Campground and the nuns. Each had found Christianity to be a powerful base from which to lead their lives. They found strength leaning into it. Each was dedicated to serving God and others and each was married for life. Dorcas, Letitia and Donna to Christ and Norma to her husband, Jack. Their clarity about the purpose of their lives was out of the ordinary.

At noon Naomi met us at the Waldeck Public Boat Access, where we packed everything into the Jeep. While we packed, Heather jumped up on top of the Jeep and sat in the kayak putting extra gear in any available space. Each time a car drove by she struck a pose and began to do the parade wave to the passing car. I am not sure what the people in the passing cars thought, but Naomi and I thought it was hilarious.

When every possible open space was packed, Heather came down from atop the Jeep and squeezed herself into the remaining space in the back seat, between the paddles and the tents. It's a good thing she is small. Packing the Jeep and leaving enough room for all three of us to ride was like setting up a clown car. We stuffed in more than a person might think was possible. Like a typical clown car

Women's Wisdom

Use your heart in your life. Be humble. Be grateful for all the simple things. What I find is that the people that are humble are the strong ones. That is where the riches in this physical life lie. Be thankful for the things the creator gave us because there isn't anything that is man-made, especially spirituality. —Barbara

Be careful what you pray for you. Be very specific in the tiny details concerning what you ask for. The details are important. If you pray to not be so angry or to have patience, know that you are going to get a lot of opportunities to practice that particular request. You will have lots of opportunities to see how strong you are and how much progress you have made in that area, or non progress if there is such a thing. —JoAn

I had a neighbor who came over about a week ago and said, *"Do you believe in your guardian angel?"* I said, "Yes my guardian angel has saved me many times." He said, *"Do you know the name of your guardian angel?"* I said, "No. How would I know that?" He said, *"Well have you prayed about it? If you go to bed and pray asking to know the name of your guardian angel it will come to you."* Well, I tried that and when I woke up in the morning the name Francis came to me. That would not be a name I would ever think about, so my guardian angel back here [pointing over her shoulder] is named Francis. —Alice

My personal spirituality believes that there is a plan in my life for me which is unfolding as I live it. When I look back I can see it. I am trying to let God do the controlling. I know that I can't just sit by and do nothing. He expects me to do something. Through recovery I have learned that you live a day at a time and in the present moment because that is all I have and all I need. It is okay. I know I have faith that God's Will will be done. If I am supposed to be around here I will be. I will use the experience to be a better person and to help others. —Bonnie

I think I have a spirit and that spirit is the core that defines who I am today. Sometimes your world comes crashing down on you. Things happen to us in life that change us. God doesn't have a plan for us; we are the ones that are in charge of our own plans. God only gives us permission to do the things that make us who we are. —Sandra comedy routine, when we stopped and opened a door something dumped out—every time! People at campsites watched in quiet amusement as we continued to take more and more gear out of the Jeep. From a distance it looked rather chaotic. To some extent it was, but Naomi had it under control. She knew where everything was at all times—with the exception of Heather's sunglasses! Naomi refused to take any responsibility for them. When Naomi took over this job (from Doug,) she became territorial. When we tried to help, she'd sternly say, "Just step away from the Jeep." Most of the time she couldn't see out the windows past the gear, but only once did she back into a post and dent the bumper.

Heather's spot in the Jeep

From Waldeck's we headed back to Sandy Lake where we had been just two days ago to meet Doug, my son Wade, my brothers, Mark, Mike, Brian, Bruce, Gary and David, and several nephews. The guys were having a boy's weekend and we were about to crash it. We wanted to surprise Wade for his birthday. Just the thought of seeing Wade lifted Heather's spirits. Wade was all she could talk about while we paddled. I was excited to see Doug who helped set up the surprise meeting for Wade.

We got to Sandy Lake before the guys arrived, took showers at the comfort station, hid on the south side of the park, and waited. Suddenly there were Doug and Wade with Heather. They found her while she was on the phone, which surprised both her and Wade. We helped them find their campsite and set up. It was wonderful to spend time with my husband, who was affectionate and attentive.

My brothers began to arrive. All had stories to tell about difficulties on the journey to the boy's getaway. The people at the campground desk had told Brian we were not registered here. So he drove to various other camps for two hours. Eventually he came back to scout all the sites here until he found us. Others had flat tires or trouble locating the camp.

We spent the evening sitting around a fire talking, laughing and eating. Bruce surprised Wade with a birthday cake decorated with 29 plastic toys, one for each year of life.

During the evening Doug and I slipped away to our tent for some intimate moments and a nap.

Women's Wisdom

For me, spirituality is about the universe providing. Put out there what you want. It may not come in exactly the way you think it is going to come. That is not our job; our job is to put in our request. It is like my mentor, Carol, says, *"So you go into a restaurant and you put in an order. Do you go back to the kitchen and watch to see if they are making it right or not and tell them what to put in there? Or do you put in your order and wait for your food to be delivered? You receive your food as you ordered it. So put in your order to the universe. It will be supplied in one way or another. Maybe not today, maybe not tomorrow. But as long as you hold that vision it is headed toward you. Then be willing to receive it when it comes."* —JoAn

Really enjoy the moment. I believe we make plans for our lives. God laughs. You need to really enjoy where you are in the moment; go with that flow when it comes because there might be another plan for you. —Deborah

It seems like I was always in this world, (the Native American world) and still in the white society. So when we were on the reservations I remember a lot of ceremonies there. Then when we moved to church school where we had to study the catechism it was okay. To this day when you talk about spirituality I can accept anybody's concept of what spirituality is. I believe a lot. I have learned a lot from both. It's not which way is right or wrong. I think you gain a lot from what ever your personal beliefs are. I know I am lucky that I have a knowing about both the Native American practices as well as my father's Christian practices. —Sharon F.

Nature was the umbilical cord that kept me connected to beauty and truth. Marrying and having children taught me patience and love. Loss taught me acceptance. My spirituality strengthened. Life influences my spirituality and spirituality my life. They are not separated. —Susan

As an adult I think there is a myriad of problems in the Catholic Church as an institution. There is no way I could begin to defend the Catholic Church in an argument with someone that is down on it. Personally I am getting some of my strength from that denomination. But I would definitely tell my kids all I know about it. I want them to be men and women of God and to know God. I want them to think of turning for some spiritual guidance when they make decisions in life

June 26, Saturday, Day 22

I woke, was out of the tent by 5:30 am, and on my way to the water to sing and make an offering for the gathering to be held that evening. As I finished, I saw Wade, and my nephews, Mark Jr. and Nick heading out to go fishing. They were shadows as they moved through the morning mist and soon disappeared into the center of the lake.

Back in the tent, I fell back to sleep with Doug's arms around me. There was no safer place on earth. I was reminded of Elaine's wisdom at the Leech Lake gathering.

We need the men to protect us while we do our work.

My brothers are generous a group of men with good humor that makes me want to be with them all the time. By 9 am the sounds of my brothers starting the fire and rustling up breakfast enticed us out of our tent. Bruce treated us to one of his famous potato and egg concoctions. Wade and the boys fried up the fresh fish they had just caught. What a delicious treat! Good food and even better company.

Heather's father, Ted, arrived as did her sister, Christina. Ted was very excited about the trip. The concept of women stepping forward in the world thrilled him. He is a philosophical man who loves his daughters deeply and was delighted to assist in any way he could. He and Wade spent a good deal of time chopping firewood for us.

After some effort we gathered everyone together and took a picture. Several of us headed to the dock to see Dad's old fishing boat that Brian had brought up. I was surprised to see it because I thought Dad sold it with the cabin on Lake Clitheral in northwestern Minnesota. Brian and Bruce had replaced the seats and restored it. It looked great. I spent a lot of time in that boat as a child fishing. We said goodbye to the guys as they all headed out fishing. Naomi, Heather, Christina, Ted and I headed to the outskirts of Aitkin to the Mississippi River Campground to set up for the gathering.

The campground is on the bank of the river which stretches 200 ft. across here, 288 miles downstream from our starting point. It is quiet here with only distant sounds of traffic. We set up for the gathering. Ted headed to his camp so he would not disturb us. A little after 7 pm a car pulled in bearing a reporter named Ann from *The Aitkin Independent Age* newspaper. After she said hello she apologized that an email glitch had prevented her from promoting the gathering. With that news, we anticipated that no one would come. She quickly interviewed us, took photographs, said she would write about the gathering, and drove off.

Women's Wisdom

that are big. I feel it is comfortable for me to ask them, "Where are you at with your God?" And if they don't want to talk about it that is okay. But it is okay for me to ask.

As a teacher, a mother and a community elder you want to help young people have the tools that they need to get through life. You want them to have education to be literate and to know how to get along with people. To me, the bigger piece is to have that inner strength that you get when you have a sense of something greater than you. I truly don't think it has to be Christian. It can be Buddhist or whatever. It just has to be something. If you don't have a relationship with God then you could just fall apart. It is our responsibility as loving people in the world to give that to young people too. There is a piece of me that has to put the responsibility back on myself instead of pointing at a 22-year-old that is not going to church and saying he or she is terrible. Instead, what did I not do or what could I do to help them to see the tremendous impact that spirituality can have in their lives? And I think it is okay for me to share my journey (which I am still on) with them. —Jan

When we pray we are always taught to be grateful first. To have balance in life you have to be grateful first so that later on if you have to ask for something you can do that. —Elaine

I never really thought I was a spiritual person until somebody told me I was. I was raised Catholic so I thought spirituality was the Father, the Son and the Holy Ghost. There wasn't really anything beyond that. It wasn't until I heard a song on the radio about glory in the meeting house, glory in the fields and I said, "Oh yeah, that would be me out in the fields." —Terry O.

If you feel as if you can make up your own mind about things then you, well at least, I was more inclined to reject religion. I found it to be very restrictive. I think more in terms of spirituality, which I would define as my relationship with everything. Religion never did that for me. What spirituality did was broaden the choices I had. I didn't have to go by the 10 rules unless they really suited me. I got to examine them that way. Put your paddles into spirituality. —Vi

We were about to invite Ted to join us when two women drove in. Amy and Weezie were charming. We had a wonderful time with them. They wrote a small press magazine called *Homespun*, which highlighted women's creativity. They distributed their magazine all over the country. They interviewed us and took photos for the magazine. Then we tuned the tables on them and asked our gathering questions. The theme from this gathering turned out to be: *Don't be afraid to take the chances that are offered you.* Amy shared,

I guess I have always been a seeker and have looked for the truth in every philosophy without limiting myself to, "Oh I am sorry, that idea is out of bounds." A few years ago I became a Baha'i. It's a universal world faith that recognizes the wisdom of all the world's teachers. One of my heroes is the Dalai Lama, because he can laugh. So, I think spirituality is kind of an evolving thing where you discover more about yourself and about the world around you. Religion is a really narrow box. Spirituality is the big picture. Spirituality is how you address all aspects of everything around you.

As for the river of life . . . you know there are times when you think you are going upstream when you are really going downstream. You are getting hung up on sand bars and tangled in tree limbs and capsizing a few times. When I was 14, I thought I was going to be a veterinarian, so I worked in an animal hospital as a volunteer, which meant I cleaned cages.

Then I decided I was going to go into elementary education. I went to a two-year college in Missouri, then on to Madison, [University of Wisconsin] because it was the most radical school I could find in the reciprocity program with Minnesota. I dropped out eventually, mostly because I wanted to be making a difference in people's lives. That was my path. School just seemed to be getting in the way.

I answered an ad in the back of the Mother Earth News *and was hired by an outdoor education center in upstate New York. In addition to forest ecology, we taught colonial crafts like tin smithing and candle making. I taught these little kids from Brooklyn and Long Island how to make fire pokers in blacksmith shop. So there was probably a gang of little kids running around New York with fire pokers. It was a really cool program for these kids who had never been out of the city, who had never seen a cow, let alone milked a cow.*

Life is what happens while you are making other plans. (Amy quoted a familiar phrase.) I went back to Madison, worked for an underground newspaper, called Take Over, *and drove a truck delivering comic books and magazines to all the head shops and comic book distributors in Madison and Milwaukee.*

Women's Wisdom

When I talk about higher power, I take on a very personal relationship with it. I say today that this relationship is one I never would have gotten in church. Church is a community I want to be involved with, but I don't believe my spirituality could ever have grown without some of the tough times I have gone through—knocking my head against the wall enough times to start listening to something. —Bonnie

I had it explained to me that we all have our own spiritual journey and religion is there to support it. Religion is man-made, but our spiritual journey goes to the core. There can be other things that support our spiritual journey, whether it is prayer, whether it is communion with the out of doors, or the fellowship of others. It is like a map. I think things get messed up when you make religion and spirituality one and the same. If you can keep them separate and have the one support the other life can be very rich. —Nancy R.

I don't think I ever knew what spirituality or a spirit was until I got pretty old. I don't think I was connected to that part of me, but I do feel connected to my spirit now. I know that I have a spirit within me. I can't define it, but I think I have a spirit, is the core of which defines who I am today. I think I have always believed in a higher power. I have believed in God. I was raised a Christian, but I never really thought about spirituality and what that was, the spirit within us. But I have done enough reading and joined enough discussion groups to realize our sprit is the outward showing of us as a person. That is how I define it. This may sound egotistical, but I think I am full of spirituality. I think I know where it comes from. It comes from my heart and inner beliefs which make me a person that is complete. —Sandra

I think spirituality is an evolving thing where you discover more about yourself and about the world around you. Religion is this really narrow box and spirituality is the big picture. It is about how you address all aspects of everything around you. I think religion often gets in the way of spirituality. The importance of being receptive, of not limiting yourselves is what gets us back to spirituality. It gives us the ability to be an open, receptive force and pull everything in. We live in such discouraging times right now; you have to focus on people who are doing really good things and glean that positive energy. It is just too easy to get sucked into the negative. —Amy

Then, I moved to my parents' place on Bay Lake. I was the first person to live there year 'round. I stayed for two years. My grandparents built the place in 1938. It was a good decision because it forced me to be by myself, to not depend on other people, and to listen to my own voice.

Then I got a job at a newspaper in 1978. Unfortunately I am still there. So now, for my fiftieth birthday, I am quitting my fricking job. I have to do this. It's really scary because you get addicted to a regular paycheck and to having health insurance. But, I can't do the eight-to-five anymore.

No, I didn't follow the path I expected. But I think life has been more interesting than if I had. If I had gotten my education degree and taken a job as a teacher, I probably would still be waiting for retirement. I guess the idea is to be open to what comes your way and to know when enough is enough. We talked about the metaphor about painting with watercolors—it is all about knowing when to stop. If you don't know when to stop you can turn the entire piece of work into a muddy mess.

Having such a small group gave us more time to talk, reflect and connect. I felt I could relax and did not feel the pressure to keep things moving. Everyone had a delightful experience.

After Amy and Weezie left I noticed the wind had abated. Ted joined us at the fire, and the five of us relaxed. The girls were afraid I was disappointed about the low turnout. I reassured them that I trusted everything had worked just the way it was supposed to. If the women wrote about us in their magazine, that evening could turn out to be the biggest gathering of all.

June 27, Sunday, Day 23

At times, a woman's body and camping do not mix. A menopausal woman whose period resembles a flash flood is one of these times. During the nearly sleepless night, my period came, and blood soaked into my clothes and bedding. I tried to clean up without waking Naomi. Despite the rain tapping on the tent, I trudged to the outhouse.

I woke to find I'd done a poor job of cleaning up in the dark. Immediately my mood turned foul. Naomi woke, looked concerned and asked if I was okay. Not wanting to get into details I told her everything was fine. "Okay," she said hesitantly, then dressed and left the tent. I faced the challenge of managing my heavy flow while sitting in a kayak. I was grateful I'd get my period only once on the trip and decided I wouldn't let my mood ruin the day for me or for the group.

Women's Wisdom

When I feel out of sorts and unbalanced I know if I go into the woods everything is right. I can just step on that ground and the path is right there. What ever is going on becomes right. —Peggy

I have tried different churches. I have tried different groups and I have yet to find one where I can totally be who I am. I am the person who throws out *off remarks* here and there. What I find is that people are trying to compete with each other. They compare and judge. To me that is not what it is about. When it comes to organized religion I can't deal with the negativity found in the churches. I had one woman say, *"I would have thought you were a Christian if I didn't know you grew up Catholic."* Evidently I am knowledgeable, but came from the wrong place. How can you judge the depth of somebody's religion because they don't go to the same building? I know I am very spiritual. As a matter of fact, I have a date with God the week after I get home. We are going to meet at a Caribou [Coffee Shop]. He is going to sit down and explain to me why I have gone through these last nine years. For six months I told him I hated him. What are you doing to me? Why is this happening? And then I came to grips with things and I said, "Let's sit down with a cup of coffee and you can explain things to me. I will not question it until then because I was told never question what happens to you. There is a reason."

Years ago there was a store named Kohl's Furniture. The advertisement said, *All roads lead to Kohl's.* I got lost in South St. Paul one night and where did I end up? In the parking lot at Kohl's Furniture Store. I said, "That's right. We are all on a different road to Kohl's." I will find out if I am right or wrong someday.

God spoke to us last year on the boat. Our motor wasn't running and there was a storm coming in and I kept saying to the guys, "When are we going to get done fishing? We got to get to shore." Finally I said, "Oh God will you just make up your mind." All of a sudden there was a bolt of lightning and everybody threw their fishing poles down and starting rowing. Boom! There was the answer. —Mary G.

I smelled smoke. Ted had built us a fire, and everyone was enjoying morning coffee and cocoa while water heated for oatmeal. Heather decided to let her sister, Christina, paddle in her place that morning. On the way to the put-in point at Waldeck Public Access, Naomi, Heather and Christina chattered about their lives. Once again, I felt the generation gap between us. I didn't have similar experiences to share, but I did listen and learned about them and what is important to them. Apparently, relationships are the most important, all kinds of relationships.

Saying goodbye to Naomi, Heather (who would meet us downstream) and Ted (who would head home now), Christina and I hit the water just as pair of eagles soared in the breeze high above us. They circled, effortlessly climbing the sky as if following some magical route upward. Paddling ceased while we took in their dance in the infinite blue. Today a swift current pulled the kayaks around bends in the steep-banked channel. I felt relaxed on the river that morning and moderated my usual pace for Christina.

Christina was surprised that the river water, (which ran so clear until Schoolcraft,) had become muddy near Aitkin. She enjoyed the fast current, but found the "first class rapids" to be a disappointment, as did I.

Rounding a curve in the river, we first heard and then saw a small herd of cows on a 12-foot embankment heavily wooded with oak and maple trees. A white cow bellowed continuously. From the distance came

Christina with the cows

Grandmother Stories

Debbie's Story

I would like to share a story I wrote about the trees. I feel it is important because we are talking about earth things.

When I was a little kid all I can remember the trees being valuable for was bugs. We had box elder trees nearby our yard. There were box elder bugs in the trees so I thought trees were for bugs. That is all I knew and thought for a time. Then as I got bigger, I discovered I could climb those trees. I didn't care if there were bugs in them. The trees always had limbs on them and you could take a nap up there. Then as I grew older I started to enjoy a walk in the woods and the coolness I felt running amongst the trees.

When I was in high school I wanted to work in the trees. I remember telling the school counselors I wanted to be a forest ranger. I remember them laughing at me and saying, *"Girls do not do that kind of work."* I was rebellious just because they said that. Whenever I heard something I did not want to hear it created a rebellion. But as you become older you realize those are healthy rebellious things. So I had a goal to work in the trees. Then I got married and decided the trees were for building a house. Then I had a rocky marriage and I escaped back to the woods again. Walking in the woods and being with my kids—I knew that was my escape.

When the weather was really hot we did not have air conditioning. Global warming came upon everybody. But you could go to the woods to be cool and stay cool. The woods became valuable to stay cool. Then I went winter camping and experienced the trees in the winter. It just amazed me that at 25° below the trees are warm. And I thought, "Every one of these is just a little step and experience." Then I moved to Ely and enrolled at Vermilion College to learn all the tree's names.

Alice's Story

I went to college to get my education. I was a biology major. However, because of the difficulty getting the classes I needed, I wound up in elementary education. Then, circumstances found me in special education, a field I would never ever have chosen by myself. There was a higher power directing that. I was one of the first special education teachers in the St. Cloud district. I worked in a couple of schools for a couple of years. Then I was transferred to the hospital. I worked on the answering moos. The cows all turned, curious to see us approach. As we watched the white cow lead the others up the riverbank. We were so enthralled that Christina nearly drifted into a mess of trees in the water. When I yelled, she frantically paddled to safety. We were still laughing at the near collision when, around the bend, we spotted three cows trotting toward us through the woods. One mooed in response to the white cow, now far behind us. We realized that they were frantically trying to catch up with the main group who did not wait for them.

Cows and people: aren't we all trying to find our place on the planet? I thought about last night's gathering, when Amy spoke so eloquently about her life and my thoughts spun back to my childhood.

I attended Catholic school through the fifth grade. Each day I was shamed just for being me. If I so much as forgot my pencil I'd get a severe berating in front of the class. I was left feeling as if I were a mistake and I should always apologize for my existence. I still struggle with that feeling at times, even though I know I have every right to be here—like everyone else.

We spotted a soft-shell turtle basking in the sun. I remembered Amy talking about the importance of living alone to discover who she truly was. Turtles are often alone and seem to prefer it that way. If being alone helps us to find out who we are, then turtles must be rather evolved creatures. Draped lazily over a rock, this creature was the picture of evolution in its most serene state. She barley lifted her head as we passed.

The map showed we would soon reach a riffle and a flood diversion downriver. By then I was used to riffles, but had yet to experience a flood diversion, which is a wall similar to a dam. The difference between them is that the water level is predetermined and there are no gates. When the water rises above flood stage, which is higher

Christina discovering the flood diversion

than the top of the flood diversion wall, it flows over the top to an area, that in this case appeared to be a swamp, that could handle the overflow

Grandmother Stories

mental health and chemical dependency floor with the young people that came in. It was the most fulfilling career anyone could have. It was not without stress, but it was very fulfilling because I got really close to all my students. I would sit in on the staffings. The students knew I knew their story, so we could talk openly about things. We connected on a completely different level than most teachers are able to do in a classroom. I wound up teaching in a hospital with all these needy kids. It really made me understand that this was directed. I know over the years I have touched many lives. Every once in a while I run into one of my former students and I get a big hug. It is just neat.

Barbara's Story

I was raised in a little shack out here where there were ceremonial grounds. When I was maybe three years old or so we moved to Cass Lake and lived there for eighteen years. We didn't have plumbing. We did have water towards the end. It was a two-room house. The only way I knew to get out of the house was to graduate and I didn't like education. I was made to feel "less than." The mayor's daughter, at that time, called me a dirty Indian. It was a disgrace. It was just that way. The whites and the Indians. You had to lie to feel safe in your home. You couldn't tell what was really going on anywhere.

I lived in a home of violence. The people on the outside didn't' know because it was a well kept secret. My mother was a very passive person. I believed she would protect me and my sister. We were never hit or spanked or anything like that. It was emotional abuse. What I saw was all I had to direct my life. It was my reality. It was a very limited perception of what life is, so I walked into a life of abuse. I saw physically abusive relationships. I thought to be strong meant that I didn't talk. I didn't have a voice. I would walk to the store with my head down. If anybody looked at me I would turn beet-red. It was my goal to get out of there without being recognized. My train of thought was that to be a strong woman I had to keep my mouth shut, take the beating and go on the next day. And I went through life like that for four years. I had a daughter at that time and I came to a point of, "Is this all there is to life?" I had no concept of what life was.

At one point we were in an apartment building. He had beaten me and the cops wouldn't do anything. I couldn't open my eyes—just a couple of cracks. It was a way of life. I woke up the next morning and preventing flooding downriver. The day before, the girls had been warned by a neighbor in camp to be careful of the flood diversion. The current was very strong.

We were on the lookout as we neared the flood diversion. Soon we could see what looked like a dam made of rocks in the distance. We approached cautiously. We realized the river depth was so low no water was being diverted. The current around it was nonexistent. Again the trepidation I felt based on what someone said turned out to be unwarranted. I wondered how I could discern the difference between what is valuable information and what is another person's fear being handed to me to carry. After a quick break on the edge of the flood diversion we paddled on in silence, absorbing in our surroundings with heart and eyes.

The quiet was broken by voices downriver calling, "Marco," and we shouted back, "Polo." We turned on the two-way radio and heard Naomi and Heather calling to tell us where they were waiting. After many miles of driving, they couldn't find the boat landing where we planned to meet. They resorted to stopping at a spot on the bank where they could park the Jeep close to the river. Naomi laughed and warned, "It is not the best spot in the world."

We rounded a bend, and there were the girls, high atop a muddy cliff. They waved us down with the butterfly flag we had brought for just that purpose. All I could think was, "I am glad I don't have to climb the cliff." We paddled to shore. The current was strong and we dug our kayaks into the mud so they wouldn't be carried away. Christina climbed out and immediately sank into the mud to her ankles. After a great deal of effort and laughter she made it up the bank. Then she headed to work at Target, her feet encrusted with Mississippi mud. Heather slid down to the water to take her sister's place.

Christina commented after her paddle,

The sun came out, the wind was just a whispering breeze on my face, and those eight miles passed by all too quickly. Nancy's got a good pair of arms on her! I found myself having to push hard just to keep up while she was setting the pace!

Her words "good pair of arms" kept creeping into my mind and made me feel proud. I realized I could let go of the thought that I was not keeping up with the younger crowd. I felt myself relax. The pressure to perform was released. What a blessing. You never really know who is going to say something that has a significant impact. I never expected to hear that from one of these girls.

Grandmother Stories

put a chair up against the door so nobody could get in. I looked at myself in the mirror and I thought briefly "This is not real. My face is all ballooned up." Something spiritual in me told me, *"You have to stay away from him and get away."* There has to be something better than this. Even though I was told there was nothing they could pick him up for, there was nothing wrong with me either. He believed me when I said I put a warrant out for him and he left. After that I didn't know what to do. I carried so much pain.

I went back to Cass Lake and began drinking day in and day out. The tears came. I found my voice. Feelings came out that had been covered up so long and I had so much pain. About a month of drinking day in and day out I called my daughter's father to come and get her because I knew in here (pointing to her heart) I could not provide her the kind of life she deserved. He came and got her and raised her ever since. From then on, all I knew was drinking. All the people I knew drank. I was terrible at eating; wine came first. I found a partner that had drinking problems too. I remember one time I was sitting in my rocking chair just thinking this must be the way it is. All I am going to do is eat, drink and breathe and then I'm going to be ashes.

I had no concept of a God. Me and my sister were made to go to church after my grandpa died and I could never understand that concept. It was too foreign to me that there is this guy floating around in the air with a beard who has blue eyes. I had no idea and I still don't understand what it is all about. As I said, it is right for some people. They have that concept and they have that connection to that God. I could never get it.

After some of the years of my drinking (26 years of chronic alcoholism.) I was an adult when I realized Gloria's sister Barb, (they were our neighbors at Cass Lake) was my role model. She was ten years older; she came and helped me at detox. I respected her. Somebody doing something with their life. I tried to go to detox one time. I was incoherent and I couldn't walk. My coordination was all out of balance. My eyes were dilated and I was bleeding out of my eye. They held me on both sides. She said, *"Barb, I can't bring you in here."* She put me in the hospital. They gave me four shots and I guess it took a long time to put me in bed. Barb said, *"We have given you five injections already. It is enough to knock out a horse and I can't do much more right now."* The next morning they told me I was going to see a psychologist.

They told me I was on the point of D.T.'s [delirium tremens]. I knew from my partner that it takes a long time to come out of that and

Past the next bend Heather and I discovered the boat launch for which they had been searching. Heather said they could not even find the road to the boat launch. The parking area was a patch of weeds and flowers. The dock, had washed away in the current. Only concrete blocks remained, sticking out of the water in disarray like children's toys.

Our map showed many creeks that fed into the river, but we often missed spotting them, as they resemble oxbows. Approaching Aitkin I wanted to find the Sissabagamah Creek. With some diligence I did. It was, however, more of a trench with downed trees, woodland debris and only a trickle of water. I could only assume that in the spring it fed the river more than it was doing now.

After paddling 19 miles, I was tired when we landed at camp back in Aitkin. I didn't have patience for our new neighbor, who was full of questions. I took a nap as the girls talked to him and his niece, Stephanie. After dinner our group shared a quiet evening around the campfire, gazing at the water. Naomi wrapped her sarong around her head in a rather glamorous way (for camping) to keep the bugs from annoying her. The smell of smoke filled the air and the sky transform from the bright blue of the day to vivid shades of pink, orange, and red. We watched a football drift past us on the river.

Naomi with improvised bug gear

June 28, Monday, Day 24

Naomi headed home for a couple of days because the next few campsites were not car accessible. Heather and I left Aiken campground ready to paddle and camp three days on our own. A canoeist named Pete put in near us with an exquisite homemade wooden racing canoe. The colors of wood strips varied a great deal and making it elegant. Pete paddled downstream with us for about a quarter mile. He seemed very happy to have paddling companions. Before he turned to head back up stream to practice, he warned us of a dead cow in the river just ahead. I nodded at him, trying to grasp the idea. How does a cow end up dead in the river? Heather and I looked at each other and let go of the whole idea of the cow.

It was warm, clear and calm, a good thing, since my kayak now felt like a barge. It was loaded down with all of the gear that Naomi normally carried in the Jeep. We paddled past hardwood forest, farms, and homes. Some

Grandmother Stories

sometimes you don't come out of it. I was practically skin and bones, but in here something began crying. I knew if I shed one tear mentally, I was going to loose it, and I didn't want these people controlling my life. They said, *"You're going to see a psychologist this morning."* I could barely walk around yet; it was November with icy winds. I thought, "They will make me see a psychologist and they will send me away and I didn't have any control of my life."

I had a sober friend come to visit me the next day. I was so close to loosing it. I had one person that cared about me. It was dark and gloomy and I couldn't cry. I thought maybe she would help. I said, " I am going home." She said, *"You can't, you had better stay here."* I said, "No." So in my hospital gown I made it out the door in the freezing icy windy. I laid in the back of her car. I was so scared. I thought they were going to come and get me and take me away. I knew I had lost control over my life. I went back to drinking that same day.

I had no concept of the traditional way, but concepts were starting to come to me in different ways. So many different things happened. A wake up call for me! There is life for me somewhere.

One time when I was drunk and I was in town. (I always tried to make it home.) I passed a home and a man called me over to the porch that one night. *"Come over here, girl."* He knew I was drunk. I went over there and he went inside. I tried to get on the porch, I fell off and broke my ankle. I called for help and no one came. They were partying in there so I knew it was up to me. I walked five miles on that broken ankle to get help. It was those kinds of things in my life that showed me that it is up to me.

The creator gave me this life you know. I am the one that has to take charge of where I go in this life. It doesn't matter if I am alcoholic or not. I have a different concept of what life is about. Life is about that we can heal ourselves. Our skin scabs over and we have the tears to keep that pain away. The laughter, too, feels good and lets that stress inside go. The creator gave this to all of us. Alcohol is just something that passed through our people so quickly and devastatingly because everything had been stripped away from us. Our way of life and our roles were taken. Language and ceremonies were taken. What is left? We covered that pain.

I am a chemical dependency counselor, and I hate to say this but, the way I look at life, the creator didn't give me this life to *fit* into society. I already had my place in society like the birds and the squirrels. There are many people who don't have an education, but what they were beautiful architectural constructions, while others were small cabins or trailers that were seldom used or in need of repair.

We noticed a football floating in the water near shore. I assumed it was the same one we saw yesterday evening. Heather paddled over to pick it up, thinking it would be another fun present for Naomi. It reminded her of Tom Hanks' volleyball, Wilson, in the movie *Castaway*. This would be our Wilson. But the name Wilson wouldn't do for a women's trip, so we brainstormed names. Penelope became a quick pick, but we wanted it to have an adventurous name, so we gave her the middle name of Trouble. We weren't sure why, but we liked Pearson as the last name. Penelope Trouble Pearson. It was tucked away in the cockpit and we paddled on.

We were joking about our new companion when we spotted a striking large reddish brown object in the water ahead. We couldn't make out what this intriguing item was so we paddled closer. Soon the stench confirmed what we had begun to suspect. *"Knox-Menards!"* we both yelled. It was the dead cow. At that point we were up-wind and the stench was bad. I feared the odiferous experience awaiting us on the down-wind side of the rotting carcass.

The bloated cow was caught in a tangle of trees. Its hide was still thick with winter hair that was attractive in the sun, but the smell was dreadful. I pulled my bandana over my nose as a filter and I paddled as fast as I could. Heather kept pace. I could see from the look on her face she was holding her breath and needed to exhale. She gasped, and a sour nauseated look crossed her face. She paddled faster. Soon we could breathe normally again, but we were both afraid the dead cow water might splash on us. Heather asked how far I thought we would have to travel before the river wasn't contaminated with dead cow water. I had no idea, but we decided to paddle a few miles before getting out of the kayaks.

Once we were past what we dubbed "muddy cow water," we stopped for lunch on an outcrop of rocks. There we were joined by a cute soft black and white dog. Her tail wagged so vigorously she could barely walk. She was interested in our lunch, but happy with the loving Heather gave her. Soon she heard a car on the nearby road and bounded off toward home. Heather was a dog magnet on the trip. This sweet girl was one of many dogs who found Heather as we traveled.

Grandmother Stories

have is so powerful. They are connected and that is what that piece of life is all about, getting that connection back in here [hand held over heart] and with all creation around.

And that message: I had my daughter and I didn't raise her. Her dad came and got her. I didn't get pregnant for all those years. When I finally sobered up I talked about it to the spirits and the leaves. A year after I was sober I got pregnant, boom! My son's dad and I had met 13 years before. We were together for eight years and I never got pregnant. We lived together and sobered up apart. We stayed away from each other for eight years and came back together. The kids are 17 years apart.

Before I got pregnant with my son I was having dreams about children. I knew that one was my daughter and there was another smaller figure. I didn't know if it was a boy or girl. I had that second child and a second chance at life. It made me open my eyes to how precious this physical life is. We have so much opportunity and privilege being connected to one another. Cherish everything around us because there is a deeper level of understanding of life than the day to day commitments! The significance of this life is so powerful. When I knew I was going to have another baby I knew this was my chance. A second chance at this physical life. We are the givers of life.

I did the best I could. We have to honor that and be grateful for that. Because I was open to everything I am changing the cycle of violence in this family. I had to work on that myself because I had so much shame from the conditioned thinking. And I kept thinking to myself, "The creator is going to give me this life." I knew the creator gave me all the strength and power I needed to make any change that he wanted to have in me. I had to generate that in myself and believe in myself. I gave myself time outs from my son and told him "Mom is giving herself a time out and I count to ten like I tell you to count to ten. Mom's working on things too." I raised him a whole different way than what I knew from the way I grew up.

I don't believe in systems because systems make us little cattle. Natives don't fit into the system. We are not brought into this world to look at things like everybody else.

So my son says, *"Mom, we are going to make it through this."* Right now I don't have the money, I have completed the circle. I started out my life without money and that is where I am now. I am living a simple life and he is the one that is the strong one. *"Mom, we can make it through anything."* Whenever I cook he tells me thanks.

Just when I thought Heather was unshakable a crayfish crawled out from under a rock while she was getting back into her kayak. She shrieked and jumped back wildly alarmed. I could not believe my eyes. Defensively she said, "I hate those things. It is my irrational fear. They just look evil! Like they are out to get you!"

We paddled on. I kept looking over at her in disbelief. Eventually we both laughed.

We felt the headwind pick up. I looked ahead and was greatly discouraged. The river was like a large lake with high waves coming at us. The intimacy of the small river I had come to trust and love was behind us. I knew we had to paddle the final two miles of our 22-mile-day and I wasn't sure I could make it. I kept yelling to Heather, disappointment in my voice, "It looks like a lake. Look how wide it is. It looks like a lake."

Heather scrunched up her forehead and looked at me as if to say, "What were you expecting?" We dug in, determined the wind wouldn't beat us.

Two miles later we landed at Lone Pine Creek campsite to discover another shoreline thick with muck. Soft mud oozed up over the top of my sandals and between my toes. It was the type of mud that grabbed hold and claimed your shoes. As I struggled to get my foot loose without loosing my sandal, Heather snickered. She had managed to get out of her kayak 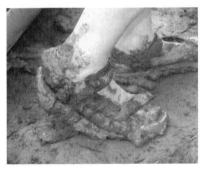 without being claimed by the earth. I had to pull on my legs with my hands to pull my feet free. Then I grabbed some sticks to place on top of the mud so I wouldn't sink again.

We pulled our gear to safety, after which exhaustion won and I lay down for a nap. I noticed my expectations and needs continued to decrease. It was taking less and less to make me comfortable. I fell asleep on my Crazy Creek chair even though it is much shorter than my body. My head rested on my hard deck bag. I was content.

I woke from my nap thinking about what I would do when I got home to generate income. I was determined not to hop back on the treadmill that had been my life for so long. What would "not jump on my treadmill" look like? I didn't know.

Artwork is always near, if not at the top, of my list. I have learned that I'm not motivated to create unless the project is meaningful, joyous, or

Grandmother Stories

We had a new house built. I told my boy if for any reason this house is taken away, if mom can't make the payments some how I will provide a roof over your head. I will always take care of you. He understands that. He understands and talks to me about the spiritual things in life and he gives me feedback.

Use your heart in your life. Be thankful for the things the creator gave us, especially spirituality.

There is one thing I would like to add about my mother. I saw her as a real passive person. Because she didn't have a voice either. I thought she was a really weak woman. She passed away five years ago. After she passed away I could see all of her strengths were right there, but that wasn't what I had been seeing. Her strengths were to feed people, to put a roof over their head if they needed a place to stay and to be kind to them no matter what. I'd seen her do many things for people. It is the *way* we see things.

Mary O.'s Story

How has spirituality influenced my life? I wasn't sure I wanted to answer this question. I am still not sure. I had a dream. I wasn't sure if the dream was prophetic or just expressing my own fear of discussing where my spirituality is taking me. I am concerned because it frightens some people. It is new for me to share this because you kind of do have to be careful.

I started out Catholic and went to twelve years of Catholic school. But my spirituality was not attached to Catholicism. My father made me go to confession every week when I was 7, 8, 9, and 10 years old. I remember at 10 going to St. Theresa's Church in Highland Park and being with Father Gibbs. I was going to confession with the chapel veil on and said, "Bless me father for I have sinned. My last confession was one week ago." He stopped me and said, *"How old are you?"* When the priest asks you a question from the confessional, wow! I said, "10." *"Why are you coming to confession every week? You don't have anything to confess."* He was right. I was making things up. I was saying things like I got mad at my mother. He said, *"You do not need to come every week."* By this time I was trembling and scared to death to go home because my father was an alcoholic personality without being an alcoholic. Everything set him off. I could say the sky was blue and that was wrong and he wouldn't speak to me for a week. Scared to death, I brings hope to the viewer. When I paint pet portraits, I want to capture the personality and spirit of the animal. I work in eclectic media; clay sculpture, stained class, watercolors, pastels, and acrylic paint. I've illustrated books, designed logos, and painted on walls, cards, and canvas. I was surprised to find that on this trip, I wasn't interested in sketching. The drawing pencils Doug gave me had, so far, been riding in my pack unopened. To be fair with myself, I was generally too tired at the end of the day to draw. Even writing in the journal took determined effort.

Perhaps I would take the entire length of the trip to clarify my direction for the future. I hoped when I got home I would see the world differently and begin to live in keeping with the lessons of the journey.

By now we were no longer wearing fleece, but still wore long sleeves to protect us from the bugs. The picnic table at which we sat was constructed out of two-by-fours. Whoever built it had missed the course on basic human anatomy. I have long legs but my feet swung freely above the ground. While sitting at the table, the top reached as high as my shoulders. I felt like a small child. Maybe the table designer was extremely tall. The table was a worse fit for Heather. We sat on top of it.

Later I sat on the edge of the bank and peacefully watched the river drift past. As the sun began to set I absorbed the subtle changes in the colors of the water, trees and sky. In moments like this the world is more magical than I can begin to describe. Serenity permeated everything. It reached into the depth of my being. I allowed myself to become immersed in the experience until there was just enough light remaining to find my way back to the tent.

When I climbed into the tent, I found Heather with a new friend. She was playing with a tiny gray spider. In the light of Heather's head lamp, their game consisted of the spider perching on top of the end of one of her fingers and then leaping faster than we could see to the tip of a finger on her other hand. I joined her in watching this event for several minutes. Soon I became a new landing pad for our tiny friend. We watched closely, and could see her prepare to jump. She crouched down slightly and become very still, perhaps gauging the distance, before making each leap. She seemed to enjoy the challenge of each jump and Heather was particularly enamored watching her meet each challenge. Before we crawled into our sleeping bags for the night we let her go safely outside of the tent

One of my wrists was beginning to show signs of the wear and tear of constant paddling. It constantly ached and was tender to the touch. With two weeks to go, that troubled me.

Grandmother Stories

told him what Father Gibbs had told me and he started yelling. He was mad at me and mad at the priest because I should be going to confession, blah, blah, blah.

I would say at the age of 9 my concept of God was that God was like a mountain with all the various beliefs and faiths and religions in the world. The mountain was surrounded by a forest and all the beliefs and faith and religions were paths, different paths through the forest. They all ended up in the same place. So it never made any sense to me the that Catholic church kept saying One Holy Catholic and Apostolic church. We would have to go to Mass and Catholic school. And then I had the good fortune to have lay teachers for religion at St. Joseph's Academy. By the time we were sophomores we were introduced to all sorts of religions. We had to study every other religion in the world and that was eye opening. That was a huge piece of my journey. By the time I was out of high school I had stopped going to church, even at Christmas. My father said I was an atheist. Little did he know how prophetic he was!

I could find no umbrella under which I could function. I was always drawn to Native American spirituality, but I felt like an intruder whenever I wanted to attend anything Native American or take a class. I didn't know if that was my own personal sense, or if it wasn't the right fit, or if I was a white person intruding on something that is sacred for them. Perhaps its a combination. I read a lot about it. I was always drawn to nature. I have owned my own home for twelve years. I turned the back yard and deck into a haven. I have flowers and gardens and trees everywhere. I am very earth centered. If I worship anything it is the earth—trees especially.

For many years nothing held me: New Age, Native American, Buddhist a little. I studied a lot of different faiths and I never quit seeking. I have always been a seeker and a questioner. I never felt like I needed to belong or call myself anything. Labels seem so limiting.

It has been three years since I fell into where I am now. I honestly can't tell you at what point it happened. It just evolved. I am Wiccan. That is a new thing to say. It is like coming out. It is very like being gay, which I am not. I don't feel free to wear my pentacle, even in my shop. I imagine I would have customers walk in, see it and turn around and walk right out. I am in an Irish Catholic neighborhood which is also a big part Jewish. There are Lutherans there too. We forget that they are there. It is a smattering who managed to sneak in. [Smiling]

An article I read was very interesting because it says Wiccan is a

June 29, Tuesday, Day 25

I was determined to win the battle against the mud. During breakfast I plotted how to get back into the kayak without taking a layer of goopy earth with me.

The sticks I had stood on yesterday had either sunk or had been washed away. I slid my kayak off the bank and down to the shore. Then I rolled small logs down the bank next to the kayak to make a walkway and confidently stepped out on it and sank up to my ankles in the goop. As I struggled once again to pull my foot loose, Heather documented my defeat with the camera.

We both got into our kayaks and kept our feet hanging over the sides. The goal was to wash our feet off in the river before we reached the rapids just downstream.

It really gets your heart racing to take on a stimulating challenge first thing in the morning. We floated downstream, feverishly rubbing our feet in the water, and leaving a muddy trail of water behind us. We finished just in time to find that the rapids were little more than a ripple.

Just past the rapids an eagle perched on an over-hanging tree. I passed directly under her and she watched me cautiously. I was thrilled to get so close. Around each bend we saw one osprey after another. One swooped down to harass a duckling momentarily separated from its mother. I yelled and it turned away.

We passed under a crackling, buzzing power line which towered many feet above us. We felt a vibration, and the hair on our arms stood up. Being so close to the electricity felt eerie and unsafe. Heather noticed two peregrine nesting platforms built on the towers that held the cables, one on each side of the river. Both nests had birds in them. I wondered what being near all that voltage did to them. I know it is not healthy for people to be that close to high voltage lines all of the time.

Grandmother Stories

very personal decision. You do have to be careful. It is a recognized religion by the US government. There are Wiccan police officers and people in government. But you have to be careful in this climate. My goodness! I would be burned at the stake by some people. I find it very sad. I know that part of my journey is to continue to share this information. I find especially the people who have known me a long time don't have any concept that I am Wiccan. If you thought for many years that I am decent, kind, loving, and environmentally conscious and following a good path what difference should this made? I guess the hesitation is because so many people don't understand it.

I say Wiccan rather than witchcraft because that term really freaks most people out. They think immediately devil worship and you have to say, *"No that is a Christian creation. We don't believe in the devil or Satan. I don't worship something I don't believe in."* Speaking this is actually very wonderful and freeing. I can't explain the passion I feel for even a blade of grass. I stepped on that mayfly and I stopped and did a blessing and said I was sorry to the mayflies. I nursed a dying butterfly for three days and wept when it died. I don't kill spiders in my house. I talk to them and give them the rules of the house and only one in twelve years has ever not followed the rules. They can't drop on my body or crawl on me, or get in my food, or get into bed with me. Other than that they can live anywhere they want. It finally feels like I have come home and I am where I am supposed to be. The only creed for Wiccan is *"Harm Ye None."* Well that is pretty basic and I am not there yet. I grew up with a lot of anger which has been part of my journey. That is my boogie man. We all have some sort of demon. I don't believe in a heaven or a hell or a God. I think there is power in the universe and I think there is a universal consciousness.

My personal credo that these last three years is "I refuse to live in fear." I believe basically the entire country runs on fear. Corporations, run on fear. Whether it is fear of embarrassment, fear of loss of money, fear of looking foolish, fear of death, and fear of something. I con-stantly struggle at not living that way. My own personal journey is to not live that way.

We lollygagged, as Naomi would call it, relaxing in the sun. We drifted past an otter playing in the water. She didn't seem to notice us. All along our route turtles of varying sizes hung on downed trees, rocks and the bank, basking in the warmth.

A deer snorted at us from shore. We saw the doe with her little one on the bank, the fawn still with its spots. It watched us float by with curiosity. Mom snorted and the two disappeared into the tall grass.

We stopped for lunch, finding a bit of shade in the hardwood forest. Heather felt something run over her foot. Next to her she saw a skink hiding in the grass. This tiny, dark, smooth and shiny lizard had a delicate structure that made her appear vulnerable. From the tip of her tail to her head she was all of four inches long. She made no attempt to run from us, which is true to their elusive nature. We were both surprised to see her sitting so calmly.

After lunch we paddled easily, not wanting the day to pass too quickly. The sun on the trees lit up the summer-green foliage. Ancient oaks lined the shore, their exposed roots in the water and their thick branches reaching for the sky. I found myself wanting to climb to the top of an oak and enjoy what the birds experience each day. I began to design a tree house in my imagination. In one of the tall red or white pines on our property I could construct one when I got home. I wanted to sit up high to enjoy the splendor of the sunrises and sunsets, to fall asleep to the gentle rocking of the wind. I'd build it from scrap lumber and figure out how to attach it without hurting the tree. Trees had become especially meaning-ful to me on this trip. They offered shelter, shade on sweltering days, and homes for birds and animals we so loved.

A heron launched itself from a treetop, her wide gray wings impressive as they brushed the branches. It had always seemed odd to see the her-ons up there, as if they were not meant to use such high perches. Maybe I developed my perception of them as water walkers from sighting them often in the shallows prior to the trip. It wouldn't be the first time I'd devel-oped a belief based on insufficient information, nor would it be the last.

I thought about what Amy had said about fearlessly taking advantage of chances and enjoying life right now. I felt a sense of pride as I realized that is exactly what I was doing. I could very easily have given up on this trip, but I had been offered a chance and I took it. It was bringing me riches I could not have dreamed of even during the planning.

As if to celebrate my awareness dragonflies danced in the air around me. Hundreds of them darted about. One huge dragonfly landed on my

Grandmother Stories

Millie's Story

My husband retired seven years ago. We have five children and the 18th grandchild is on the way. Don, like many men, wanted "to motorhome." We traveled part-time for many years. It was a very enjoyable phase when we were camp hosts at a campground on the coast near Santa Barbara. Four of our children were born in California so it was a *remembering* experience. However, during that time I realized I needed more focus rather than just letting life happen. I felt drawn to seek a spiritual director. One requirement I found was monthly sessions. Extended traveling and meeting monthly with a spiritual director were not a fit.

That was four years ago. About the same time we sold our fifteen-year residence, located on the Mississippi River at Pine Point near St. Cloud. Our original plan was to "full time motorhome." As time to leave neared, Don was the one who couldn't let go of the house and sell everything. We ended up purchasing our biggest house ever in Sartell across from the high school. (Hardly a retirement home.) Our plan was to use it as a transition house thinking we would eventually know what we would like to do and build a retirement home within two years. Now, four years later, we are still in our surprise home and very content.

After a year of journeying with a spiritual director, I was invited to begin a four year program to become a spiritual director at a local monastery. I will begin the final year in September and am doing very well. To my surprise, my passion has given stability to Don's life as well as mine. We still travel but now fit those travels into the school year schedule. A wonderful blessing has been that Don and I are realizing that pursuing our individual interests stimulates and bring newness to our relationship and has fostered a healthy approach for identifying and maintaining the *I* in the *WE*.

Peggy's Story

The spiritual journey has been an interesting one. I see it as a circle now because I was raised Christian—Lutheran in an all-white small town. I had this picture of how life was supposed to be, but when I was about 12 years old I knew something was different about me. In the Lutheran church we go through confirmation. Before we did that

kayak to ride the river with me. I studied the iri-
descent greens and blues on its back. Its black
slender wings were a stark contrast to everything else around her. Then suddenly she was
gone to join the others.

The day began to heat up. Padding in the sun
took its toll, fatigue set in quickly, and I began
to focus only on finding Half Moon campsite. According to the map, we
should have seen it already. We were long past a sign that read, "Campsite
50 yards." Finally fatigue won out. We headed for Half Moon boat launch
where the sign said, "No Camping." We unpacked our Thermarest mats
and took a nap in the shade.

Later, as we wandered around the boat launch searching for an out
of the way place to make camp, we noticed many of the large trees were
deeply scorched. Some of the small trees had been burned completely. At
the top of the hill we found signs of a party spot, with empty beer bottles,
debris, burned wood and coals in a makeshift fire pit. The energy level
on the hilltop felt unsafe so we decided to camp next to the launch, even
though it meant we would be more visible from the river.

We unloaded most of our gear, but did not put up the tent. I couldn't
relax. I had a sense I was breaking the rules, and we'd get caught. I had
been taught to always follow the rules because there was a good reason
for them—even if you didn't have a clue what the reason was. Every time
a boat passed I felt more uncomfortable. Then a truck pulled in. I was
convinced we were in trouble. The driver of the truck got out and started
throwing a training bag into the water for his dog to fetch. He watched
us for a while and then introduced himself. His name was Stan, his dog's,
Mandy. He came to the landing often to exercise her. He told us everyone
missed Half Moon campsite and ended up camped here. Half Moon campsite was back in the woods. You had to pull your boat up at the sign we
had seen and take a path over a boardwalk and up to the top of the ridge.
As he talked we felt more comfortable about spending the night here, and
began putting up the tent.

Noting the burned trees, Stan said arsonists had come through several
times a couple of years ago. I thought that must be why there was so much
negative energy here—the trees were not happy.

We continued to talk while Stan threw the bag for Mandy. He asked us
questions about our trip, curious that a couple of women would take on
this challenge. Previously he'd seen only young men camping here. As he

Grandmother Stories

each of us met with our pastor individually. What I said to him was, "I understand being confirmed as a Christian, but I don't understand the Lutheran part. Why isn't being a Christian enough?" He said, *"Well then maybe you shouldn't get confirmed."* That really wasn't an answer. But from then on I started seeking because I was trying to find spirituality. I had a real foundation, a strong faith in God from my parents and my grandmother. The stories I heard gave me comfort, but it was a limiting belief. *"Okay you are confirmed a Lutheran."* But that separated me from anybody who was anything else. That did not feel right.

So when I was in college I explored lots of different religions. Eastern religions and a little bit of the Native American. Then I was married to my husband for 22 years. During that time I was approached by Jehovah's Witnesses. I embraced that. Looking back, I understand why. At that time my life was so controlled in so many ways. The Jehovah's Witness life really fit for me. That particular religion has very specific ways and specific beliefs. It just kind of fit with the rest of my life and how I though I was supposed to be.

I had five sons. They grew up and as young teenagers began to be out in the world. They began to see that how their dad treated me, and treated them, was not right. They started to confront him. This gave me a little more courage. To make a long story short, I ended up leaving him. To my surprise, all my children turned against me. They wouldn't see me for two or three years. That was hard, but I knew in my heart I had done the right thing.

I met a Lakota woman at the shelter. She and I have since adopted each other as mother and daughter. She was a young woman but she taught me many things just by her example. She would tell me *"This is the way you do things."* She told me about the spirits, and the trees, and plants, and the animals. It made so much sense to me. When I was feeling out of sorts and unbalanced I would not have to put it into words. I knew if I went into the woods everything became right. So when someone says that the spirits are here [in the woods] that fits my life's beliefs. They put words to something I believe.

Then I got to know a man who honors and respects women. That was so different because I had so much more control and independence. In fact I got mad at him once when I worked at the casino. I was coming home at midnight in a big blizzard. We live out in the woods on Oak Point. Driving home I thought, "Oh gosh he is just said "young" he looked at me as if to say, "What is a woman of your age doing out here?" After we refused the beer he offered, he said he wished he had ice cream or something for us. He was determined to assist us in some way. Heather lit up at the mention of ice cream. Stan didn't miss the cue and asked if we knew how to find the Dairy Queen in Brainerd where we would be tomorrow. He told us to park our boats on the left side of the river under the second bridge and to walk up the hill. We were both delighted with that information, and after a couple more tosses of the training bag for Mandy, Stan wished us luck and said farewell.

As we prepared for bed, Heather told me my back muscles were very defined. That was fun to hear. I'd like to think all this work was having some impact physically. We both wanted to jump on a scale and see if we were losing weight. Even though we were working hard, we were also eating peanut M&Ms (they didn't melt in the sun), and lemon drops. We wondered what the effect of exercise plus candy was on our bodies.

We crawled into the tent, and I began to recall all of the animals we had seen. It was a day rich in eagles, herons, peregrines, hawks, turkey vultures, deer, otter, rodents, skinks, turtles and many smaller birds, including an oriole that flitted past us and perched in a tree, and the dead cow. I fell asleep still a bit anxious about our campsite, but comforted by the thought that nature had been embracing us and keeping us safe. This night would be no exception.

During the night, our sleep was interrupted by people camped up on the hill. They kept yelling at their dog, Fred. Fred didn't listen. The loud voices and the roar of the four-wheeler they were playing with continued late into the night. I tried to sleep with a mixture of fear and anger towards our unwanted neighbors.

June 30, Wednesday, Day 26

As Wednesday dawned I felt more tired than ever. We were on the water by 7 am and planning a 27-mile paddle. Conditions were absolutely calm. Heather's reflection on the water was a perfect mirror image. Despite our wanting to push hard to avoid the wind and heat later, we were drawn to paddle gently and soak in the serenity of our surroundings.

As we drifted, a pair of loons swam just ahead of us. A small creature, perhaps a young beaver, with just her nose out of the water, also swam in front of our kayaks. It didn't dive like a beaver. When it tried, it immediately bobbed back up. It was smaller than my fist; I could not identify

Grandmother Stories

going to be really worried about me." I get home and he was sleeping. At first I thought he could care less. But then I realized it was because he knew I could handle it. He had faith and trust in me. That is what I really wanted.

Sister Dorcas's Story

I thought of being a wandering missionary with a knapsack. Religion was sort of my teen age rebellion because my family had none (no religion), at least not formally. But my father turned out to be a Mason. I didn't know that until the day he died. He never went to church and I never heard anything about it.

My mother was brought up in the church, but she never went. Her god was beauty. That impacted me I am sure. She was a dancer. She fell in love with ballet at eighteen. But she thought she was ugly. Her cousin called her "long toothed mule face" and I think she believed it. She was really a very attractive woman. She danced beautifully and didn't marry until after she finished dancing. When she couldn't dance anymore she slowed down enough so someone could catch her. She loved sunsets and everything beautiful. She was an artist, too.

Then my sister dragged me to see The Nun's Story when I was just out of high school. It was a stupid movie. A very poor portrayal of the religious life, it was very negative and self-effacing. But I wanted it. Within two years I went to the convent and eventually was professed. Once you are professed, real life begins. I was shipped out of the convent to a girl's boarding school. Relationships began to be something that I had to work with. I wasn't trained to be a school teacher and that was the professional work the sisters did at the boarding school. I wasn't teaching and was so very isolated. I cleaned and washed dishes and arranged for the special needs of the sisters of the convent. That was my job. I was there all alone and it was hard.

Then, after never having gone to a camp before in my life, I was put in charge of two dormitories full of kids at summer camp. I cried through most of the first summer. They were 6- through 12-year-old girls with 13- to 15-year-old teenage girls who were counselors. I had two dorms full of these girls. Twenty kids in each one, with counselors and counselors-in-training. That is where I learned what short-sheeting a bed meant. The one good thing was that we were still wearing the habit. It was a great disciplinary tactic. When the kids were noisy in

it. Perhaps it was a large mouse or a baby muskrat. It continuously tried to dive to avoid me, but popped back up again like a fishing bobber. I paddled away to keep from upsetting it further, then watched it continue across the river and disappear into the tall grass on the far shore.

At first the river was narrow relative to the lake-sized patches we had paddled, and perhaps five times wider than when we first started the trip. I liked being close to the trees and animals and connected to the natural world where the river was narrower. When it widened, I felt we were up against a superior force, which of course we were. Being close to shore let me believe I was somehow safer.

Our drifty trance ended as we entered a wide section of river where the gentle breeze turned into a head wind, tossing waves in our path. For miles we saw herons stalking the tall grass that grew out into the middle of the shallow river. A very large heron made an awkward landing in the top of a tall jack pine and settled in. Eventually it took a regal stance. Cormorants perched on logs near us. An osprey dived, came up with breakfast, and flew off toward the trees.

In the next narrows we encountered several families of ducks. A mother escorted her ducklings away from us towards shore, leaving one in deep water, spinning in a panic. It dove as I paddled past. Suddenly the duckling surfaced right next to my paddle. Startled, I burst into laughter. The duck quickly disappeared again below the surface. I stopped paddling to avoid hitting it and waited until it surfaced at a distance and found a safe route back to Mom.

In the next open area we faced the headwind again. Cabins on shore made that patch appear even more like a lake. Near Brainerd the shore was lined with cabins, houses, docks, and boats. Downstream a skier sheared the water behind a boat. As we approached the city, the highway, loud with morning traffic, cut next to the river.

We passed under a highway bridge and approached Potlatch Dam with trepidation. This was one of the major dams in our path. Our map indi-

Grandmother Stories

the dorm at night all I had to do was walk in wearing my habit. I didn't have to say a thing.

You were expected to do what ever you were asked to do. That was part of the old rule. One of the sayings is that *"You learn to believe that you could do whatever, in the providence of God, you are told or asked to do."* Letitia was there as well. We put into place a lot of good changes at the camp. We changed activity offerings and the way that things were done. The music changed, the whole chapel thing changed. We modernized it.

I never would have dreamed of where we ended up. It is better than anything I could have imagined and far different from anything I would have imagined. Much more fun, much more free. Letitia and I became fast friends at DeKoven [Episcopal Retreat and Conference Center]. She is probably the closest friend I have ever had in my life. I would not have experienced a lot of things if I hadn't had someone else to do them with. I mostly instigated, but she was willing to go along.

Gertrude's Story

I am going to have my brother-in-law screened to see if he has Alzheimer's. I married his brother and three of us lived together. That was a mistake from the start. We could have moved and lived somewhere else, but my husband didn't want to leave the farm. He and his brother were the owners of that farm, so we lived together. My brother-in-law had a grudge against me since the day I married his brother. We lived like that for 49 years. We live in separate houses now but there is a garage we have to share. He keeps making my car dirty. So what should I do about that? I don't know.

My spouse was diagnosed with dementia three years ago. He knows that if he does something wrong he will have to go to a nursing home. So he is fairly good. But I am going to have a social worker come out and tell his brother he has got to stop making my car dirty and breaking stuff. It is costing me money. It is for no reason other than to make me miserable.

cated the portage around the structure was very close to the dam. We cautiously paddled past a row of buoys with large signs on them warning of danger, and anxiously hugged the right riverbank. Ahead, were the bright orange buoys Stan had told us were next to the portage. They too bore signs warning of imminent danger. We were just about on top of the buoys when we spotted the portage and paddled for shore. Heather said it was a little too close for comfort.

With a view of the dam and Brainerd's water tower We pulled up and enjoyed lunch in the shade. In the heat of the day our conversation turned toward Dairy Queen and a nap. We had paddled 13 miles. The calm air and water of early morning seemed like they were days away.

While resting in the shade I realized that facts previously without meaning now held my interest, such as distance above sea level. Previously, sea level did not have a direct relation to my life. But on this trip, I found myself curious at each dam how far the water level had dropped. At the headwaters in Itasca the river was at 1475 feet above sea level. I learned before the trip that the Mississippi River loses half of its height well before it leaves the state of Minnesota. Overall that is an average drop of about 7 inches per mile, which means by the time the river reached Potlatch Dam it had already dropped 200 feet. That was difficult to grasp.

After lunch we each made four trips across the portage with our gear and kayaks. The portage was a fenced area with freshly mown grass and pavement, well designed for portaging. To our delight we found a bonus—well maintained outhouses. Penelope (the football) had to stop and pose by the undertow sign warning boaters to stay away from the dam. Heather found the picture of a person being spun around under water rather scary.

On the other side of the portage we discovered springs bubbling up in the shallow water through pockets of clean gray sand. Everywhere else a brownish fungus grew on the rocks just under the surface. We plunged our hands deep into the ice-cold water and churning sand and found no solid bottom. I found it spooky; Heather found it exciting. If the water level had been any higher we would have missed those springs all together.

Back on the water we paddled through several exhilarating rapids thinking about the Dairy Queen (DQ) and forgetting the heat of the day. At the second bridge we tied up our kayaks, safe from the strong current, and started up the sandy embankment. It was a stiff climb. We took time to admire the graffiti under the bridge. An eight-foot rainbow floated above someone's five-foot high initials done in round indiscernible letters decorated in bright colors with dots and arrows. On one of the pillars was a cartoon drawing of a man with big sunglasses. There were flames coming off the sunglasses and the word King written large across his chest. There were a lot of signatures and swear words sprinkled among them. If I did not pay attention to the words for what they meant and just focused on the colors and designs, it was quite a work of art. The colors and shading took some talent.

The DQ sign stood like a beacon at the top of the bridge. We were stunned by the unaccustomed sound of major highway traffic just a few feet away and stood watching it like deer caught in headlights. Then we bolted for the DQ window to order Blizzards and ice water. I instantly got a brain-freeze headache and decided to eat more slowly. We sat at a picnic table feeling grateful we were not driving in the heavy traffic that buzzed by us. We asked a very bewildered girl to take our picture with the DQ sign in the background. She could not understand what the big deal was about DQ.

The yard next to the DQ sloped down toward the water. It looked like a much safer way to get back to the river. A sign on the lawn said "Boys' Home." We cut through the 'boys' yard and found a path that led under the bridge. We imagined it was the boys who had painted their big bright initials, peace symbols, and anti-war slogans in bold, expressive colors on the bridge concrete.

After our DQ break we paddled more rapids before many sand bars slowed us. We skidded our kayaks over the tops of them or were grounded and forced to get out and tow them. At Brainerd, the river is 330 feet wide, with very high banks. From our vantage point, there was no sign of a thriving city. We passed several islands in the river, one of them quite eerie. What was that sound? Lots of birds calling? We guessed the island might be a rookery for some species of bird, but mostly it sounded like wounded animals growling at us. I kept expecting to see a pack of mad dogs or a cougar pop out and spring at us. It was like the sound track of scary movies when you know some creature is going to attack the lead character. But we passed by the island and spotted nothing on the shore or in the trees to help us understand what we heard. Soon our focus shifted to finding Kiwanis Park at the south end of town where we planned to take a nap.

Tired enough to be slaphappy we swapped jokes and kept laughing whether or not they were funny. Most weren't. We paddled to the far end of the park, where we found a sandy beach with some shade wide enough to lie down. I have no idea how long we slept, but it rejuvenated us.

At 3:30 pm, the heat was sweltering. We put on long sleeved shirts to protect us from the sun. To stay cool, we periodically dipped our arms in the water, soaking our shirts. I squealed each time the water streamed down my arms and hit my armpits. Unfortunately I had to dip my arms more often than I liked because the shirt I was wearing was a quick-drying fabric.

Downriver we found fewer signs of people and more peace and quiet. A bald eagle dove for fish, but came up empty. A turtle on top of a beaver dam worked particularly hard to scramble down to the safety of the water as we passed. The river view was stunning. We giggled with delight when we hit sandbars or shot down fast water.

I began to wonder if my question about what I should do when I got home was the right one. It occurred to me that I already believed things would happen the way they were supposed to on the river. What if I held the same would work back home? That's what the women at the gatherings were suggesting. I would need to pay attention and follow my heart. I felt newly confident as I pondered the benefits of living from that philosophy. I wanted to believe I could take my newfound peace home. I visualized it penetrating every aspect of my life.

We stopped at Baxter canoe campsite where we had planned to camp and had a bite to eat. We decided to keep moving even though the campsite had a spectacular view of the river with a sparkling set of rapids. Neither of us wanted to set up camp here when our itinerary had us paddling only six miles the next day. With 21 miles under our belts, (or kayaks) we set out again.

Around each curve in the river we were treated to the sight of deer. Ahead the water glistened and we saw the silhouettes of dozens of deer on the shoreline enjoying a cool evening drink. At the confluence of the Crow Wing and the Mississippi Rivers, we startled a couple of deer that ran across the Crow Wing River to get away from us. It was stunning to watch them bound through the water and disappear into the woods. We pulled in to our campsite around 6:30 pm and set up our tent immediately.

Our fatigue made the thought of expending energy to cook dinner humorous and we laughed. We walked the mile to the ranger station to register and plodded up to the building only to find it was closed. Back at camp in the peacefulness of the evening. Heather wrote in her journal,

Someday I would like to make a movie based on true experiences from my life. Here is a scene for my movie: A beautiful evening, the setting sun shines golden through the trees as Nancy and I walk down the middle of the road at Crow Wing. The world is calm, deserted. The stillness meshes perfectly with our mood, which is that of mellow acceptance. We walk slowly. Exhausted to the point that we don't care that we just walked two miles for nothing.

Heather had more steam left than I did. She washed her hair and went for a hike while I got into my sleeping bag and quickly drifted off to sleep.

July 1, Thursday, Day 27

I woke at 5:30 am and left our tent to sing for the day's gathering, the fifth one of this expedition. A stunning sunrise greeted me. My heart was full of anticipation as I sang and watched the sky change colors from pink to orange to blue. In the quiet, I wondered what wisdom the women would bring when they joined us around the fire that evening.

When I was able to pull myself away from the mesmerizing view, I headed back to the tent to nap. By 8:00 am we were up and happy to see Naomi when she arrived at 10:00 am with a big grin on her face. She brought letters from home and a care package for me from Doug. I really needed that right then The timing was perfect.

The girls set up Steph's (Naomi's roommate) tent to replace Heather's. Steph had bought the tent at a discount store. No matter what they did it always looked like it was on the verge of collapse. I heard Heather exclaim that it was scary to be in. She began making a list of the qualities for her new "perfect" tent. The betrayal of her old tent, after all their time together, still haunted her.

The girls headed to town. I walked to the park office to register our group campsite and surprise Doug with a call. I got the surprise. Doug wasn't in his office. Hiking around the park, I startled a woodchuck running down the trail in front of me. A bright green snake on the dirt road saw me and struck a frozen pose, curled tight with its head rising up from the center, eyes watching me. I walked all around it, and it still didn't move. I couldn't even see any signs that it was breathing. It seemed so vulnerable in the middle of the road. I stood motionless and stared at it thinking, "Oh honey, this isn't working for you. I can see you." The snake's length reminded me of the Mississippi: Its narrow tail represented the beginning of the river, and then it widened and curved like the bends in the river. I sensed Ms Snake was there to tell me something. Perhaps her message is that no action can have negative results. She thinks remaining motionless will help her become invisible, when in fact a better option would be to take action and get into the grass where her coloring would help her hide. I identified her later as a smooth green snake.

The trees at St. Croix State Park are not as tall as those in Itasca, especially compared to those we saw in the Little Winnie campground. This is a much younger forest with thicker ground cover. When I passed the boat launch I heard squeals of glee coming from the river. Three canoes were making their way up river, each carrying two adults and two children. The clanking of the paddles on the side of the canoes, and the many near misses hitting each other, indicated to me they were amateurs. As they broke into singing a round of "Row Row Row Your Boat" it was clear they were having a good time. It took a lot of energy to get up river, but I don't think they cared.

I tried calling Doug twice, but there was no answer. Disappointed, I walked the trail leading to our campsite and nearly stepped on two fuzzy brown woodchucks. We didn't see each other until I was almost on top of them. I jumped and all three of us screamed. The little round creatures scurried into the woods and disappeared.

Continuing down the trail I found Heather's sun glasses—again! She had been searching for them this morning. She managed to lose them almost daily now.

I had walked more than five miles and it felt good to be using my legs instead of my arms. I realized doing things requiring mental or emotional endurance was normal for me. Physical endurance had not been my forte. Often I pushed myself to reach a goal. For a change, on this trip, I was taking care of myself. I was stretching, taking vitamins, eating, and drinking well. While stretching the night before, I noticed I could no longer touch my wrist to my arm when I bent my elbow because muscle got in the way. I thought, *"Whose arms are these?"* Never before had they been in that good shape. My arms were firm, strong, and unrecognizable.

I also realized why I preferred the kayak to the canoe. Not only was it more fun to paddle and glides through the water easier, but it released me from internal dialogue about whether I was pulling my own weight. In childhood I learned to be vigilant in doing my share, making sure I wasn't a burden on anyone. In a canoe if I needed to rest and wasn't paddling as hard as my partner, I would slow her down. In a kayak I'd just get left behind and could catch up later. In a kayak I am right down at the surface of the water and part of my environment. I love that feeling.

Driving back to the ranger station I finally reached Doug by phone. We were enjoying a wonderful conversation when Heather's friend, Leslie pulled up in her car. I quickly ended the call to take her to our campsite. As I drove back, with Leslie following me, I felt bad. I'd ended my time with Doug in order to take care of someone else. Frequently when something breaks my focus, I forget what I'm doing, no matter how important it is, and take on that new focus. I decided to begin to change that habit by calling Doug to apologize.

Heather was ecstatic to see her friend. Leslie had been her support car driver when Heather, her sister and cousins paddled a stretch of the river last year. Leslie planed to camp with us for a couple of nights.

The gathering brought six women to our camp. Alice and Nancy R. would be paddling with us the following day.

A particular type of woman was drawn to the gatherings. They had adventurous natures—that either came naturally or that happened after life had brought them a challenge which they had survived. They were excited to be at the gathering, but didn't know what to expect. They came from different backgrounds. They enjoyed listening to the life journeys of each woman.

As I prepared for the gathering I noticed my confidence had grown. I trusted the process and spoke confidently. It felt good to let go of worry. I hoped that habit was becoming ingrained.

As it happened, Nancy R. was spending her birthday with us. Alice brought her a birthday cake. As we cut into the cake Bonnie said it was her birthday—her sobriety birthday—so we celebrated for her, too.

We began talking about spirituality. Nancy R. shared,

Probably the best metaphor for me has been from an experience I had in the Boundary Waters several years ago. I was in the bow of the canoe, and my friend Mary was in the stern. She is an expert canoeist. We were approaching rapids—they were pretty good rapids. I said, "Mary, I've never paddled rapids. What do I do?" She said, "Your job in the bow is to just keep paddling and to note any big rocks. I, in the stern, will get us around things. All you have to do is keep paddling." I thought, "I can do this." I'm paddling and I start to feel the current. It gets really exhilarating, but there is a big rock ahead of us. Well, I have to save us! So I stick my paddle out and we broadside and stay that way through the rest of the rapids. As we get into calmer water I sheepishly turned to Mary. She said, "That's what I meant by keep paddling." That stayed with me because I have only to keep paddling in life. I don't have to worry about getting around a rock. I need to trust my stern person. To me that is my higher power, my God.

Bonnie added,

I know that the wisdom I have today has come through many many mistakes and experiences. It has been through trials. It has not been through the good parts of life, because then I become complacent.

I was brought up in a Christian home. But when I really became spiritual was when I went through a divorce. I was visiting with my pastor. I said, "I just want him to be happy, even if that means we split up." I had accepted that I was a part of the marriage and I was a part of the divorce. For the first time in my life I had not just put the blame on the alcohol on his side. You know it takes two to make a marriage work and two to split it up. So that was my first experience of a cloud being lifted. I admitted I was also a part of this failing marriage.

Today I believe it is every trial, every crisis I have gone through that has given me the knowledge I need. In November I was told I had gastric cancer. I am eternally grateful I had experiences behind me. That gave me the strong faith to face this crisis. Today when something tough comes up I say "There I grow again." I don't look at tough times as a bad thing. I just look at it knowing I am going to learn. I am going to be a better person. I am going to be able to help others.

As we talked about advice for our young women, Alice said,

I watch all this Brittany Spears stuff. I am happy we have our family raised, and I am not trying to dress teenagers. We didn't have much money. I sewed a lot of the clothes our children wore. They were content with that. They didn't have to have a certain name on it to wear it. Things have changed, and not for the better. In those early years when our children were really small I used to go down to Munsingwear in the cities to buy rolls of fabric. I made all their underwear; I made all the clothing that my children wore. My husband brought home maybe $98 every two weeks. With four children and a house payment, it was hard. I could stretch a pound of hamburger a long way.

All of our children had jobs at home as they were growing up. We had a schedule up on the wall. You could trade a job with somebody if you didn't like doing it, but the job needed to be done. We didn't show any partiality for male or female. The girls shoveled snow and the guys washed dishes. My youngest son was sewing clothing for his French teacher when he was in high school.

Gretchen, who had been a midwife for 20 years, talked about what makes women strong.

Lately I've been thinking it's just the way you are made. You have your period every month. I heard somebody say recently that you had to endure that. And I thought, "Oh, well I suppose that is one way of putting it." I never really thought it was a horrible thing, but it does carve out a different way of looking at life than the guys have. And you don't have a choice. Your body says, "Okay, you are going to try to run this thing, but it is not yours to run." And then you are carrying somebody else around in side of you. It still brings me to tears. It astounds me and everybody in the room when a baby is born, every single time. It's so much bigger than words. It profoundly affected my soul. My husband was standing right there next to me, but he didn't get it. (The group laughed.) He said, "I'll just try to bring in some more money, I'll be back. I really love you. Keep doing what you are doing. I'm just glad I am not doing it."

Nancy R. talked about wanting to be remembered for not being afraid.

Six years ago. I had a traumatic cross-country ski accident. I was alone. It took me four hours to crawl out of the woods. I had a leg broken in two spots. It was dark and got down to eight below zero that night. I have frostbite knees and surgery scars, but the point is, I never was afraid. Every time I got tired, a voice said, "You're not dead yet, keep moving." I kept thinking, should I be writing notes in the snow? Are there wolves around here? Do they think I am dinner? Should I yell? I kept hearing, "You're not dead yet. Keep moving." It was a full moon. I wasn't afraid. I never panicked.

Alice added,

I went to see Nancy a year after that. I was privileged to walk that trail with her. I couldn't believe it. The terrain was straight up. It was straight down. It was straight up. It was straight down. She'd been crawling.

Nancy R. stated emphatically,

I pushed my skis ahead. I couldn't leave my skis. After the accident, I couldn't sleep one night. So I wrote my story and I called it the Night Crawler.

A lush, green, heavily wood trail created a magical corridor on our way to the river. Each woman tossed her aspiration stick into the water; then we stood for a moment taking in the view of yet another magnificent sunset with deer drinking at the shore.

After Bonnie and her friend Kim reluctantly said goodbye the rest of us sat talking by the fire past midnight.

July 2, Friday, Day 28

Heather and I paddled out from the park, having had made arrangements with Nancy R. and Alice to meet us at Fort Ripley landing downriver. They would paddle the last 10 miles of our 18-mile day.

Although the weather forecast thunderstorms, the day turned out sunny, hot, and humid. We paddled a length of river with Crow Wing State Park on our left and Fort Ripley Military Reservation and State Game Refuge on our right. Two signs sat together on a background of pristine wilderness saying, "State Game Refuge" and "DANGER Military Reservation No Trespassing." It struck me as peculiar. The two signs seemed to be at odds with each other.

Camp Ripley, established in 1848, is a 53,000-acre training facility for the Minnesota National Guard. The Guard practices combat operations there. The Minnesota State Patrol also trains at Ripley, along with athletes who compete in winter biathlons. C-130 aircraft land at an Army airfield there. Despite the small arms and artillery fire nearby, Camp Ripley is also home to wolves, bear, deer, and an environmental program that tracks those and 48 other mammals, 565 plant specimens, 126 bird species, 41 kinds of fish, 65 species of butterflies, plus reptiles, amphibians, and mussels. Along with the Department of Military Affairs, the Minnesota Department of Natural Resources helps manage the state game refuge and studies deer and wolves there. Researchers have found wolves denning with pups inside the firing ranges. So I guess it does work to have them in the same place, but it still strikes me as peculiar.

The water is shallow along that stretch of river, and there are many boulders in the riverbed where Nancy R. and Alice joined us. They got off to a rough start. Trying to avoid some small rapids, they paddled towards shore where it was too shallow and rocky. They grounded their canoe on a large rock 20 feet off shore, then rocked, lunged, and argued about how to dislodge themselves. They got free just in time to get stuck once more. Their canoe sat deeper in the water than our kayaks. Paddling effortlessly, I could only empathize and try not to reveal the humor I found in it. Their communication and humor about their predicaments were inspiring. One

Paddling team: Nancy R., Alice, Nancy, and Heather

of them always seemed to find the positive. As the day progressed they got a lot of opportunities to find humor.

We spotted deer drinking at the river's edge. The deer encountered mud similar to what we had back at Lone Pine Creek campsite. They'd climb the bank with goop caked to their legs, looking like they were wearing high top boots. We saw raccoons, osprey, cormorants, ducks, and turtles. We caught a large turtle off guard in a shallow place in the middle of the river. She dove, and her wake welled up six to eight inches as she swam or perhaps ran across the bottom. It reminded me of the way I have seen torpedoes ruffle the water in the movies. Heather saw it, too. We were both stunned by the speed at which the turtle moved through the water. I was glad Heather had seen it because it was hard to believe.

We passed through many rapids around the islands, most of which were not shown on the maps. We could explore their sandy beaches and breath-taking woods but felt we needed to stay on course. Around the islands, we had to pay close attention to spots where the currents converged, and quickly adjust for sudden surges of power.

At one point I approached a strong rapid and spotted a big rock in my path. I was convinced I had it all under control, but the current spun me sideways and took me right over the top. I dropped off the rock with a sudden plunge. Heather said my kayak and I disappeared from sight. I landed upright and felt a huge shot of adrenaline surging through my system. I yelled to the others to avoid that spot, but the sound of the water was greater than my voice. The rest of the paddlers didn't need a verbal warning. Just watching me disappear prompted them to avoid that area.

Naomi, Leslie, Nancy, Nancy R., Denice, Katie, and Alice

As the day progressed, we encountered many other rapids, which were approached with equal parts exhilaration and trepidation.

We took out at Fletcher Creek Landing and had time for a nap before Naomi arrived 45 minutes later. Nancy R. and Alice were noticeably tired, but still smiling. They had a much tougher day than Heather and I. We headed to Lindberg State Park where we would spend the night in a camper belonging to my sister-in-law and brother, Denice and Bruce. Denice and my niece Katie, age 13, would be spending the next three days with us.

On the way to camp we passed the main entrance to Fort Ripley. Directly across from the entrance were several bars, an adult bookstore and exotic dancers. As Naomi turned the corner on to County Road 115 she said with sarcasm, "Isn't it ironic this is right here?" It was more than ironic to me. It stood as a symbol of how many people in our society still see women as objects to be used but not respected. It was so blatant right outside a government facility.

When we got to camp at Lindberg State Park, Denice and Katie had set up the camper and instituted their plan to pamper us. We were off to a wonderful start, just having a soft place to sit, in the camper away from the fierce bugs. Denice and Katie made us a sumptuous meal of beef and broccoli on rice, and strawberry shortcake. Heavenly!

Sleeping in the camper were Denice, Katie, Naomi, Heather, Leslie, and me. With six of us in the small camper it was cozy. The talking went into the evening but it was not difficult to drop off to sleep. Heather's mother, Lorrie, joined us and pitched a tent at our site. She was in the camper with us for everything but sleeping. Nancy R. and Alice camped at another site.

Relaxed and well fed, the girls got squirrely and giggly. It was contagiou—we enjoyed a lot of laughter. Katie hung on Naomi and Heather's words, soaking in every moment.

I noticed that I connected with the girls differently than Leslie did, who easily talked and giggled with them. I was more of an observer. Perhaps I connect better than I think, or just differently. It would not be the first time my perspective of myself was off. We sat at the fire for a while, and then headed to bed.

July 3, Saturday, Day 29

The next morning we found it difficult to leave the soft beds of the camper, get motivated to pack, and hit the water. Nancy R. and Alice were sore from the prior day's adventures and decided not to paddle today. Nancy R. said their day on the river had been challenging, but one of beauty, fellowship, and exhilaration in the company of wise women. She wrote,

You are in the flow of the universe. The universe will reward you.

She loved that we celebrated her 63rd birthday at the gathering on July 1st. Alice wrote that sharing the thoughts and experience of the women at the gathering were blessings for her, and she would carry the embers of the fire on her next canoe trip. I was sad to see this fun pair leave.

As we said goodbye to them the day's paddling team assembled. Christina (Heather's sister), who had joined us again that morning, Lorrie, Leslie, Heather and me. We finally made it to the water at 11:30 am. Paddling was slow with a novice paddler in the canoe. Lorrie was learning. The slower pace helped my right wrist, which was constantly sore. The beating it had taken on the unrelentingly windy days stressed it severely. On those windy days I couldn't wear my wrist brace because the brace didn't allow my wrist to bend as needed for feathering the paddle.

When the paddle is feathered, the blade in the air is level with the surface of the water and does not catch the wind. The other blade of the paddle is in a normal position for making a stroke in the water. Over time, a greater amount of physical exertion is needed if the paddle has not been feathered. Feathering a paddle requires turning my wrist with each stroke,. This, combined with repeated bending, pushing and pulling, had

Paddling team: Nancy, Lorrie, Heather, Leslie and Christina

stretched the tendons that connected the wrist joints. Today's slower pace along with and elastic wrist wrap gave it some much-needed rest.

Leslie tried the kayak and really liked it. With the three Jeskes and Leslie on the water, we laughed a lot. Leslie and I found we had many things in common. We talked about the gathering and what we got out of it. Leslie said it was hard to put into words. There was so much going on at so many levels. What she heard loudest was, *"Don't take what you have for granted."* We both agreed that it's far too easy to take what we have for granted.

Gretchen, who spoke about young women, had touched both of our hearts. She said,

Young women need to know they have value. We need to encourage them.

Besides taking what we have for granted, it seems we are also very good at pointing out what is wrong with our youth. They need interactions with adults who value them so they can be nurtured and grow healthy. We talked about our attempts to value youth in our daily lives by mentoring or listening to them.

Our paddling brought us to the Little Falls Dam portage. While taking the boats out to portage them, I accidentally knocked Leslie into the river. We had lifted the kayak out over a woman who didn't seem to understand she was in the way, even though we said something to her. As I lifted the bow, the stern shifted, and Leslie toppled over another kayak into the water. I turned around just as her feet flew into the air. She popped out of the water pretty well soaked and burst out laughing. We were glad the weather was warm. Portaging the boats warmed her up, but her pants were wet the remainder of the day.

Denice and Katie surprised us by meeting us at Bell Prairie County Park for lunch. Then we saw Naomi a little further down shore. During lunch we received a history lesson from an elderly man named Dave, who told us about logging in the area. Logs left behind had sunk and formed many of the islands around which we were traveling. It is hard to believe the islands with their rich foliage and tall mature trees started with a few sunken logs.

Leslie fresh out of the water

After lunch we began paddling amongst the log islands. The water was shallow. Our boats took different routes through the sprinkling of islands. When we came out the other side we debated which way we were to go. Directionally I had gotten completely turned around. The water seemed to be going in more than one direction. It turned out Heather and Christina were navigating correctly and saved the day.

At the end of the day we rounded the corner into Pine Creek Boat ramp. Naomi was soaking up the sun on top of the dark brown bridge. Hanging from the bridge was our butterfly flag.

A gentle rain began to fall just as we settled in at camp. The mild downpour made the air smell fresh. The tight quarters of the camper became a bit of a challenge with six people in residence. Naomi was tired and had a tough time at the end of the day. She yelled at me, much like she did as an adolescent. Heather stared at her in shock. With so many people around, I didn't feel I could really talk openly to her. So I left to go for a walk, angry and hurt. This old behavior from her was hard for me to accept.

On my walk, I sensed I was being followed, but every time I turned around no one was there. It did not feel like it was a person in the woods. Perhaps it was a forest spirit following a few steps behind me. I had no idea what it might be, and it further irritated me. I wanted to be alone. I didn't need another puzzle to solve. The woods were thick, the trees predominantly oak, maple and ash. There was a heavy canopy that blocked a lot of the light, but the ground cover was lush. Even though it was a vivid refreshing green, it left me feeling closed in. By the time I got back to camp the forest spirit and the woods themselves had distracted me and I let go of my reaction to Naomi's behavior.

The next day, Naomi and I talked about the stress of being in a large group, where we didn't know everyone. I told her I understood the pressure of navigating personalities. In the past I had always been a safe target for her frustrations, but it was not alright for her to fire at me anymore. She apologized. She realized what she had done. After so much time alone she was having a hard time dealing with all the things going on within. The addition of so many people in a tight space with all the it activity put her over the edge.

For my part, I struggled to find a balance between wanting time alone and wanting to fit in with the group. Sometimes I felt sad that more of my friends weren't participating in the trip to show support. As much as I tried not to, I took it personally. Heather's family and friends seemed to be everywhere. It made me realize that Doug and I lived a rather isolated life. We don't socialize with many people. So why should I expect them to show up on the river? I wondered if I wanted that to change.

In this particular crowd there was much for which to be grateful. I didn't think our supporters had any idea how delightful they were making this part of the trip for us. Lorrie cooked dinner for us and brought Baker's Square pies, just as she had done when we were in Itasca. The members of this expedition at this campsite had become independent. We seldom ate together, but we enjoyed each other's company that night. I showed photos of the trip, downloaded onto the laptop computer from my camera. There was lots of laughter, questions and stories.

Before bed, again needing a break from the intensity of the crowd, I went for a walk. I wanted to relax and let go of my unnecessary responsibility to see that everything went well. When I got back, Leslie was building a fire. The two of us sat and talked while she dried her pants from the afternoon's plunge into the river.

Leslie said she saw me on the water as a strong, thin, powerful woman.

Although I've heard similar words before, I couldn't take it in. No matter how many times I'd heard it, I didn't believe it. I knew I would be able do so much more in my life when I was able to embrace that powerful view of myself. I drifted off to sleep repeating what she had said in hopes that it would penetrate.

July 4, Sunday, Day 30

After another scrumptious breakfast, we headed out onto the water with Christina and me in kayaks and Heather, Leslie, and Lorrie in a canoe. Lorrie took the stern this morning to learn to steer. It was challenging new experience for her. She did well. We paddled under cloudy skies with a gentle breeze at our backs. Singing camp songs and laughing. We sang "Stay on the Sunny Side of Life", several rounds of "I Met a Bear," and one I had never heard of—"The Princess Pat." We passed lovely homes along the wooded shores.

After about 10 miles of incredibly delightful river, we said good-bye to our paddling partners at the Blanchard Dam, the largest hydroelectric dam on the upper Mississippi. We would see Leslie and Lorrie later that afternoon, but Christina was heading home. They took out on the east side of the river and we paddled to the portage on the west side.

The portage around the dam turned out to be more challenging than

Portage around Blanchard Dam

we had anticipated. The trek down totaled only 125 yards, but it was a steep hill to an obstacle course of eight-foot boulders and chunks of concrete larger than us. I always seemed to be exhausted when it came time to carry the kayaks. I was concerned about my wrist and the weight of kayak on it as we struggled through this rough portage. The portages weren't anything like those in the Boundary Waters. The Boundary Waters portages often have obstacles too, but they are 'nature made' and somehow more manageable than the enormous chunks of concrete. One of the portages on this trip required us to pass through a cow pasture, opening and closing gates as we went.

As soon as we started down the river, the sun came out. The terrain changed. Instead of houses, we passed long stretches of woods and fields and threaded our way through many islands and rapids. Heather and I took turns either gliding effortlessly through the rapids or bouncing off boulders and occasionally getting stuck. Some times we had to get out of our boats and walk through shallow water. I grounded myself so badly I easily stood in my kayak striking a pose. We wished our recent companions could have been with us for that fun, gorgeous stretch of river.

The water was clear and the shore was sandier than it had been upstream. At some spots in the rapids a grayish brown algae-like plant grew on the rocks and bottom of the river. It would easily break apart into millions of pieces and make the water appear dirty when my paddle touched it. Whatever the plant was, I was thinking I did not want to have to get out and stand in it. Just at that moment, I grounded myself. There was only one way to get loose—get out. I placed my feet in the water and stirred up that grayish brown goop. I tried to focus on the intense beauty that lay ahead

of me, but I could still feel the little particles dancing around my toes and ankles. I got back into the kayak as fast as I could, and not very gracefully. In my haste to get out of the goop I just about flipped completely over.

The beauty along this stretch seemed never ending. The islands, now a regular part of the river, made the river feel more contained. I was adjusting to how the river was growing, and finding myself enjoying it as much as I did days before when it was much narrower. An eagle dove for fish. Turtles lounged everywhere. A really large fish jumped. Where the Swan River converged with the Mississippi it created a large shallow bay and sand bar. Out in the middle of the bay someone had set up a volleyball net and a referee stand. I imagined the spectators all had inner tubes or other flotation devices in which to sit in as they watched a game. I savored the uncommon experience of paddling a kayak under a volleyball net!

Nearing Two Rivers Campground there were several docks along the shore. They were just ordinary docks to me, but every once in a while Heather would exclaim with glee, "Look at that one." It looked no different to me, but Heather had worked for several years as a welder for a company in Ely that makes docks. The docks she was excited about were docks that she had probably helped to construct. One dock had her particularly excited and she went over for a closer look.

I paddled on ahead to our take out spot while she inspected the dock. As I pulled into shore she caught up to me. Two Rivers Campground was a private facility with mini-golf, which Denice, Katie, Lorrie, Naomi, and Leslie enjoyed while they waited for us. The long sandy beach that we landed on was next to the expansive campground, full to capacity. Two Rivers also offered tubing on the Platte River. The seven of us decided we had to enjoy the relaxing fun of floating down the river on an inner tube before we headed to camp.

Picking the tubes was a complex process for our crowd. Each woman had to sit in many tubes to try them for size before they selected the 'right one.' After the bus ride to the start of the tubing area, we energetically clambered down the hill and into the water. Naomi was a little too energetic. When she plopped down on her tube, she flipped over backwards getting completely soaked right at the start. When she tried to get in again, she went over sideways and came up laughing. By that time we were all laughing so hard we could barely settle into our tubes. The third time was a charm and Naomi was floating in her tube along with the rest of us.

Katie, who had never been tubing before, was scared at first, but was soon enjoying every moment of it. This was a first for Lorrie and Heather, too. Lorrie's tube was too big to maneuver. She got stuck on every rock and floated into every downed tree along the way. It was hilarious to see her attempts to steer her tube. Her hands and feet barely touched the water, so her valiant efforts were often fruitless. At one point we were convinced a tree was going to get the better of her, but she managed to maneuver around it by hanging on to the tree and using it for leverage. Lorrie knew we had a code word for when we needed help, so each time she got in trouble she'd yell, "Home Depot." She could not remember "Knox Menards." Each time Lorrie yelled, "Home Depot," Heather and I would bust into laughter. The rest of the group was baffled. We tried to explain but we were laughing way too much to speak clearly.

Anyone in our group who hit a sand bar or shallow spot yelled, "Butts up," to warn the others, and followed it with "Butts down," when she was free again. In several spots I floated gracefully over the shallows while the rest of our group ended up in a big pile. I did not know what I was doing differently than they were.

There were several other groups of people out on the water with us. We passed a rowdy group of drinkers. After great effort to avoid them, Naomi got stuck in the rapids with them. We could see from the smile frozen on her face that she was quite uncomfortable with the inappropriate things some of the men said. One young man in the group got between her and the others, shepherding her along to the outside, reassuring her, and apparently protecting her from the rest. She did not look relaxed until she was away from them and with us.

Shortly after Naomi's encounter with the rowdy flotilla, a couple of people in front of us started screaming. A water snake had joined their group for a moment. One of the girls, who was terrified of snakes, had it swim over her foot as it attempted to get away from the crowd. The girl somehow managed in her panic to stand up on her tube to escape the snake. She was able to balance up there for a long time. A couple of people in our group saw the snake and chose not to say anything to the others, knowing it would scare them. The snake disappeared quickly and was never really a threat to anyone.

Occasionally when we tumbled through a rapids, the gear we held in our laps would get washed overboard but would magically end up in someone else's possession at the bottom of that particular rapids. Lorrie ended up with Denice's water bottle. Thinking we might get hungry before we were done floating, we brought food to snack on after our long day. The food was carefully placed in a waterproof bag called a dry bag and attached to one of the tubes. When it came time to eat we discovered the dry bag was anything but dry. The crackers and other treats had turned to mush.

We'd been told our flotilla would take 45 minutes, but when we reached the take-out point we'd been on the water for three hours. We were tired, hungry and ready to head back to camp for fajitas. When we arrived back at camp, Denice commented on how special she thought it was there were three mothers and their daughters sharing this experience. I agreed.

Dinner was delicious. We sat and laughed as we relived our tubing adventure. Then everyone went to bed early, completely exhausted.

Lorrie wrote,

I haven't laughed so hard for a long time. Facing fears in the canoe, with Heather and Leslie being so supportive, was awesome. My confidence and trust were increased tremendously because of their gentleness, which is something I need right now to help heal my spirit. Water Women Wisdom is the most inspiring venture I have ever been part of. I'm so proud of Heather and Nancy and happy you found one another and created this adventure for yourselves and for all women. Thank you. Thank you. My eyes are joyfully tearful. I love you Heather Lee. You are my inspiration and all that I am reaching out to be. You are living life to the fullest. What else could a mother ask for?

Nancy and Heather, may you have minimal 'Knox Menards' (No 'Home Depots'). Reach for your stars, but keep your feet in the kayaks.

July 5, Monday, Day 31

Everyone crawled out of bed stiff from our tubing adventure. We laughed at each other as we lurched, stumbled and groaned our way around the camper. After I got dressed I headed to the camp office to find a phone. I called WELY radio back home for a interview about the trip. It was a short, entertaining conversation. The MCs, Mike and Joany, were fun. Mike's questions were, as usual, off the wall. He asked,

Did you catch any redhorse and fry them up?
Could you ride any of them?

What about lassoing one and letting it pull you downriver?"

Joany did a good job reeling him in.

Back at camp we said a lengthy good-bye to Leslie, Lorrie, Katie, and Denice, (who where headed home). They really wanted to stay with us and we would have like that too. I found it odd to think that in an hour we would be in the serenity of the river while they were in traffic. I liked our agenda much better.

Naomi drove us back to Two Rivers Campground. Then Heather and I paddled downriver but up-wind. We met Naomi for lunch at Stearns County Park. Heather told us she had been thinking about Zeus, the Greek sky god. She proceeded to have a talk with him about the wind and let him know that she had quite enough of it and would greatly appreciate it if he let up for a while. She went on to let him know that the wind was serving no purpose at the moment so it was a waste of his energy. When she was done talking to him she turned to us and said, "That should do it." After lunch the wind calmed considerably. Heather just smiled.

We paddled past lush woods to start with, but as we approached Sartell, the number of houses increased and eventually became prevalent. We chatted, rating the houses we saw. Our rating scale was based on how enormous or quaint the building was, whether it had a rolling lawn that looked like country club or if the natural plants were allowed to flourish. When it came down to it, we favored the smaller ones that left the bank of the river looking natural.

As the day progressed, more boats appeared on the widening river, especially speed boats. I got more practice navigating waves from their wakes. At one point, a boat headed our way at full speed and looked as if

Nancy with Penelope on board

it would collide with us. It was clear the driver didn't see our kayaks because he had not once looked in our direction. Luckily for us, the passenger spotted us and pointed us out to the driver. I made a mental note to take extra care watching for boaters who weren't paying attention.

We paddled hard, keeping the pace so we'd be

sure to reach Sartell in time to set up for the gathering. As we reached the center of town where the Champion Dam is located we could not avoid seeing an enormous baby blue and slate blue structure. It was International Paper Company, which is attached to dam. The colors made me think of Pepto-Bismol. If Pepto-Bismol was blue this is what it would look like. As we approached the blue monstrosity, it made the dam all the more intimidating. I could hear Heather repeating over and over, "We are getting too close and I don't like this. Knox Menards, people." Each time she spoke it with a little more trepidation in her voice. We landed much too close to the dam and found Naomi who waited to greet us with warm pannini sandwiches. We headed north back to the Sterns County park to eat lunch and take a quick nap before setting up for the gathering.

The park maintenance man, John, greeted us. He went out of his way to help us set up. He was quite talkative and proud of his job. I had asked if we could scrounge some firewood from the park. Immediately he left in a truck and showed up a short time later wearing a blaze orange jacket and riding his John Deere with a load of firewood for us. The girls teased me that he was flirting with me.

In between the assistance we got from John we set up for the gathering under the shelter. I started the fire in the Smoky Joe grill, which both Naomi and Heather had encouraged me to get rid of each time Naomi purged the Jeep. After all, she had to have room for the glorious gifts the river would provide. Now the little grill was earning it's space in the Jeep.

Soon we greeted the first arrivals. Alice, who paddled with us and had been at the Crow Wing gathering joined us again. This time she brought a friend. Six women were seated with us around the fire. It became clear that the energy of this group was very different from the others. People spoke with hesitancy and skepticism. Gertrude, who was the oldest, had experienced a very hard life and came to complain bitterly. No matter what we talked about or how I tried to focus the discussion, it always came back to what was wrong in her life, as though she expected we could fix it. She shot down all encouragement or talk about healing, growth or support. Her attitude was that her life was awful and hopeless. At the end of the gathering Gertrude said, "So, what was this all about?"

When the conversation didn't focus on Gertrude, it turned to religion. Some of the women were firm that Catholicism was the way and the light, and the church was the center of their spiritual lives. Others discussed their various spiritual paths. All were uncomfortable at times, but it was definitely a rich discussion.

Millie talked about her life with husband Don after he retired. They moved and she began a four-year program to become a spiritual director at a local monastery.

Millie began,

At a recent workshop, a speaker disclosed that her four adult children make choices that she struggles with. She said she finds peace with self-talk, reassuring herself that God isn't finished with her children yet, nor with her.

I thought the speakers statement was powerful. It reminded me that when I have expectations, I am the one who becomes miserable, not my children. I'm working hard to let go of those expectations.

For me, religion is a cult or a denomination which people join. Spirituality is who a person really is. I like the image of the onion. As it is peeled we get deeper into the onion, but it is necessary to go around time and again to get to the center. The same is true with us humans. We adults keep coming back to some of the same issues that impacted us in childhood. Throughout our lifetime, like the onion, situations arise that cut away at us. If we are graced, that cutting gives us a deeper understanding of ourselves and our purpose in life. This is growing spirituality.

Jan shared,

I feel that as a teacher, a mother and a community elder, I want to help young people develop the tools they need to get through life. I want them to have that inner strength you get when you have a sense of something greater than yourself. I truly don't think it has to be Christian. I think it can be Buddhist or whatever. I just think it has to be something. It is our responsibility as loving people in the world to give that sense of faith to young people. I have to put the responsibility back on myself.

Maureen added,

I think there is an element of seeker in people. There are many good people. In that seeking, I have come across many people who have influenced me and my growth. That continues even though the world is more complicated. I was just told by my husband's mother that her mother said she was ready to die because the world had become too complicated, too rough and harsh. However, I am still seeking and learning a lot.

In the middle of the gathering a van pulled up and a man got out. While Naomi went to greet him I saw two women and a child get out of the van. When he got closer I recognized him and jumped up leaving Heather to run the group for a few moments. I reached them as he hugged Naomi who looked very confused about this stranger who was glad to see her. They were my godparents, Jim and Val (who goes by the nickname Larry). I couldn't remember the last time I had seen them. I talked with them briefly and excitedly made arrangements to meet them in the morning. Their daughter Beth and a granddaughter were with them.

Jim and Larry had eight children with whom I'd played on their dairy farm as a child. I had the opportunity to visit them for two weeks one summer. They even "gave" me a cow, (which I named Francy), to care for while I was there. Growing up a city kid, I was thrilled to help bail hay, bring the cows in, watch them be milked and get to see the inner workings of farm life. I was totally surprised that they had tracked me down, and immediately felt immersed in the unconditional love I always received from them.

After they departed, I turned my attention back to the gathering and it ended shortly after. I had found neutrality challenging at times because I had to work at looking past the stringent religious dogma that was being presented. Generally I was able to find what was underneath the dogma, and feel the deep spirituality and belief in a power greater than us, which is at the helm of spirituality. These caring women openly shared themselves.

From my traveling companions there were sighs of relief when the gathering was over. Gertrude reminded Naomi of an adult in her life who is bitter, angry and difficult to communicate with. Heather found the "narrow" attitudes of the group almost more than she could bear.

We packed up and headed to Heather's friend Andrea's house for the night. Andrea, Heather, and Naomi stayed up talking while I showered and went to bed exhausted, but feeling a sense of pride at a job well done.

July 6, Tuesday, Day 32

Naomi and I started the day at a coffee shop with my godparents, Jim and Larry. Jim has the same sense of humor and heart-warming smile as my Dad, (who died ten years ago). Jim made me feel as if Dad were with me. We talked about my siblings and then about their eight children and about Francy the cow. They were both so excited to see me—I felt amazingly happy. Jim and Larry looked at me with such affection. I realized on a deep level that I am loved by others, some of whom I rarely see.

As the day progressed I moved from a heartwarming experience to the practical side of life, laundry, a nap, and lunch. Then I headed to the mall to get my sunglasses fixed. They had been crushed among the gear—the lens kept popping out. As soon as I started driving toward the mall, the world closed in on me. I felt vehicles coming at me from all sides. Inside the mall was no different. It was overwhelming chaos. In a shopping frenzy, people fawned and gawked over little plastic things with no real value. Kids told their parents what they *"had to have!"* I had disconnected from the pull of advertising and the "wanting" we live with, but thought, "Oh, I've done that too." Sadness and anxiety welled up in me. I couldn't get out of there fast enough. It is impossible to avoid the fast pace and commercialism in our society, but that is what I knew faced me when I got home.

On the way back from the mall, I realized that after a two-hour jaunt into the urban world I was crabby and particularly irritated. The feeling was unfortunately familiar. It was enough to make me want to retreat from the world all together.

Later, we went to a movie. I really didn't want to see *Spider Man,* but I wanted to be with the group. I no longer can enjoy movies where people or animals are injured—it really bothers me, even if it is only "fantasy." I know what I am seeing on the screen is not real, but the violence affects me at a deep level. I dream the violence in all its colorful detail for a couple of nights after. I know those images have affected how I respond to the world. If it is affecting me that way, I can safely assume it affects others that way as well.

Back at the house after the movie we were greeted by the only animal we saw today, Andrea's dog, Milti. He had left us a note that he wanted me to consider a piece of wisdom for my book.

Eat when you're hungry—bring lots of food.
Stop often to go potty
Bark loudly to scare off the church people.
Love, Milti

July 7, Wednesday, Day 33

It took us quite a while to find a place south of the Champion Dam to put back into the river. It was clear "they" do not want to encourage traveling on the river. There was no easy access. When they placed boulders on the shoreline to stop erosion, the fact that people would need to traverse the rocks while carrying boats and gear could not have been a consideration. We finally entered the river near the Veteran's Park.

At this point the river is about a quarter mile across. The prediction was for rain, which is what it had been doing since we got to Andrea's two days ago. We decided we did not want to camp in the rain. So instead of camping on Boy Scout Point, we would paddle three more miles to Clear Lake water access. Naomi would pick us up there and we would stay at Andrea's one more night.

For the most part we found serene water. But as we passed through Sauk Rapids, we entered a patch rated as Class I-III rapids. Adrenalin was already surging as I paddled fast to keep up with the rolling current of the river. I could see the rapids ahead and I caught a glimpse of Naomi running along shore attempting to capture this moment with her camera. The current carried us past her too quickly. I paddled hard and watched where Heather went ahead of me. We headed for any V-shaped water that we could see and kept a keen eye out for rocks protruding from the water. Riding the Vs generally helped us avoid any white bubbling water where the rocks lie near the surface. It was a short run, but it was one blast of churning bubbling water after another. Coming to the end of the run, during the last maneuver, Heather avoided a spot churning white with massive waves. I aimed to the right of it where Heather had safely gone and found I had unintentionally shot straight into it. With a shriek, I took a cold wave into the cockpit and kept paddling hard. Soon I was in calm water joyfully right side up. All I remember thinking during the adrenalin rush was, "This would have been a good time to have used the kayak's spray skirt." We were both hooting at the end of the run and wanted to go back and do it again.

Heather asked me if I could have handled that run at the beginning of the trip. I said emphatically *"No."* I remembered my encounter with the tree that just about dumped me. My balance and skill level had increased dramatically since we started. The kayak had become an extension of me. I had spent so much time in it, that I could anticipate the effect of every subtle move I made and did not have to think about it.

The adrenalin reduced to a normal level, we stopped at the Munsinger and Clemens Gardens, just before the St. Cloud Dam. The gardens featured roses, shade plantings, perennial beds, a white garden, swings, fountains and statues. The many gardens varied from informal to classical European. Blooms that day were stunning yellows and oranges, blues and fuchsia. Each bed carried a color theme, which the design of the plantings brought to an amazing

Canada Anemone

peak. As we moved from one garden to the next we were treated to a variety of sweet fragrances that filled the air. It was a spectacle of color we found difficult to leave.

We jumped back into the kayaks for a short paddle to the dam. When we got there we pulled our kayaks up and secured them, then crawled up onto the sidewalk like a couple of sea creatures, which is probably how we looked to the folks nearby. They failed horribly as they tried not to stare. Heather mentioned how amused she was at our "river-rat" appearance. I had to agree.

Portaging the kayak around the dam was hard on my wrist. Each time I lifted any weight the ache intensified. Ibuprofen wasn't cutting it anymore. I accepted that pain, too, would be with me until trip's end.

The sun came out in the afternoon. The warmth, calm, and stunning scenery found us drifting on the water. I didn't want to paddle and interrupt the serenity and splendor. Switchbacks and mud had become a thing of the past. The shoreline was predominantly sand and rocks. We began to see different vegetation in the mix along shore. Giant Cottonwood trees appeared everywhere. knew this adventure would be coming to a close in less than two weeks.

Peppered with rapids, the river narrowed around islands where the water surged in spurts. The islands were covered with lush, green foliage, tall trees, and inviting nooks and crannies. I knew better, but I liked to imagine the islands were pristine and that people had not yet set foot there.

The women we met in Sartell kept coming to mind as I paddled. Gertrude did not fit the usual profile of women who came to the gatherings. She challenged me. But the more I thought about her, the more I knew that it was perfect she was there. She represented a great number of women who have had a hard life and have become bitter and emotionally closed off. The world they live in is so limited that when options are presented they can't even consider them. Their perceived limits are immediately applied to all suggestions. They can instantly list several reasons why something won't work, leaving them with no options. Those trying to help them keep butting against a wall. People eventually just stop trying and the person is left alone.

Gertrude clung tightly to her religion and professed all of the answers could be found there.

If only everyone else in the world would just follow the rules of the church everything would be all right. They just need to go to church and follow the Ten Commandments.

Her faith, as she expressed it, seemed to be a mixed blessing for her. It gave her a structure from which she could find security, rules to live by and a place to belong. But it also put her in a position of being dependent on others behavior (following the rules) for her to be happy and the world to be a good place. It is unrealistic to think everyone will follow one set of rules or one dogma. So how can she ever really be happy?

The other women's discussion of how spirituality and religion are separate opened doors to other options and ways of seeing the world. Their philosophies provided room for a greater tolerance of the differences in people and their needs. Some expressed a desire for people to see things their way, but knew each person had to find her way. As they spoke I heard so much compassion for people.

I paddled on as a familiar sense of isolation settled in on me. I wondered what provoked it. Did thinking about Gertrude bring it on? No, it was too familiar. I have always carried this sadness with me and have been unable to unearth its source. I could list many things in my life that may have added to the feeling: Mom's death or my first failed marriage, but I don't believe that is the source. Perhaps more time alone would help.

The need for quiet time alone, and to not feel isolated contradict each other. When I feel isolated I also feel lonely and I want to be more connected to and known by my companions. I seek solitude so I can reconnect to and be known by myself. Knowing myself was the key to rooting out the source of the sadness.

Naomi, grinning from ear to ear, was waiting for us at the Clear Lake boat access. It was still afternoon when we returned to Andrea's house in suburbia. People walked by pushing baby carriages. Lawn mowers could be heard around the neighborhood. Earlier in my life I spent a great deal of energy striving for this very lifestyle. It no longer represents a measure of success for me.

My thoughts turned to the list of things I wanted do in the Twin Cities before we headed home in two weeks. I genuinely wanted to see Aunt Charlotte, had to see the accountant, and needed to connect with Barb. Aunt Charlotte, lovingly known as Auntie Chuck, was Doug's aunt. Each time I saw Auntie Chuck I left feeling empowered to do anything. With a big smile on her face she listened intently and was amazed at anything I did. She hung on every detail and loved to see photographs. She once told me she was sure I would end up being the mayor of some town—and she thought I should be!!

Auntie Chuck was now struggling with poor health, battling bone cancer. Time with her had become precious. My deep desire to see her, my need to see the others, and take care of business began to create a familiar feeling of being on a treadmill. It was easy to keep her at the top of the list. Accountants will always be there and Barb would understand.

July 8, Thursday, Day 34

At Clear Lake we paddled past woods, a few houses, and sandbars that beckoned us to soak up the sun, the gentle breezes, and the peace of the day on the beach. We saw turtles, and more turtles. A little one perched on a larger one's shell. Both disappeared into the river when I approached. Later, Naomi told us about watching an osprey dive out of the sky into the water and fly off with a fish. She was rather excited. She had not seen as much nature as we had so these moments were extra special for her.

One of the benefits of islands is that we had many opportunities to choose where to paddle. Sometimes we didn't stay together. As we approached Monticello, we should have chosen the other side of the island. Three quarters of the way down the length of the long island, a sign was posted on shore indicating the river was potentially dangerous ahead due to undercurrents produced by the Xcel energy generating plant looming in the sky to our right. We had seen the stacks with the white strobbing lights miles back. The swift water eliminated our option to turn back. Anxiously, we continued forward, approaching an ominous-looking structure rising from the shoreline. It looked as though it could start pumping huge quantities of water at any moment, but it did nothing. The current did not change as we passed the generating plant. We felt relieved and assumed the plant was not doing what ever it does to create the dangerous under currents. I asked Heather what else she thought they might be doing to the water. She said she didn't know. Simultaneously we pulled our hands up the neck of our paddles so we would not touch the water.

I found myself doing a countdown of the remaining days on the river, wanting it not to end and, at the same time, looking forward to going home. One of the draws home was an opportunity to build a tree house. The shape of the tree and the location of the branches would determine a lot of the design. I look forward to sitting up there and watching the sunset, or the sunrise.

I had spent 34 days, 24 hours a day, with Heather. She's a sweetheart, but a change would be good. I imagined she was ready to be with her friends, too.

I thought about many things on the water and came to some meaningful realizations. Often they didn't make it into my journal; they had been erased by fatigue at the end of the day. I had to trust they were filed away somewhere in my brain and would resurface when I needed them.

I wondered, after all of this activity, if I'd get restless at home. Heather said she would keep her kayak on her car so she could jump in and head for water anytime. Going home was starting to take on an interesting aura of adventure for me. What would it be like? How would I handle it?

This part of the river was exciting. There were lots of rocks and strong currents to navigate. We were both happy for the challenge. We stopped for a break on Oak Island and heard Naomi's voice drifting across the water. She was yelling "Marco."

We responded with "Polo," but she couldn't hear us. As she continued to yell "Marco," we set off to find her, following the sound of her voice. She was sitting on one of many large boulders out in the water at Snuffies Landing. She had been berry picking since this morning and had a bright red sunburn and ten pounds of strawberries. We sat on the boulder at the edge of the water and ate the sweet, ripe berries until we couldn't eat any more. Our fingers were red with strawberry juice. Refreshed, we paddled on as Naomi drove ahead to our next campsite.

After more of the stimulating scenery and occasional rapids, we pulled into camp at the Montissippi County Park about 2 pm. This park had many people milling around, which heightened our awareness that we had to keep our kayaks safe. We chose a spot just south of our camp and hid the kayaks in the woods, dubbing them the "Wild Jungle Kayaks."

I took a long nap before dinner so I could feel fresh and focused for the gathering. The air smelled sweet and fresh, the breeze kept the bugs down. The river moved rapidly and cottonwoods rustled in the breeze. There were people walking around, using the boat launch and fishing pier near us, yet it still feels peaceful. I dug out the now valued grill and began setting up for the gathering. Heather approached wearing her bright orange sarong and looking rather exotic carrying an armful of wood.

I always dressed up for the gatherings. I wore a purple print skirt that I love. As the facilitator, showing up in my paddling attire never felt respectful of the purpose of the gatherings or of the women who attended.

The first who arrived for the gathering were my sister-in-law, Sandra, and her friend, Arlene. Mary G. arrived right after them. She used to be a clown with Doug and me when we lived in Hopkins, MN. Doug and I had taken clown classes and joined a club called Comedy Caravan, where we met Mary. Mary's clown character was Melody, a tenacious and mischievous being. Doug's character was Oops E Daisy, MD, a perpetually clumsy doctor. My character was a 6-year-old girl named Precious, basically shy with long straight pink hair, pink tennis shoes, a tiny heart shaped nose. While we were members of Comedy Caravan we performed in parades and at festivals. My favorite clowning activity was visiting hospital patients. We clowned for about three years.

Mary G. and I posed for a picture doing an old stick gag. She held a stick up in the air and said, "This is a stick-up." I held one out in front of me and said, "This is a yardstick. I'd found it in the yard." Goofing around with her made me want to try out our old bits on the junior high kids I worked with at home. They would find them corny, which would be the point.

After clowning around we enjoyed the fresh homemade bean dip, chips and bars that Mary G. brought. Sandra and Arlene offered us cookies and bread. The evening's discussion was littered with laughter as we talked about happiness, being your own person, and taking the time to learn who you are before settling down into relationships and other life commitments.

Two of these three women had undergone major life changes as wives, mothers and homemakers. One's husband divorced her after she and her four children followed him around the world. Another's intimidating husband had a stroke at age 48, leaving her to raise their kids, the youngest of whom was 14.

Sandra began,

Sometimes your world comes crashing down on you. You have to find out what makes you happy. Things happen to us in life that changes us.

I think my advice to them (young women) would be to figure out who you are even though you are busy with children, husbands, and community commitments. Figure out who you are and what you are made of. Figure out what makes you happy before you have to face some trauma in your life, such as divorce or death.

Some people make poor choices. Then they sit and whip themselves for days and months and years. What purpose is that? So you made a bad choice. Get over it.

Another bit of advice I have for young women is never, never lose your sense of being a child. It's okay when you are 29 or 49 or 69 to get down right dumb ass silly.

Mary G. talked about what constitutes happiness.

It is that feeling of peacefulness or contentment that everything is flowing in life. Look at animals—cats particularly. They are happy all the time. They have no stress in their life unless you move your foot too fast when they are walking by—then they go straight up. So they have—what?—ten seconds of stress. Then they take a nap.

Arlene shared,

You make yourself happy by what you do—first off for yourself and then for others. Always put yourself first, not in selfishness, but in good self care. Then everything else is going to fall into place.

Mary G. contributed,

Be yourself. Don't change who you are to fit in. If people don't like who you are, get out. Move on if you have to be somebody else to be with those people. I think that goes whether you are with a man or a group of friends. If you change yourself to fit with somebody, that is not going to make you happy with who you are, or make you like yourself.

After more laughter the evening concluded and we said goodbye to these special women.

Later I lay in my sleeping bag and pondered the women's words. Perhaps the sadness that I chronically struggled with needed a dose of focused happiness. I needed to transform the energy into something healthier for me. Outside the tent, louder than the drone of the distant freeway, I heard the sounds of bird wings in flight and bird song in the trees overhead. A deer snorted repeatedly from the woods. I fell asleep, wondering if the deer thought we might actually be frightened into moving.

July 9, Friday, Day 35

After a night of rain, the sky threatened to unleash more downpour in the morning. I mentally readied myself to paddle through it. Again the deer was outside our tent and wanted us to move on. She snorted several times as I lay in the tent. The girls slept through it. Getting up on rainy days is a slow event for us.

We ate breakfast in the parking lot next to the car: away from the mosquitoes. Back in the woods where our tent was set up, the mosquitoes were hungry and relentless. We packed up our gear in record time. Those blood thirsty little buggers can be very motivating.

On the water Heather and I paddled for a long time in comfortable silence. The threat of rain dissipated, as it had on many other days. The skies cleared and the sun peeked out from behind the clouds. Fast moving water made paddling easy and a cool light breeze kept us company. We crossed many ripples that appeared from a distance to be rapids. I had begun to approach rapids with respect and excitement, my fear had faded as my confidence increased.

Along the river were several rowboats occupied by fishermen. I was used to watching guys fishing from motorboats, so seeing the oars in use with no motor in the boat was strange. Then I remembered how, as kids, we'd get around on the lake in an old green wooden boat equipped only with oars.

We passed another "creepy" sounding island, similar to the ones in Brainerd. Just when we decided the noisemakers must be ravens, a heron flew out of the trees, emitting the same wild, eerie call. Mystery solved. Our haunted islands were heron rookeries.

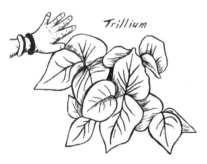

Trillium

Passing another island downriver from the rookery I spotted the largest trillium I had ever seen. I was so impressed with its size I made Heather, who was quite a ways ahead of me, paddle back so I could get a picture of it with her hand beside it to illustrate the size of the plant. I wanted people to be able to get a sense of the true size of this hugh plant. I wished my plant-passionate daughter, Jo, was with us. This would have been an exciting moment for her. I wondered if the flower it produced was normal size or if it was large as well.

At the town of Elk River the Mississippi bends into a sizable switchback with large islands in the center. The current moves and swells in many directions around the islands. It is a picturesque scene, but as has been the case with most of the towns, we didn't see much it. Just past town, the river straightened again. We arrived at Babcock Highway Rest Area at noon. We were grateful we had made such good time because it had begun to get very warm.

We had paddled fifteen miles in three hours, arriving at our pick-up point three hours ahead of schedule. Naomi planed to pick us up at 3:30 pm and we were sure she was out of walkie-talkie range, so I walked the mile into Elk River to find a phone and call her for a ride. I found a phone at the Sunshine Depot Sports Bar, got her voice mail and left a message. I would have felt better if I talked to her directly, but I knew that for Naomi her phone is like another appendage and she checks messages often.

The walk to and from town took me down a busy four-lane highway where the traffic made shocking racket. On the way back a very loud, school bus-yellow tractor with a mower attachment followed me along the shoulder of the road. I kept checking to see if it was gaining on me as I was more than willing to step aside to let him pass, but he did not seem to be catching up. I wished I could get away from all the noise, but we were stuck traveling the shoulder of the road together at a walker's pace. Even with the tractor bearing down on me, I stopped to claim yet another special gift, a screwdriver, for Naomi.

Back at the rest area I found Heather lying in the shade and joined her. I contemplated what happiness meant to me and discovered I could not find a satisfactory answer. If happiness is a choice as Sandra, Arlene and Mary G. suggested, and if happiness is what we strive for, then why don't we all just choose to be happy? The only logical conclusion is that we enjoy our misery. But that makes no sense. I strive towards happiness daily, but what did it really look like? I'm sure I must carry some kind of definition for the word as it applies to my life because I sure know when I am not happy. I drifted off to sleep in the shade of a maple tree attempting to clarify the definition of happiness in my mind and heart.

As the afternoon proceeded, Heather and I played by the water where many small turtles sunned themselves, and we wandered around for what turned into three and a half hours. The temperature had become swelter-ing and my patience with waiting grew thin. The heat exhausted us. Naomi did not get the message until 3 pm. She had been only a three-minute drive away in Elk River at a friend's house just a few feet from where I made the call and had left her phone in the car.

The air conditioning in the Jeep was extremely refreshing. It helped offset the stress from the ride through rush hour traffic. We arrived at Naomi's home where I found a card from Doug waiting for me. It was funny and I was excited to get it.

I went out to dinner with Barb. My wish to have a conversation with someone my own age was granted. She talked about how much she enjoyed her time with us on the river and was eager to hear about our adventures. As the evening progressed, she talked about her unhappiness at work, the stress she felt, and how her company kept expecting more and more. I wanted to give her words of advice, but none came. All I could do was listen. Her feelings echoed others I'd heard along our path. I remembered Andrea and her husband John, who didn't like their jobs, and Gertrude for whom life was profoundly painful. I felt sad there are so many people who feel stuck in such hard places. They reminded me of that treadmill I want to avoid. My determination not to climb aboard strengthened.

July 10, Saturday Day 36

I was uncomfortable during the night and did not get the rest I wanted. In the morning it occurred to me that I'd been sleeping better on the hard ground than in the bed at Naomi's, at the motel, or when I was at home. After breakfast we drove back to Elk River.

Christina, Heather's sister, had considered joining us again (paddling a canoe), but decided to meet us at Elk River with a canoe so Naomi could paddle with Heather and me. The three of us set out in cool, sunny air and on calm water. It was a delightful morning. Soon we were among herons, lots of them—herons in the water, on shore, in the trees, and flying overhead. In our amazement we stopped paddling and floated so we could watch the herons land, gangly-legged, in the trees or fish for their breakfast along shore. In one stretch of river I counted 48 herons in sight at one time. Around every curve in the river there were more and more of them.

Paddling a few miles downriver we passed the home of one of the teachers who works in the same school as Naomi. Deb and her husband Jim sat on their dock waiting for us. They invited us in for lunch. During casual lunch conversation Naomi mentioned that her friend who was scheduled to shuttle us to our car, was unavailable. The girls hadn't planned to tell me because they felt they had it worked out. Their plan was to call a taxi cab. I pictured us sitting at a landing trying to figure out how to get the canoe and kayak on a taxi cab. I was irritated that the girls hadn't told me earlier and I grew silent. Naomi recognized right away that I was upset. If they had kept me informed I could have made arrangements with someone I know in the cities to help us. I realized they were trying to fix the situation on their own and take some of the responsibility from me, but I was still upset. Deb and Jim solved the problem by offering to shuttle us, and we eagerly accepted.

Refreshed by lunch and time out of the sun, we headed out again into the beautiful day. Before too long we encountered a headwind, which made paddling a challenge, especially for Naomi in the canoe. Her muscles were not used to this. As the day progressed we occasionally pushed against white caps. I watched the wind take a toll on the girls, who sat higher in the canoe and caught more wind than I did in the kayak.

Just past Clouquet Island, close to Anoka, the number of boats on the water increased dramatically. The stationary fishing boats weren't a problem, but the speedboats and jet skis created a challenge. They chopped up the water until the surface looked like a giant waffle, sending wakes our way from every direction. We could again see that some of the drivers were paying no attention to our little boats. As we passed one of the fishing boats we asked what was going on and discovered that we had paddled into the middle of Anoka's annual festival and bass fishing contest.

Not much farther downriver we noticed a large round man in his senior years in a pontoon boat. He appeared to be naked. When he passed us we could see he had on a Speedo that could not have been any smaller. He smiled at us and it felt creepy. It appeared he got some pleasure out of having three women look at him. Unfortunately we got to see more of him than we wanted to as he paraded his boat up and down the river many times that day. The girls began to refer to him as "Dirty Naked Man."

We spotted a flock of Canada geese that we were to see several times that day. We knew it was the same flock because among them was one white goose whose bright white feathers made her stand out amidst the others. She seemed out of place to us, but they all seemed quite happy together.

We stopped under the Highway 169 Bridge in Anoka and walked up to the SuperAmerica store for ice cream. While we savored our frozen treats, we watched in awe at the recklessness with which some people were navigating on the water. The waves were chopping and colliding in every direction from the wakes of all the boats. The situation was complicated at this location because the Rum River, which feeds into the Mississippi, was just yards from the bridge. The Rum River had boats coming and going from it as well. There were a couple of boats anchored in the shade below the bridge. The occupants were calmly fishing as if all the commotion around them did not exist. The occupants of another boat were clearly irritated by all the traffic. I wondered how they could catch anything.

Perhaps the fish in this part of the river have adapted to churning water and noise.

The farther we paddled from the bridge the less traffic there was. We began to focus on getting to the Coon Rapids Dam where Deb and Jim were to meet us. The wind continued to toss waves in our direction. Fatigue was showing on Naomi's face. Concern for Naomi was showing on Heather's face. This made the final stretch seem even longer.

Approaching dams no longer generated trepidation for me. As long as we approached with respect and paid attention, there was nothing to fear. At the speed we travel there would always be enough warning and time to do to keep ourselves safe. With the Coon Rapids Dam boat access in sight my thoughts were interrupted as Dirty Naked Man cruised past us one last time, still grinning.

The boat launch at the dam was teeming with people of all ages. It looked as though everyone in town was out enjoying the day. Deb and Jim were waiting for us, all smiles. They had spent the day at the Anoka festival. They thanked us because if we had not needed a ride, they would not have gone to the festival. They gave me a ride back to the Jeep and related their adventures at the festival.

After they dropped me off, I drove back to get the girls. They had been entertained by all the characters coming and going at the boat launch. We struggled to secure my kayak and the large aluminum canoe onto the Jeep. We put the canoe on first thinking that the larger heavier one should be on the bottom. But the kayak would not fit no mater what we did. The canoe had to come down. We needed a new approach to our puzzle. Determination gripped us. We placed the kayak where the canoe had been. Then we angled the canoe on top of the kayak. We stood back and admired

Heather and Nancy with canoe and kayak
on top of Jeep

our accomplishment. Heather cinched it down so tightly that nothing could have possibly moved.

Back at Naomi's, we sorted and repacked gear for the last few days of our expedition.

As we unpacked, Heather and I commented on how hard Naomi had paddled through an emotionally and physically demanding day. Heather commented that the 17 miles felt much longer due to the wind. Naomi felt better listening to us. She said that she felt like a wimp and that she should have done better. Her shoulder had hurt badly by mid afternoon. She now glowed pink with sunburn and her legs were a ripe apple color. We told her we were impressed with her endurance. We decided to treat ourselves to pizza for dinner.

July 11, Sunday Day 37

Thunder and lightning woke me at 4 am. I feared the weather would keep us land-bound. I reassured myself that the storm could blow over in a couple of hours, and went back to sleep. When I woke again at 6 am, I heard thunder and saw an occasional flash of lightning brightened the morning sky. The weather report said the skies would clear up, so we packed our gear and headed back to the Coon Rapids Dam.

We put in at the south end of the Coon Rapids Dam Regional Park, safely away from the churning water that poured from the dam. The water dropped about 20 feet there. We lumbered down the rocky embankment with our gear in the pouring rain all the while watching the sky for lightening. The lightning continued but was blasting further off in the distance. Our intuitions said we would be fine, so Naomi headed home. She reminded us repeatedly that she was headed back to her warm dry bed.

We paddled quietly close to shore for a few miles hoping we would be safer from the weather. Serenity settled in as the thunder faded. We passed homes, wooded areas, and city parks along the banks. As we paddled I felt myself getting colder and wetter under my rain gear. I refused to believe that my trusty rain gear leaked. That jacket and pants had kept me dry through many a storm on many camping excursions. When the sun came out, we pulled off the water onto one of the islands that are part of the Islands of Peace to strip off our outer layers.

The Islands of Peace were founded in 1971 as a tribute to the men and women who served America in times of war and peace. The slogan etched on an arch where you enter the trail down to the islands read *Where peace is a way of life every hour of everyday for all those willing to share the experience.* The three islands have mature forests of maple and basswood trees, and high population of birds who raise their young there. It has long been a home to a pair of bald eagles.

I was less than peaceful when I discovered I was soaked to the skin. My rain gear had totally failed. I'd have been in serious danger of hypothermia if it had been colder or if the rain had continued. I felt betrayed. The thought of buying new rain gear at this point, so close to the end of the trip, made me angry. I took off the kayak's spray skirt, dumped a considerable amount of water out of the cockpit, and began the drying process. Down on the pebbled beach Heather was conducting her own drying process, but hers was much less involved.

As we continued paddling, the river paralleled Interstate 94. The chaos of the city I had once lived in captured my attention. On the other side of the freeway wall people sped by in their cars as we peacefully paddled our kayaks a few yards away. I perceived the Mississippi as a vein of serenity and beauty that runs through our country, through towns and cities on its way to the Gulf of Mexico and the greater waters of the Atlantic Ocean. This and other rivers around the world subtly provide balance wherever they flow.

It occurred to me that a vein of serenity and beauty could be found in people, as well, no matter what they present on the exterior. These veins are not always visible, and sometimes we have to work to find and enjoy the serenity and beauty in people or our environment. It has always been worth the effort to discover that vein in people or in nature.

With these serene thoughts occupying my mind, we rounded a bend, and there was the hazy familiar skyline of downtown Minneapolis. We stopped paddling for a few moments to take in the view. Then we found a

Minneapolis skyline

sandy beach and took a quick break across the river from the Minneapolis Water Works, a stunning red brick structure. We paused there because we knew our experience of the river was about to make a dramatic change. But we were in for an unexpected surprise.

Until then we had been the only boat on our section of the river. Ahead, a speedboat circled repeatedly. We could not fathom why it would continue to circle as it did in the same spot. It was not until we got closer that we could see it was pulling three skiers. They were practicing impressive maneuvers and sailing off a ski jump. They spun in circles in the air as they flew off the jump. We paddled slowly past on the other side of the river to enjoy the show. Occasionally one of them would fall sending water splashing high into the sky. I expected the boat would have to stop to pick them up as we did when I skied at my Dad's cabin. We were impressed at how quickly and easily the boat was able to pick up a fallen skier without stopping. He barely even slowed down. We marveled at their skill and were grateful for the private show. We found out later the Minneapolis Auquatenial was to happen the following weekend and assumed these guys were practicing for a show they would do during the big annual festival.

Drifting along enjoying the show I spotted an older African American man on the shore also watching. His sweet face smiled a toothless grin and energetically nodded at us as we went buy.

Soon we passed barges that lined the banks of the industrial area. Trees were few and buildings many. This was a different world. There was an expansive metal salvage yard with a giant conveyor belt, a lumberyard, and other industrial buildings. The area was all a-buzz with trucks and cars moving about in controlled chaos. The docks were designed for large boats and barges and we were but a speck among them.

Leaving the industrial area we entered downtown and came around Nicollet Island, called "Curling Waters" by the Dakota Indians. It had once been inhabited by railroad yards, grain mills and "working-men's taverns." It is said rowdy drinkers could be dropped through trap doors into the river. Today's Nicollet Island featured wooded parkland, lovingly restored homes, with flowers and beauty everywhere. This is where we got our first sighting of a paddleboat.

As we approached the upper St. Anthony Falls lock, (our first), we passed under a series of bridges with vastly different architectural designs. There were several impressive bridges along the span of downtown Minneapolis. They included suspension bridges with huge cables, not so impressive rusty boxy shaped iron bridges and, my favorite, the Stone Arch

Bridge. It was constructed with native gran-
ite and limestone and consists of 23 arches.
It was originally built for the railroad but was
revitalized and was now used primarily for
pedestrians and bicycles.

We spotted the bright yellow painted on
the end of a concrete wall that lead to the
lock and paddled straight toward it. The
builders of the locks consider each lock to
be one of the steps in the "Stairway of Water"
on the Mississippi River. Without these locks
and dams, safe passage for the large boats
and barges would not be possible. As we
approached the lock I saw anxiety on Heather's face. We had both seen the St. Anthony
Falls in the past and had great respect for its

Heather in lock
holding onto float

power. Neither of us wanted to make a mistake here and get swept over the
falls. The lock's traffic light was not lit, and we feared the lock was closed.
Paddling closer we found the cord hanging from the wall to signal the
attendant and we pulled it. The traffic light came on and the attendant
answered. He told us we would need to wait 15 minutes for the lock to fill.

We held tight to a ladder on the side of the wall that extended from
the lock and watched as the water rushed past us and into the lock. Along
with the water, a lot of debris and trash swiftly moving past. This was the
first time we had seen much debris in the water and we were stunned
and disheartened. Soon the light turned yellow, and the enormous gates
opened toward us. When the light turned green we cautiously paddled in,
feeling particularly insignificant compared to the size of the structure.

The friendly attendant explained the first three locks had floats built
into them so small boat users like us could safely hold on as the water level
in the lock changed. The floats sat in vertical slots in the concrete wall
of the lock. We paddled up to one of the floats and Heather reached in
to grab the rusty metal handle while I held tight to her kayak. As we held
our kayaks in place the water level in the lock slowly dropped 50 feet. The
water was released into the river below through channels at the bottom of
the lock. The water did not churn as much as we had anticipated, and we
eased our grips. I had wondered if the locks would operate for such small
craft. We discovered they operate for any size craft traveling the river.

The attendant became very excited when we told him we had started

Women's Wisdom

Basic Wisdom

I don't feel very wise at 60. I am still wondering when that wisdom is going to come. —Terry B.

Truly, I am going to start with wisdom. I believe that I get wisdom everyday from every single person I meet. I am very grateful for that gift and I look for it. I almost expect it everywhere I go. Be it at the laundromat, it will be something that I am going to learn. —Deborah

I never knew a definition for wisdom. I thought it was a wise guy, wise acre, wiseass. But wisdom is nothing more than knowing the things that I can change and the things that I can do something about. It isn't a big mystery. If it was, I couldn't have it. It would be too big for me. So it had to be small enough and easy enough so I could have it. Other wise I would be on the outside. I want to be on the inside with others and connected. Really, wisdom is being smart enough to know what you can do about something. Knowing your business and what is your neighbor's business isn't a real big deal. —Sharon W.

I think that power and wisdom are two of the words people tend to not understand. Wisdom can be mistaken for intelligence and power can be mistaken for authority and control. —Peg

I think about so many of those eastern countries where the women have been in servitude for many years. I come at this from my own perspective and wonder how they can feel like a person when they are covered up to a point where they are a non person. Only their eyes are visible. —Alice

Are we ready for a woman president? It really hit me because I look at this world and get so upset. No, wait a minute—the balance is off. We need both in charge because we need nurturing and thinking. I think we need to have women in influential positions to bring out their aspects which help this whole universe. —Nancy R.

I believe women are the wisdom of the world. I would like younger women to spend time with older women . . . younger women and older women like this type of gathering tonight. —Roxana at Itasca and planned to paddle to Red Wing. He said it was a highlight of his summer when "seafaring folks like you" came through his lock. He kept talking to us as we descended. We watched more debris bubble up in the water. He said the lock could hold two hundred-foot long barges and that as we moved downriver the locks were much bigger so they could hold more barges. The barge traffic further downriver was much heavier. As he spoke we heard another attendant radioing the next lock's crew that we were coming. Soon we were too deep within the lock to hear him anymore, although he kept talking. We felt even tinier as we descended to the bottom of the lock.

The gates at the far end of the lock were gray with large wooden beams spaced horizontally across it. We assumed the wood beams were to absorb the impact of boats that hit it. The water was full of trash, and the concrete walls were covered with a dark brown slimy substance. We waited for some kind of signal that we were at the bottom but none came. The downriver gates in front of us slowly began to open away from us. Unknown to us, on the other side of the exit gates, people waited in an observation area overlooking the lock to see what exciting boats would emerge from the structure. When the gates opened we saw their surprise when our two little kayaks paddled out towards them.

The Lower St. Anthony Falls lock was just a river curve away and soon was in front of us. The crew was ready. These attendants were also excited about our trip and were very friendly. That lock dropped only 30 feet. We were beginning to feel more relaxed about the process. Navigating the locks wasn't nearly as scary or hard as I had expected. Relieved, we continued downriver.

Exiting Lower St. Anthony lock we found ourselves in fast-moving turbulent water. Carefully I glanced back over my left shoulder and saw the water rushing furiously over the dam. Around a bend we reentered a world of trees, and stopped for lunch on a wide sandy beach on the campus of the University of Minnesota. High riverbanks and trees set off our prominent view of the Minneapolis skyline. There was a lot of activity along the shore at the campus: people walking, biking and sitting in the shade enjoying lunch. That was the Minneapolis I remembered.

We paddled to the Minneapolis Rowing Club landing, anticipating an easy end to the day, only to discover Naomi could not get to us because the road down to the water was gated. The idea of hauling the kayaks up the steep hill to the Jeep was eliminated right away. We decided to head downstream for easier access, but the open doors to the Rowing Club boathouse captured Heather's attention. She stopped dead in her tracks

Women's Wisdom

It is something that we can experience with each other. We don't have to stand there and act like we know what we are doing when it comes our turn. We don't always know what we are doing. We have to have somebody there saying, *"Well I don't know either, but I am with you."* —Gretchen

A woman understands a woman. I think it has to do with life-bearing. We are strong because we have had to go through a lot. We have never really been alone even though it may have seemed like it. There has always been another woman who has gone through the exact same turmoil at the exact same time. We can draw strength from that. When we are at our highest and happiest. When it is a joyful time, there is a woman down the street or in the grocery lines that is enjoying a wonderful time. We prop her up too. It is a *we* thing when it comes to women. It is a *we* thing. We are never alone. —Sharon W.

We live in such a *yang* or male dominated culture, sometimes with so much aggression and not much wisdom. One of the things we manifest well as women is nurturing wisdom. We make all the difference in a family, in a community and in a country globally. —Rebecca

Life Perspective

Always celebrate on your birthday. —JoAn

I used a metaphor with my husband who died of cancer. It is this: there is a great possibility I could die before you. I could get hit by an 18-wheeler. I call it my 18-wheeler metaphor. There are no guarantees in this life. We lose our life. We don't live in the now, because we think we can do it tomorrow. To appreciate what we have right now is really the gift. The spirituality to understand this, and assimilate it and really appreciate the things that are given to us is the gift. The gift of this gathering is very very great. —Sally

I did what made sense at the time. It is not a matter of what I didn't do, it is a matter of a person's journey. What matters is what I am doing now on this journey. —Millie and stood speechless gazing through the door at the many racks of rowing shells. I saw sheer lust in her eyes. She'd dreamed of being on a rowing team and loved the look of the sleek, hip-wide shells. They were about 25 feet long, brightly painted in silver, red, white, and blue. The rower sits on top to row. I don't know any more about these shells but I couldn't imagine how I would keep from tipping into the river.

After waking Heather from her trance, we headed downstream. Boat traffic picked up as we approached Lock and Dam No. 1 near Minnehaha Creek, my childhood playground. A couple of boats buzzed near us to get a closer look. The drivers did not realize what effect their wakes have on kayaks. We approached the lock and paddled under the Ford Bridge. Looking up we saw big sections missing from the bridge, as construction crews made repairs. It was odd to be able to look through the gapping holes to the sky on a bridge I had crossed many times.

Then I noticed an immense wall on the west bank that I had not remembered seeing as a child. It covered the entrances to many sandstone caves that we explored as children. I must admit I did not spend much time in them myself because caves scare me. When I was a teen there were many efforts made to close off the caves because kids were getting hurt. In one case, I recall someone died in the caves. The stone was so soft that it was not difficult for the kids to dig a new entrance around the old concrete barrier that had been constructed years ago. The new wall was definitely a long-term solution. There were no signs of the caves along this stretch anymore.

Feeling like old hands at this lock business, we got in line with three other boats. The light turned from red to yellow and the gates slowly opened. Two boats exited, the light turned green and we entered the lock. Lots of people on shore watched. We held on to the float, which in this lock was shoulder-high. The bigger boats' crews grabbed onto mooring lines tossed to them by the lock attendants.

The water level slowly dropped 30 feet. I became anxious to see Minnehaha Creek just south of the lock. Just up the creek is Minnehaha Falls which drops 53 feet. Anticipation grew as the gates in front of us opened. As we filed out into a boat-congested area I went to the right to see the creek. Heather paddled left to avoid the traffic. Areas in and around the locks are "No-Wake Zones" for safety reasons. However, one of the motorboats that shared our lock behind me roared out at full speed, swerving within a few feet to my left. The boat's wake came flying at me, and I managed to turn fast enough to avoid flipping. Angered by the event, I got quick retribution. A sheriff's boat posted just outside the lock flashed its

Women's Wisdom

As a grandmother one of my recommendations is to simplify your life as you get older. I don't seem to have completely acquired the talent yet. I had an illusion that when I got older and my children were raised and on their own, when I didn't have all those responsibilities and I was about this age I would have this wonderful amount of time appear from somewhere. Time in which I could do all those things I had wanted to do my whole life. All the projects would have their space and time and they would unfold. Well it just has not quite unfolded that way. I am 56 years old with 6 grandchildren. I have more projects popping up and blooming in my life than ever before. One of the things I learned along the way is that we have so many preconceptions about life and how we think it is going to be. It reminds me of a quote by Mark Twain, *"Most of the things in my life never really happened."* All the things I worried about and preconceived are just illusions. Sometimes we are so focused, we loose sight of the most important fact that we create our own lives. Creating our own life is our greatest piece of art, our gift to ourselves and our families. Take back your power and intention and create your life! —Rebecca

Life is a journey we need to take. It is a journey that will include all that you have experienced and all you will experience. Our job is to learn along the way. —Nancy R.

Decide how you want to live your life and then find the job or the method that will allow you to live that life. If you don't listen to the voice inside you, you can miss your opportunity. It may take you longer to get there, but as long as you get there before you are breathing your last what is the difference? —Mary O.

I retired as a teacher of Physical Ed after 25 years. At 64 I started this new adventure. I went from teaching to guiding women canoeing in the Boundary Waters Canoe Area. —Barb

One thing we have to try to instill in our youth is our traditions and our culture. Our children shouldn't be imitating gangs. They think it is all glamorous. —Sharon F.

blue lights and gave a burst on its siren. The speedboat was waved over. I couldn't make out what the sheriff's deputy said, but I know my kayak was part of the conversation because he pointed at me. He handed a piece of paper over to the speedboat driver.

I paddled toward the creek and quickly realized the water forcefully rushing from the usually calm creek would be too strong for me. The waves it was creating were the biggest I'd seen thus far on this trip. The current was moving too swiftly for me to pull to shore before hitting the creek's turbulence, so I turned and made a mad dash across the river, hoping the big boats would see and avoid hitting me. I reached the other side where Heather was safely waiting. We paddled a short distance to Hidden Falls boat access, pulled our gear on shore and watched the crazy boat traffic. It was reassuring to know the next day was Monday and that most people would be at work and not on the river with us.

Hidden Falls Crosby Farm Regional Park is on the opposite shore from Minnehaha Falls Park. It is named for a small waterfall that is hidden in a ravine and a farm that once existed there. The source of this falls is an underground aquifer which pours from the earth at the top of the ravine and makes its way to the river. I saw it once when I was a teen exploring this side of the river.

After several attempts to reach Naomi on our walkie-talkie we gave up. We borrowed a cell phone from a man who was enjoying the park with his family. She was relieved to hear from us because she had not been able to find the rowing club and had been at a loss as to where to find us.

A few minutes later Naomi helped load the kayaks onto the Jeep. We drove to the shelter at the other end of the park where we would hold a gathering the next night. The shelter's unusual design included overlapping and connecting square roofs. Some boys were using them as skateboard ramps, while other boys videotaped the action. I guessed from their skill and ease up there that they were experienced and comfortable riding the roofs. It looked risky to me. The mother in me wanted to make them all get down.

We drove to the home of my brother Brian and his wife Jayne and found Brian busy laying paving stones. Jayne showed us to our rooms, where she had laid out new towels, shampoo, shavers, lotion, and lip protection. Jayne wanted to pamper us. After we showered, they took us to Sergeant Pepper's restaurant for dinner, then back to the house for ice cream and to share photos of the trip. As I drifted off to sleep I took a tally of the day. We had navigated nineteen miles, three locks, and survived major boat traffic.

Women's Wisdom

I grew up in a family where I was not really encouraged but also not discouraged. I was allowed to be just who I was. I was allowed to grow to be me. I grew up with eight brothers and was allowed to be one of the guys or be a girl. I could be what ever I wanted to be. I was free to grow. That was a good time for me until I was in my early to mid 20's. From then until probably just within the last five or ten years I was kind of locked into going with the flow. I was living other people's spirituality and not really trusting my inner voice. I think the whole business of navigating the waters of life is an important thing. Pay attention! For me navigating the river of life means determining at what point you trust yourself and your own inner voice. I trusted my inner voice when I was younger, but I have mistrusted it for a long period of time in my life. It's not that you can't depend on other people, not that you can't be supported by other people. You need other people in your life to support you. But you really do have to trust *you*. You live your life day to day. Nobody else does. There are many people, a group of women right here, who have a lot of things to share, a lot of wisdom. You can take bits and pieces of that wisdom to help you navigate the river of life so you don't get sucked into the flow. Whatever direction you choose to go is okay. —Jane

The first question for me is how you find your place on the planet. This has been a path for me. I grew up in the tradition of going to church on Sunday with the family. That always felt wrong to me. We learned "we are right, they are wrong." How can the whole world be wrong? It just can't be right to be so exclusive. I guess I have always been a seeker and looked for the truth in whatever philosophy without limiting myself to, "Oh I am sorry that is out of bounds." —Amy

I don't really think you appreciate life until you get older. Young people don't seem to know where they are going. They don't know why they went that way, or which way they are going to go now. They are not looking forward to growing old. They just stumble along each day. That is part of what you learn as the years go by and you raise your family. You have ups and downs, tragedies, and sickness. It all makes you strong. I am lucky I am here. I could have "checked out" seven years ago very easily but I am still here. I am happy. I don't believe God lays out a plan for me. I have to make my own plan and it has to agree with Him. He has to believe in what I am doing. I think this way because He gave me another chance. That means a lot. —Arlene

July 12, Monday Day 38

We left Brian's at about 9:30 am and drove back to Hidden Falls. I'd lost my prescription sunglasses at Brian's and losing things puts me in a nasty mood. I searched everywhere for them and was sure they were still in the house somewhere. When we hit the water, I paddled hard to burn off the negative energy, but it didn't work.

The river experience was a completely different world from Sunday's madhouse. Wind and water were much calmer. No other boats were in sight. I'd grown up in this area. I found myself looking at Fort Snelling with new eyes. It was closer to Minnehaha Falls than I expected. My childhood trips from one to the other by car took forever. The black stonewalls felt much more like a fortress from down here than when strolling around in the fort above. The fort was built here because the Mississippi and its tributaries offered many natural transportation routes. To the Dakota nation, this area was considered sacred and the center of the world. There is a great deal of history surrounding the life of this fort. The land was purchased from the Native Americans for $200 worth of trinkets, a keg of whisky and the promise to build a trading post. It was the primary trading post until the Civil War when it was used to train volunteers for the army. More recently, it was used to process inductees into World War II.

As a small child I explored the woods along these banks, delighting in finding a spring bubbling from the ground or frogs in a pond. My brothers and I found many treasures and had many adventures here. I remember one spot on the creek where we always crossed by going over a downed tree. The log was wide, but it always scared me. I was much slower in crossing than my brothers.

Along the shore stand many majestic old trees. The ones closest to the water have had most of their roots exposed by the river's currents. There appears to be nothing under ground to support them. The weathered gray gnarled roots grew in every direction. I found each tree more fascinating than the last.

We drifted for a while watching a brilliant white egret fishing near shore. It was so intent on what it was doing that it didn't notice us approach. It stood motionless in the water staring into its depths. Suddenly it plunged its head in

Women's Wisdom

I like what we are doing here at this gathering because I think we all have a part to play to create peace. I think it is a privilege and we all need to really lift up our voices both in prayer and in support of people. —Paula

I find some of the things I thought were the most painful, and those things I didn't think I was going to get through, are the things that have taught me the most. I have used that learning from them the most and it makes me who I am. If life were just floating down the river then we would just float. Everybody needs to hit some rapids! —Terry B.

If you try to go with the flow it never really works. At certain times you always hit rapids or you hit little things here and there and end up having to navigate. —Winnie

The direction the river of life has taken me did not follow the path I expected. That difference in flow has shaped everything I am. If my life had gone on the way I thought it was going until I was 100 or whatever, I would never have done the things I have done. I'd like to share a quick story about the Mississippi. When I saw a sign a few years ago that said National Route of The Great River Road I decided I was going to drive it. I have driven both sides of the entire river road from Itasca State Park to Venice, Louisiana. If my river of life hadn't changed directions 15 years ago when my husband left after 32 years of marriage, I would never have done that. I just enjoyed it so so much. —Nancy O.

Sometimes you paddle and paddle and you don't get anywhere. —Terry B.

If you float you go wherever the current takes you and you see some stuff you wouldn't have seen otherwise. There is something to be said for just getting up in the morning and doing what the day dictates. My friend Sal would say, *"Taking in the day,"* and taking in the next day, and taking in the season. —Terry O.

At 65 the direction my life has taken has totally dumbfounded me. I didn't expect to become the person I am today. I have to say I am quite proud to be who I am. Don't let anybody else tell you what to do. Find it your own way. The answers are all within you. That is the only place you will *ever* find them. —Shaughn and came up with a small fish flopping in its beak. I was engrossed and delighted by my environment and my mood had lifted. I decided I'd be okay if I never found my glasses. We paddled into the convergence of the Minnesota and Mississippi rivers. Eerie plumes of muddy water from the Minnesota River bubbled up to the surface all around us turning the Mississippi a milky brown.

Just under a railroad bridge we pulled off to the side and let a paddleboat go past. Heather told me she'd once worked on one of those boats. One of her paddleboat adventures included getting grounded on a sand bar while loaded with passengers. After a few hours they were able to dislodge the boat and get their passengers to shore. Later Naomi told us that the captain helped her locate the boat launch and gave her permission to go into the paddleboat area to wait for us. After the "Harriet Bishop" passed we could easily see the St. Paul skyline. I recognized the new Science Museum building. St. Paul is known as "Little White Rocks" by the Dakota Indians because of the white sandstone cliffs in the area.

We radioed Naomi that we were a half-mile out. She told us the *Women's Press* photographer was there waiting. We quickly spruced up as best we could, given we were over-heated, sweaty, tired and had no mirrors or combs. When we got closer, the photographer directed us to land in a place where the light was good, though the spot wasn't good for us. Sharp metal objects protruded from the water, and the current was strong. We didn't think she had any experience with kayaks because she instructed us to move around in ways that were not possible, and she was impatient with us when we did not do as she asked. She wasn't the friendliest person we'd met thus far. Heather was glad to get away from her and her cowboy boots.

After the photo session we headed back to Hidden Falls Park to wash our faces, change clothes, rest and eat in the shade. The heat and humidity made us feel limp and useless. Christina, the *Women's Press* reporter,

Women's Wisdom

Fifty and free. Now I am free to do what I really want to do. I have tried going against the flow. The thing that keeps coming to mind is this—don't try and push the string. It doesn't work. Don't push the river either. All the things in that happened childhood, all those negative things made me what I am today; they are a part of who I am.
—JoAn

In the river of life you will find all kinds of debris. The natural kind, the deadheads, and all the stuff that is floating around. These are a part of life and it isn't always pretty. You will see the paper cups, and the trash that is the part of life we wish we didn't have to see, but does exist.
—Nancy R.

I have a real strong feeling that my whole life has been directed. It has gone in directions I had never planned, but it just kind of happened.
—Alice

I agree, there are no coincidences. It is synchronicity. It is like flags are raised and say, *"You need to go in a different direction."* I know sometimes I struggle, but when I can get this perspective it is "Oh yeah I see now where that was leading me." —Mary Jo

I believe in the snowball effect. One negative thing leads to another. The other side of that [being positive] is an even bigger snow ball. If you are nice to one person, even if it is only for a moment, it makes that person's day better. Then they might be nice to another person.
—JoAn

Everywhere I lived people were the same way. If that is what you are looking for, if that is how you live your life, that is the way it is going to be. But when you make a choice (we all have choices), when you choose to live life differently and you make your new circles, then things will change. —Elaine

When I look back at the years when I was working, my vision was always to the day I could quit, to the day I could move on and could go somewhere else. I never really sat back and enjoyed where I was at the time. I was always looking ahead. In ten years I will have what I want? —Sandy met us at 3 pm. We talked with her for an hour and a half. I was so hot and tired, it was a struggle to answer her questions in any kind of coherent way. I was relieved when Heather offered her thoughts. After she left I could not remember what I'd said. I wondered if I sounded intelligent. I didn't have any other choice but to let it go and trust that what ended up written in the article was what was meant to be.

The gathering time was approaching quickly and we began preparations. First I had to ask two groups of boys skateboarding on the building roof to find another area to skate. This appeased the mother in me who wanted to get them down. For the most part they were good about it, with just a little grumbling. Earlier we had noticed a man who had sat in the shelter all day. We debated about whether we needed to ask him to leave. He had left his post only twice to go to the bathroom. Because he was away from the area we were using we decided not to disturb him. The participants didn't even notice him.

People began to arrive: Barb (who had traveled the first 3 days with us), Deborah, and Deb (who I had not seen for years), MaryJo, Jodi and her dog, Maggie May. Maggie May was a golden retriever, very white in the face at age six. My family and I had trained her as a service dog while volunteering for Helping Paws, an agency in Hopkins, that trains service dogs for people with physical disabilities. Many of the people who receive the service dogs are in wheel chairs. Maggie May lived with our family for two and a half years. She arrived at the age of nine weeks, and could sit on command after only a week. By the time she left us, she knew 80 hand and verbal commands.

It took a moment for Maggie May to remember my voice and recognize me. But when she did she wagged her tail, wiggled and squealed with excitement. At times when I talked, she sat up and watched me intently. I could see she was tempted to break her "working" command and come to me. I had to be careful not to talk with my hands and inadvertently give her any commands.

Nancy, Maggie May, and Jodi

Women's Wisdom

We are waiting for the big things; we are planning on the big things. We are dreaming while little things happen, without our even knowing it. They are the most beautiful. —Kathryn

I honestly think everyone comes from good. We recognize it. Not everyone has had the opportunities to be in good situations all the time. Some people's opportunities have provided them with more. Regarding children, we are responsible for presenting them to other young people. We can help them by volunteering. I am still learning a lot. —Maureen

In once sense I think no matter what I would have chosen I might have ended up at the same port. But, it might have been a different journey. I think there is something in us, perhaps the soul's purpose, I am not sure. It is something innate. We may choose a more difficult road, a stupid road, whatever. But the destination is there. You will get there even if it is back-pedaling or going back and forth. I don't think you can avoid it. —Sister Dorcas

I don't think there are any wrong decisions. They are just decisions based on what we know. They are not written in stone. I used to think that before I could make a decision to do anything or go anywhere, I needed to know exactly how everything was going to turn out before I did it. Once I made a decision there was no changing it. That is not true. The part about making bad decisions is that I don't think they are bad decisions. They are decisions I make based on the information I have. They are decisions I make based on how old I feel that day. I make two-year-old decisions or six-year-old decisions some days. But I make decisions. If it doesn't happen to be what I want, then I make another decision to do something else. —JoAn

Share with Youth

When you are twenty you think every decision you make is going to last a life time, but it is just one more decision. It is either right or wrong. If it is wrong you make another one and keep moving on from there. It does not have to be forever. —Ronnie

Jodi brought three women with her. Barb brought a friend. Two women came as a result of an ad I put in the *Twin Cities Wellness* paper. Heather's cousin Mariah, and JoAn showed up. Heather met JoAn in the park earlier in the afternoon. Heather had been drawn to JoAn because of her greyhound and invited her to return for the gathering. Not counting Heather, Naomi and me, the gathering brought together 14 women, including five grandmothers.

Shaughn began,

The direction my life has taken has totally dumbfounded me. I didn't expect to become the person I am today, and I have to say I am quite proud. My wisdom is: be who you want to be. Find your joy. Find what gives you the greatest joy and do it. Don't let anybody else tell you what to do. The answers are all within you.

Jo An said that all of the negative things that happened in her childhood helped her grow into who she is today. She added,

I have tried going against the flow. The thing that keeps coming to mind is, don't push the river. It doesn't work.

MaryJo, who is an artist, shared,

I just did a show. The title of it was Vanitas. Vanitas were still life's done in the sixteenth century. The idea is that, you can't hang on to the things of this earth. They are all going to go away. I wasn't intending to cry but that is the way it is. They (the art pieces) normally have something like a skull in them, for example, flowers that were decaying, a timepiece that has stopped or a candle that gone out. Okay, so it's about not hanging on to the things of this earth, because you are not going to take them with you. For me, the theme, was, how do you grasp life in spite of its gravity? And that is why I am here. I figure, if I can spread a little joy or positive energy, that is it.

Growing up, there were a lot of people, who criticized me saying it should have been done another way. I am finding I don't need that. I need people who are affirming and supportive of me.

She added that she has become more thoughtful about how she uses her energy.

I need to do it wisely, instead of by brute force. I still get it done; it's just in a different format. I am not going to run the marathon; I'm going to walk the marathon.

There is one thing I wish I would have been told when younger: never be afraid to make a mistake. If you try something and it doesn't go the way you

Women's Wisdom

What wisdom would I like to share with younger children as they travel their river of life? I think the truly wise don't touch that with a 10-foot pole. I see the yearning for independence. I see the uncertainties and the trials they are going through. My best contribution is to stand back and say, "It is your choice. I will support you." Those are the hardest words you ever say as a mother and a grandmother. —Vi

I don't have advice for younger people because they teach me all the time. You see I was an old spirit when I was young. I was a *know-it-all* and I had an attitude problem. I wouldn't listen for nothing. Everyone else was old and didn't know what was cool and what was going on. I listen now, to the youth—all the way down to my little granddaughter. She will be three next month. One of the smartest most wisdomy things she said to me was when she climbed on my lap and said *"Grandma, your neck is falling down. Grandma your neck is falling down."* That is wisdom and it comes right out of a baby's mouth. We think about what will get us to the stars and all that kind of stuff. We think that is wisdom. Wisdom is what I think it is. —Sharon W.

I don't know about sharing wisdom with younger people. I want to do that by example. I would like the example, to be someone who had a dream and followed through on it. —Nancy O.

For anybody young or old, if you have a dream or goal, strive towards it. There will be obstacles and there will be things in the way. Never let loose of that dream or goal. Just keep pushing towards it. It will happen. Maybe not the way you wanted it to happen, but it will happen. Maybe not when you want it to happen. If you have a dream or goal fight to get it. That is part of happiness. —Arlene

I would like our young people to know the power of their voices. I would like them to know their stories, our stories, because they teach a different culture and a different way to look at life, which is good. I would like them to know their history. If a person's stories are not told, if your history is not told, then you do not exist. You go through that education system and you are not there. What are you? You're nothing. You do not exist. It is important for us to become the writers, the actors, the singers. We have to do that. We have to become the doctors so that we can tell our stories and have our own voices. —Elaine *intended, don't feel as if you failed. Learning from mistakes can give you great confidence.*

JoAn said she became more compassionate after she turned 50.
Now I look at people differently. I try to see what their pain is, and how I can help. If somebody cuts me off when I am driving down the freeway, I look at them and say, "I hope your day improves." I believe in the snowball effect. One negative thing leads to another. If you are nice to one person, even if is only for a moment, they might then be nice to another person.

Ronnie's advice was,

Decide what you want to do, and just do it. Don't let any reasons stand in the way. You are going to get to be 50 whether you do it or not, so you might just as well do the things you want and be true to yourself. You won't be good for other people, unless you are good for yourself.

Deborah added,

I have seen the benefits of taking risks. So, consciously, once a week, I do something that is fearful for me. It could be just making a hard phone call. A couple of years ago I jumped out of plane. I wouldn't do that one again.

JoAn said,

You have to laugh! Life is way too serious anyway. You know how the light turns green, and there is always somebody behind you who is in a big hurry, and they lay on the horn? I was waiting at a red light and was the first one in line. The light turned green, and my hand accidentally hit my own horn. I just cracked up. Here I was honking at myself. We just have to laugh at ourselves. It is very contagious.

The structure of this gathering was different from the previous ones. At the end, we took time for the younger women to ask questions of the grandmothers. Their thought-provoking questions delved into the truths about life.

Heather asked,

What is different about the 50s?

Shaughn replied,

It gets better. The thing that happened for me was that a little switch turned on in my head. All these things I had held in came out. If I didn't like your behavior I told you. If I liked your behavior I told you. That was really freeing. There were times when I would open my mouth and I couldn't believe what I said.

Women's Wisdom

There is one thing I wish I would have been told when younger. That is, never be afraid to make a mistake. If you try something and it doesn't go the way you intend, don't feel as if you failed. Learning from mistakes can give you great confidence.

On the other hand, if you try something new, be open minded. Don't be so rigid in your thinking that you won't allow yourself to change your idea as you pursue it. I like to tell myself to *relax my thoughts*. In other words, be open to new ideas, either your own or someone else's. Creative thoughts will begin to flow through your mind and soul. —Lorrie

I have three sons and two daughters. My hope is not only for my daughters but for their friends as well, is to be true to themselves. I hope that my sons will honor the women they are with. I have too long a history of being dishonored as a woman. Regardless if you are a woman or a man, be true to yourself. It is the essence of life. There is a very high price to pay when you don't do that. I encourage young women to not be afraid of being who they are. —Ana

Young girls are growing up trying to please everyone. It gets them into a whole world of trouble. If we could impress two serious thoughts for a young girl to remember, they are first, that she can be her own person and second, it is okay to say no. —Alice

I would like to tell young women to have more self-esteem. So many women think they are nothing unless they have a man. They think that they have to have a boyfriend or a husband or they aren't well enough on their own. If young women had enough self-esteem they could try a new life and new things while they are younger. Change careers. Don't be so caught up that you have to *do this* or you have to *do that* to have confidence. Young women are *something* even if they don't have a man. —Melanie

What I would tell girls is that a lot of things people worry about will pass. *This too will pass.* We put all our energy and focus on things we have no control over. I can see it in my own daughter. There is always this need to win. Youth is wasting a lot of energy on the need for approval. It is a waste of energy! —Gloria

MaryJo added,

I think finding female energy is strong, but it is also compassionate under-standing caring empathy. Between my 20s and 30s it wasn't necessarily there. Coming to see and recognize all the wonderful characteristics of all my female friends is a joy. It is taking on strong but still female characteristics.

Patty asked,

Do you value money differently?

JoAn answered,

Money is a five letter word. The thing that is different for me is that I don't worry about financial security like I did. There were times when I was selling everything in my house just to buy food. (Selling my plasma to buy food.) I know now that the universe supplies. There is more than enough for every-one. I lived and believed that if I became rich then somebody else was going to become poor. I didn't want to take that way from them. But it is not true! I practiced poverty mentality—afraid there wouldn't be enough for tomor-row. I shouldn't really want a lot because that would be very selfish.

Then I had a vision one night of this stream of energy and abundance. It was traveling over the city and dropping abundance. When it got to my house it said, "She is practicing poverty mentality so apparently she doesn't want any abundance. If that is what she chooses I can't go against that. I can't override that. That is her choice, so I need to just keep moving on." Now I know the abundance in the universe is unending; I have a sense that I will always be taken care of. A sense that I didn't have in my 20's. I want to spend it now. I don't want to wait until I am older. What if I don't ever get older?

Ronnie added,

I interviewed a number of older women in the course of some research I did. These were women whose husbands had been ill. For the most part, these women didn't have a job and had never worked outside their home. Notice, I didn't say they never worked. They never worked for their own source of Social Security or a means of making ends meet. There is one woman right now who is in her late 60's and has to work just to maintain her health insurance. One of the things that came out in my conversations with these women is how totally fearful they were of not having money, of living to be older and not being comfortable in terms of knowing if there would be a roof over their heads and money to pay for things.

So for me, on the one hand I worry about it less, but I also worry about

Women's Wisdom

A deadly combination is to be both impractical and cautious at the same time. I did that for a number of years in my 20s. I was impractical in terms of not thinking about money and/or the future. Money was not important to me and it still isn't. I could have been a little more practical. You might want money down the road. Put some money away in savings, a 401(k) or something. I was too cautious. I wanted to move to San Francisco but I wanted to go with someone. I couldn't get a friend to go with me. There were so many dreams I had. I wanted to be a makeup artist in the movies. I went to school for that but I didn't pursue it because it meant taking a leap. I missed a lot of leaps because I let fear stand in the way. There isn't anything more deadly on this planet than fear—except maybe apathy. Just get it out of your way; *somehow* get it out of your way. Eleanor Roosevelt said, (I am not quoting her exactly but) *"In order to conquer fear you have to look it in the face. You must do the thing you cannot do."* —Mary O.

I would give young women permission to take care of themselves in body, mind and spirit. —Nancy R.

My advice to youth is: don't listen to us so much. Listen to yourselves. What you are learning is exactly what you are supposed to be learning. What we have to say in retrospect is not quite as accurate as we would like it to be. Some of the advice people were trying to give me when I was growing up just confused me because it didn't match up to their example. Make your own way. Everything is going to be okay. It really is. It is here. It is now. It is happening. —Sharon W.

It is important that young women get to know themselves first and care about themselves first before they get into a relationship. Men and women are so different. Men will never think like we do. Get to a point of acceptance instead of trying to change people. Understand them for who they are. —Bonnie

I would want to tell younger women to keep moving forward with respect and patience for self and others. We can have it all if we are willing to dare to be different. Move slowly. Remember that the freedom you want for yourself you must allow others to have. —Millie

I would want a young woman to know that she is loved. Loved by God. Loved by people in the world. —Jan *it more because I am fairly healthy. The odds are that I probably have another 30 years to be around. I have to be concerned that there is enough money being stockpiled away for that rainy day. At the same time, it means couching it with 'I might never get there.' So I want to spend it and enjoy it while I am here. It is more about balance.*

The discussion was marvelous and rich. When it was over no one wanted to leave. Many lingered to talk a bit more with each other before they departed. Several of the women said that what we are doing is inspiring to them. Heather and I had reached a place where the trip no longer felt like a big deal. This was just another slice of life—another way of doing it. From our perspective we were paddling, feeling purposeful in the moment and on one long camping trip. We got up, packed, and paddled. Each day offered new challenges. We maintained a certain level of alertness for boats, downed trees, or a lock around the bend. But basically our days consisted of get up, get packed and paddle. We were in synch with life. The exception was that the gatherings were always extraordinary.

Bill and Melissa arrived to take us to their home for the evening. As we finished packing things up, Naomi's phone rang. It was my bother Brian. He'd found my glasses—yeah! Off we went to meet him. On the way, we stopped for a heavenly hand-tossed pizza with spinach and white sauce. The girls went to bed while I talked with Bill and Melissa.

Exhausted, I went to bed. The girls had saved the couch for me, but again I found the floor the most comfortable place to sleep.

July 13, Tuesday, Day 39

After breakfast with Bill, we headed to Harriet Island to meet Heather's sister, Christina. She was bringing a canoe which she and Heather would paddle. We did the usual gear shuffle after which Naomi declared her triumph. She crawled on top of the Jeep like in a game of King of the Hill.

We set out on the water. Naomi headed out to visit with a friend. For Heather, Christina and me, the first five miles of river was less than serene. We paddled past barges docked on shore and heard the loud airport traffic from Holman Field next to the river. I know St. Paul has more river-based industry than Minneapolis but it is not evident from where we paddled. This area has bays and backwater where much of the industry is located.

High atop Dayton's bluff opposite Holman Field is Indian Mounds Park, one of the oldest parks in the area. The Indian Burial Mounds are believed to be the burial site for an ancient people known as "Hopewell."

Women's Wisdom

I work with teen moms and pre-teen moms and their babies. The thing that seems most important every time I stop and look back is this: Did I make sure and tell them I thought they were important? They are an important person. They don't have to earn it. That idea seems to be driving me to help these young girls and young women who are looked down on. They are bearing the next generation. We have no wisdom when we put them down. It is important to try and help them realize their value so they can express it. It would be really great if there were a few of them that said, *"You know, I didn't know I was important, but she pointed that out."* —Gretchen

Don't change who you are to fit in. If people don't like who you are, get out! —Mary G.

Living on one's own, we find out who we are, what we can do, without all of those other expectations. Young women will be so amazed at what they discover about who they really are and what they are capable of, on their own. I would advise any young woman, whether or not she is contemplating a commitment to a partner, to do this. —Kathryn

Be Remembered For

Just being remembered would be fine [Laughing]. That is typical Sally. —Sally

That I was a really good gardener. I am really proud of that. Living gently on the earth. Sometimes just floating. —Terry O.

I would just like to be remembered as a joyful person. Letitia means joy in Latin. It has been one of my striving goals to live up to my name, you might say. —Letitia

I would like to be remembered as a person who was honest and had self-honesty, who had a sense of humor, who was not afraid to tell a joke or story on myself. I'd like to be remembered as a fair person who followed her heart, perhaps to the alarm of the rest of her family. —Terry O.

In more recent times the Dakota Indians used the site for their burials. The mounds in the park are fenced off to protect them.

Just below Indian Mounds Park is the site of Kaposia or Little Crow's Village. The village was important to the Kaposia people for their survival. It was also used by a group of Mdewakanton (Dakota) during the summer months. There are many sites like this along the Mississippi River, known as *"Ha-Ha Wa-Kpa"* (River of the Falls) to the Dakota.

Few other boats shared the river with us. We stopped to take a break and were on shore when the first barge of the day passed creating a three-to-four foot wake. I watched the barge's wake intently and remembered Bill and Melissa's story about two teenaged girls who had been killed about a month earlier when a barge ran over their homemade raft. Neither craft could maneuver quickly enough to avoid the collision. The story gave us pause and heightened our respect for the barges. Coal, corn, gravel— so many products, are transported on these hulking barges. They measure 200 feet long by 35 feet wide. On this part of the Mississippi, towboats push as many as 15 barges at a time. The little towboats have about 5,600 horsepower. Just one barge can carry cargo equivalent to that of 15 large rail cars or 60 semi-trucks. Our canoe and kayak looked like specks next to these big rusty hulks.

It was another day for birds. Sadly we found a bright green parrot dead on shore and wondered how it had come to be there. As we passed Pigs Eye Island Heron Rookery, we spotted hundreds of seagulls, egrets, and pelicans. Our old friends, the pelicans, seemed out of place scattered among the others. Their odd shapes next to the other birds made Heather and me smile. A bald eagle soared aloft. Because eagles had been with us nearly every day, we came to think of them as our guardians.

Women's Wisdom

I would love to be remembered like my grandma. She had friends. She had faith. She had a cheerful spirit. She lived in a little town and knew everyone that lived there. She never did anything rich or famous. She wasn't the best cook or seamstress. She did crossword puzzles and counted cross-stitch. Everyone who knew her loved her because she was just nutty. That would be just fine with me, to be remembered as the person who was fun to be with. —Jan

I would like to be remembered as someone who tried to be the best person I was created to be. To encourage and allow others to do the same is important—and that I loved deeply. God . . . Self . . . Others. —Millie

A few weeks ago my husband was sitting with a faraway look in his eye and he said, *"When you are gone there are going to be all kinds of ways to remember you. You have made all those beautiful quilts and you have painted all those beautiful pictures. You give them away and people have your pictures. What have I got to show for it?"* I said, "You have five children that have been successful human beings." But he said, *"I don't have anything that I can put my hands on."* I told him that what he had was more important. —Alice

I had a sense of humor, that I was fun, that I thought *outside the box* and that I was happy. That is how I would like to be remembered. —Kathryn

I would like to be remembered for having a sense of humor. I hope I made people laugh. I am not Mother Teresa by any means. Maybe she had a sense of humor, I don't know. She probably did. She would have had to have a sense of humor to do anything like she did. I was listening to Carl Rhiner once and he was proud to say that all of his children were non-toxic individuals. I hope I am a non-toxic individual. —Amy

I would like to be remembered as someone who had a dream and followed through on it. I didn't just sit back and say, "Well maybe somebody else will do it." Or sit back and wait for someone else, hoping they will ask me to do it. —Nancy O.

I don't know if it is important to be remembered. —Donna

On the water again, we spotted a barge approaching us from downriver. We hurriedly paddled close to shore. We positioned ourselves so we would head directly into the wake it would create. We waited, reassured that a barge could never sneak up on us. They progressed so slowly that we would have plenty of time to move to safety. The barge passed. We rode out the waves and enjoyed them. I was surprised it wasn't scarier. The process was all quite manageable.

Aspiration sticks

At the closing ritual of the gathering the night before, we had given each of the women two "aspiration sticks." Like each of the gatherings before the women burned their first stick. Since our gathering was a distance from the river, I gave the women the option of having us put their second aspiration stick in the water for them. Several chose to give us their sticks. Pausing to float on the water I took a few moments to say a prayer, and then tossed the sticks into the water and watched them float downstream. Seeing the sticks with the bright purple yarn floating in the river always made me feel hopeful.

As I finished, I heard Heather yell something to me. They had gotten so far ahead I couldn't tell what she was saying. Just then I drifted over a large wave that seemed out of place. *"Wing dam, wing dam,"* Heather yelled again. We had just crossed our first wing dam. Like other challenges of the river we had been warned about, it proved less frightening than advertised. If Heather hadn't told me, I would have missed it thinking it was just an odd wave. Wing dams are concrete or rock walls under water created by the Army Corps of Engineers. The dams angle out from the shore into the river, directing the current, controlling the course of the river, and reducing erosion. They can create enough turbulence to flip a small boat, but that certainly wasn't the case this time.

The shoreline was heavily wooded. There are stretches of sandy beach strewn with tree trunks grayed by the elements. Tree trunks were piled high on some beaches and up against the bridge abutments. From a distance they looked like twigs that had been washed up on shore. Up close the tree trunks were impressive in size, as was the power it took to pile them on top of each other. They were a reminder that the Mississippi should always be respected.

People in cabin cruisers passed us with curiosity. Some boaters cruised

Women's Wisdom

I love life so much. The one thing that scares me is death. I don't want to die. I just don't want to die. That is why I want to live to 102. Maybe at some point I will be happy with that—but the thought of not being around! I don't want to miss anything. I can't die. But If I have to die I want to be remembered as vibrant, enthusiastic, funny, supportive, caring, sassy, and intelligent—somebody who loves life, in spite of everything, I have always been an optimist. —Mary O.

There was a time that I wanted to be remembered as the top sales person. And I was. Today I want to be remembered for the only thing that matters to me—my relationships—that I was a loving, caring mother and grandmother. Period. —Bonnie

If I am going to be remembered it is because I wasn't afraid. I was secure in who I am. I think my children and my friends would say that I am adventuresome. *"You are going to do what now?"* I really am not afraid to live or die. I want to be remembered for being a responsible person, for being a kind person, being good at a number of things. Those are important too. But it really hit me that I wasn't afraid. —Nancy R.

I know I will be remembered for my art work. *Goodness, Truth & Beauty,* as John Keats wrote. Besides expressing my own soul, I tried to make people happy with my work. I hope they will see that I tried to be open and I loved. —Susan

I was asked this question just a few months ago at a workshop. At that time I said I would like to be remembered as a good neighbor. But in between that time and now, Mothers' Day came along. We didn't celebrate the holiday because as the kids were growing up we were Jehovah's Witnesses. I don't ever get cards from my children. But from my two middle boys (one of them was extremely angry over our divorce), I got a card that said, *"Happy Mother's Day Mom. You are a woman of peace."* I thought, "Whoa, even with all the violence they recognized that. They saw that in me." What better legacy to leave than to be thought of as a woman of peace? It meant a lot to me that they would pick that. That is how they look at me. I think that would be a good way to be remembered. It is a good way to try to be, peaceful. —Peggy in spotless shiny boats and were dressed in matching outfits with incredible tans. Others folks wore torn tee shirts, had tattoos and cruised in boats that showed signs of wear. I enjoyed the diversity.

At this point in the river we had to pay attention to the red and green buoys that mark the channel down the center of the river. Bigger boats must travel according to the markers. Green buoys are on the right side of the river when you are traveling downstream and boats stay to the left. Red buoys are on the left side. A saying "Boat Folk" use is: "Red on right, returning from sea." We had the option of traveling near shore in most cases. Curves in the river dictated how we navigated. We often crossed over the channel to the other side to avoid being to close to the larger boats. We proceeded with caution when crossing the river, knowing that we were not visible to the larger boats.

I tired quickly as we paddled in the heat. The sun was unrelenting and there was rarely an opportunity for shade. The breeze was warm and did not cool us. We took the opportunity to go around an island and follow a channel to enjoy some cooler air closer to the trees. Occasionally we got a whiff of dead fish or decaying plants, but it didn't last long. The cool air was worth the price.

Along the shore, and on a few islands, there were makeshift homes created out of a vast variety of things; new wood, drift wood, tarps, old windows, rope, tires, trash cans, chairs, etc. One makeshift home was particularly intriguing. It reminded us of something Peter Pan might have lived in. It was large and colorful and creatively put together. It even had a rope swing over the water.

When we landed to make camp, the first thing we did was take a heavenly two hour nap on the beach in the shade. We camped on an island site

A makeshift home on the riverbank

Women's Wisdom

Of course everybody would like to be remembered as a nice person. I would like to be remembered for having a clean house, a clean car and that I helped somebody out if they needed help. —Gertrude

I would like to be remembered as a loving mother, number one, but also as a person with a sense of adventure and an interest in lots of things. I was someone willing to take a chance on life to make it interesting. —Alice

How I would like to be remembered—I made a difference. —Shaughn

You know how a boat goes through the water and leaves its wake behind? For me as I travel through life, I am always leaving a wake behind me. I want that to be positive. I want people to say it was positive when they encountered me. It wasn't negative and it wasn't scary. —JoAn

I want to be known for two things. First is my outrageousness and never being afraid to be who I am . . . ever! Second, is that I practiced acts of kindness. —Deborah

I would like to leave this life having people remember that I had a lot of guts, and stood for what I believed, in and that somehow I was able to make a difference. —Ronnie

I want to put the wisdom which I learned from my nephew into the circle. He was probably the youngest wise person I have ever met. He left this earth when he was twelve years old. I had the gift of being with him when Make A Wish came to him and asked him what he wanted. They would grant whatever he wanted. My brother and sister-in-law could not handle being there, but I choose to be there. He couldn't decide between two things. One was to get the rookie card from Michael Jordan who was his hero (because that was worth a lot of money). Or he had the opportunity to meet Michael Jordan. I watched his face as he was deciding between the two. He looked at this lovely couple that came to tell him he could have his wish and he said, *"I want the rookie card because then that is forever."* It brought such delight. He was so full of humor. We were expecting he was going to want to meet his hero. My nephew is not with us anymore but the card is with us, and so is his spirit. —Deborah just north of Upper Grey Cloud Island that offered a small sandy beach. During the night we discovered lots of body-unfriendly roots and rocks. Our spot at the tip of the island came with a fantastic view of the lush green bluffs downriver. This site had been difficult to access. There was a big sandbar (perhaps mudbar would be a better description,) leading up to the beach. We got stuck pulling in. We heard lots of noise from passing boats, barges, and trains. The train tracks seemed to run down both sides of the river. We could hear trains pass at all hours of the day and night. but couldn't see them. We felt lucky when the wind masked the racket. It became clear that our days of campsites with picnic tables and latrines were over. Now we had nothing but the ground and the woods.

In the cool evening air we made a ring of rocks in the sand and built a small fire from driftwood, watching barges chug past. Fatigue usually precluded fire building at the end of the day, but that night we relaxed by the flames and enjoyed the sunset. As one of the barges moved up stream past us I noticed a strange phenomenon. The barge first caused a kind of tsunami effect as water pulled about four feet away from the shore when the barge approached us. After the barge passed huge waves followed. Then the water settled back to its original level.

Gazing into the fire it occurred to me that there were only three days left on the trip. I was torn between being glad I would be heading home and continuing the adventure. I look forward to returning home to Doug

Christina at fire

Grandmother Stories

Norma's Story

You see, I started out with computers. Then I left college after two and two-thirds years. I had two years in engineering and transferred into math education. My standard comment is, "I ran out of money and ambition at the same time." [Laughing] I was going with my husband at the time and I was able to live at home and go to the university. You still needed a little money to go on. At that point things were opening up and there were some pretty good jobs. This was probably 1955. I was able to get a job using my math background working with Honeywell. They called us computerists, before the company had computers. We did the computing for some of the first space ventures like the Vanguard rocket. So space things have always been very interesting to me. And then in '58 our first daughter was born so I stayed home for her. I had the joy of being able to be home with my children. I tried going back to work. I worked with computers for six months. But raising the family while working was not working real well for me.

Then I got hooked into the nursery school bit. I think that was the beginning of pushing kids very fast. It was my belief that nursery school was a play time. It was a chance for kids to learn how to just get along with each other, learn basic concepts such as how to listen to somebody else, to stop and do things and listen to stories. Another friend said they wanted to start one in Glen Avery Church and asked if I would be interested. Two of us shared directorship for half a year and then I took over as director for the next ten years.

Then, when I had two children in college and one getting close to it I decided it was time to go get a full-time job to help pay for college and things. That didn't work out and I wound up back in school. I couldn't find a job I liked. I tried one. I walked in and they put me in front of the typewriter, which drove me crazy. I should have turned right around and walked out. So I went back and got my programming certificate. I never actually programmed after that, but I worked with computers in various ways—more as a user. I enjoyed it. I used it a lot when I worked temporaries. I finally retired from our church as the accounting assistant after four years. I ran my own company along with the nursery school. I also had a day care center.

and our pets: Benny (an 80 pound mutt that looks like a Guernsey cow), Whisper (a Sheltie) and our cats Corky and Mavis. I wanted to see what would come next in my life and start another adventure on the home front. On the other hand, I wanted to keep paddling to the Gulf of Mexico, steeped in the simplicity of life on the river. I'd grown used to being in nature no matter what she handed us. I loved being away from the confinement of buildings.

My old patterns and chasing the thousand details of daily living awaited me at home. I wasn't sure I had my priorities figured out enough to override the home routines. I knew I wanted to write, make art, be with my husband and children, and do meaningful work. I dreamed of leading a more focused, intentional life. I wanted to take action and make informed, thoughtful choices instead of reacting to what was before me. So many tasks and people would be demanding my time and attention when I got home, and I didn't yet have a tangible plan for dealing with it.

Perhaps I could pay more attention to my life on a couple of levels. First, emotionally—noticing how I was feeling. If I found myself getting anxious, I'd figure out why, and deal with the reason. Then—on an intuitive level, I could get quiet and see what heart had to say. Being in the moment at home would be an extraordinary change for me.

July 14, Wednesday, Day 40

Rocks, roots and a slope that caused us to roll into each other during the night made that island site close to the worst sleeping spot on the trip. But our river view made up for it. I climbed out of the tent very early. Birds were already busy in the trees. Geese swam buy in a flotilla that included two white ones. The sun rose in a cloudless sky. Calm water called to me. I jumped in my kayak to explore before breakfast. I navigated through the narrow, shallow passage between islands. I startled fish and turtles under the surface of the water and the mud below. With each paddle stroke aquatic creatures surprised me and made me laugh as they frantically sped off stirring up the bubbling mud.

After breakfast, while Christina still slept and Heather was finishing her meal, I headed back up river in the kayak to connect with the women who would paddle with us that day.

I paddled a mile through channels, savoring the peace of being alone in that lush, magical place. Navigating by map was almost useless. It reminded me of Mark Twain's book, *Life on the Mississippi*, where he describes how

Grandmother Stories

Winnie's Story

For many years I have thought what you are doing on this trip is something that would be a great thing to do. Going down the Mississippi has been in the back of my mind since I was fairly young—probably since I first got introduced to canoes.

I grew up near the Minnesota River which was "off and on" navigable. We had a homemade canoe. When we paddled, we had to stop and cut down the branches of the trees that had fallen across the river. It made it kind of an adventure. When you are in nature you see things, experience things. I am just listening to the peepers out there right now and really enjoying them. There is something that seeps into you when you are on the water or in the woods that is kind of magical.

Gretchen's Story

I was glad to come to a gathering. I have been to a lot of women's stuff because I am a midwife. I did traditional midwifery, which is more home birth than hospital. It was a lot about going into people's homes and fitting, getting very intimate with them, establishing the kind of trust that allows you to sit on somebody's bed with her spouse next to you, and be between her legs and touch their baby.

Life profoundly effects who I am, how I think, how things go. I am 50 now and I still have a 14-year-old to raise. She has some disabilities. She is maturing slower than some other people, so I have more time with her. That is kind of fun. She is working. She doesn't want to have a bare midriff all the way up! That is handy.

I am raising another seven kids—sort of. The other kids' parents aren't [raising them]. They are such good kids. One of them is 15 and she doesn't get it. She is very straight and prim in her choices so far, but her dress doesn't look like it. I watch her mother, (who is either not sober or straight most of the time), lash out at her and tell her how she really looks. You can just watch the innocence go away. She doesn't understand that if that is the way I am then that is all that matters. So lately I have been trying to remember when I figured that out. It was a disappointing thing. I am glad I am not at that age anymore. I didn't like having to come to terms with innuendo and what was not straight forward in sexuality. That is what I think while watching Melody. She is the boat captains had to learn the river by heart because she was always changing her landscape. Ever-changing islands and shifting sand bars had made the map largely inaccurate. I maintained a general sense of direction, using intuition to guide me. Part of the magic of the place was that every time I reached a choice-point where I was unsure of the direction to take, a heron sitting in a tree would take flight to show me the way.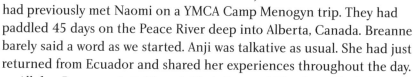

I found Naomi and her friends, Anji and Breanne at the boat launch out of St. Paul Park eager to get onto the water. Breanne and Anji had previously met Naomi on a YMCA Camp Menogyn trip. They had paddled 45 days on the Peace River deep into Alberta, Canada. Breanne barely said a word as we started. Anji was talkative as usual. She had just returned from Ecuador and shared her experiences throughout the day.

All day, Breanne, Anji, Naomi, Christina, and Heather talked about their camp experiences. I'd never gone to camp as a child so I grew quiet. I had nothing to add. I often paddled off and took the opportunity to explore the shore and reflect on the trip. I would turn 50 in October and had already begun to experience what the women had talked about: the benefits of being over 50. I value things differently now, but am still waiting for the peace of mind they talked about. I experience it occasionally and it remains with me for longer periods of time. I await the time when peace of mind makes itself at home within in my being. A smile crossed my face as I remembered Mariah's (age 18) question at the last gathering. She asked innocently.

> *It feels right now like you always have to get up over the next hill and you have to do something and then after you get up the next hill you have to do something else. Does it ever plateau? Or is it always that you have to do one more thing and your mind is always just AHHH! Does it get easier?*

The grandmothers giggled and smiled at her lovingly. There was no tangible answer to her question. We all knew we would not have an answer that would completely satisfy her or tell her what she wanted to hear. Hence the reason for the laughter! Ronnie attempted to answer her,

> *It gets easier to keep growing. Just try to stay open to learning new things. Recharge and heal and stretch yourself beyond where you think you can go. But, it is always uphill.*

Grandmother Stories

ducking under it. She doesn't want to see it yet and it is coming right at her like a semi-truck.

I did midwifery for twenty years. I got to sit around for hours on end and honor women and watch babies "start up," or try to go get them if they weren't going to "start up." While I was busy keeping their body going there was a lot of spirituality happening. But it isn't written. There is a lot of mystery. I find myself out there just doing it, because somebody has to go get that baby to start. You have to do it. It is so literal that it is just astounding. It is scary stuff. [Laughing] I have always laughed when I am scared.

Gloria's Story

Coming from outside of our circle was the chaos. I remember always hiding in the car while sitting on the seat because I didn't want the cop to see me, thinking he would take me away. As a result, when I got older I ended up with what you call panic attacks. The fear implanted itself and it was always there. I was always aware of what I saw and who was looking at me, how I behave and, don't say anything. Spirituality changed that thinking. Somewhere along the line I had this thinking about me and expressing my own feelings, my own thoughts, my own wants, my own wishes, anything that I wanted. Even in expressing my own opinion that somehow along the line I have to have permission. I don't know where the permission would come from, but it seems like I was always saying, "Well, excuse me, pardon me for living, but I got to say something." When I graduated from high school it said next to my name, *If silence were golden Gloria would be a millionaire.* I never talked. When I did start getting a little sense of being privileged so I could talk, I babbled and chattered and spoke real fast.

When I was 21 I was a chronic alcoholic. I started drinking when I was 12. At age 21 I ended up in a hospital in Illinois. There were white alcoholic ladies in there that started putting me down. First for being there, and second for being young. I was too young to be an alcoholic. (That was discounting my experience.) When I came into recovery and now that I am older, I know that what moved me was my spirituality. It was always this white God that I called upon for help and it was Christian. I never wanted to be identified as Christian, but that is what was way down inside, helping me all this time. That is why I fell back into

She was also reminded that there might be a grander adventure on the other side of that hill. I agree. It does get easier. It seems with every decade a level of angst is released that uncovers a stash of joy that has been waiting to emerge.

At times the girls and I just floated on the water, eating and talking. To get out of the boat traffic we paddled behind some islands into an area called Baldwin Lake. We took a break on Lower Grey Cloud Island. Grey Cloud Island's Dakota name was Mhpeyahota Win, after Grey Cloud Woman a notable Dakota woman who was important to her people and the third daughter of Chef Black Dog.

Moments after we were back out on the water Anji was panicky. She had been mugged and quite sick while she was in Ecuador. The experience left her feeling jumpy. At one point a barge approached from more than a mile away and she yelled with panic in her voice, "Nancy, there's a barge coming!" I tried to reassure her she was safe. She watched nervously from the duffer's seat in the middle of the canoe, feeling helpless as it passed.

As we approached Lock and Dam No. 2 near Hastings Anji panicked again. She barked out loud directives from the middle of the boat to Naomi and Breanne. She told them where to go and how fast to get there. Naomi and Breanne's calm voices got her across a wide spot in the river and we converged at the end of the wall leading to the lock.

As I paddled down the length of the wall searching for the line to signal the attendant I heard Anji again issuing directives. This time she wanted me to come back. I continued forward feeling bad that Anji's experience in Ecuador left her so fearful. That was a big change for a girl who would do just about anything. I hoped she would move through her fear quickly and once again find the adventure the world offered, something she could embrace.

We waited at the lock wall for half an hour as the lock's crew completed repair work on the structure. Anji held her breath as great gates opened. I thought I heard a little whimper from her as we paddled into the lock with another boat and got our mooring line. We clustered our three boats together and waited as the water dropped 16 feet. When the water level reached the bottom and the gates in front of us began to open Anji exclaimed, "That was rather anti-climatic." We all laughed as we paddled safely out of the lock. We could see Hastings in the distance.

At 2 pm we reached the Hastings boat launch. We took out the canoes and kayak and sat in the sand watching the traffic of jet skis and boats of all sizes coming and going. Breanne called her husband to come and pick

Grandmother Stories

Christianity. When I was down and out, I hit bottom and wanted help, I called upon the God I learned about.

I learned about God, as I understand him, in AA [Alcoholics Anonymous]. That kept me sane. I quit drinking at 26 because I was told that in another 4 months my life was going to be cut off. My acceptance of that truth was good. I thought, "This is my lot in life; this is what I was here for." I sat in a hospital bed and I was willing, ready and able to go [die].

My final days at 26. I said, "Let me relive my life. What can I say that I left behind?" My self-confidence forced me to ask myself that question. My biggest regret was not being a mother. I always felt it was an honor to be a mother. I didn't accomplish that then. But, I called upon the creator to help me and assist me. I became a mother. I always viewed that as a miracle. Because from where I was to here and being a mother is a miracle to me. Someone said there is a higher power out there, a creator out there that has other things in store for you. I was reminded that I could move past the alcohol. During the times when life had became unbearable there was always this higher power helping me. Whether poking me in the ribs or slapping me in the face, it was always there reminding me constantly. The creator was reminding me of things I didn't do. Like when I woke up in the middle of the night with a big nudge. *"You didn't thank the creator for the baby you are carrying."* Yes I did, but I got down on my knees and I thanked the creator for my baby. So those kinds of little nudges came along the way. If I am really down and out and thinking this is all there is, I will never be happy. I forget what life is all about and get in a big rut. I remember the exact words that came to me, *"God has not given you the spirit of fear. Spread that love and power and be sound of mind."* I was always on the edge of mental illness. That is what I think.

Then I looked into Lakota tradition. I went to a lot of ceremonies. I felt real good. When I brought everything together, I was able to comprehend, choose that way, put it all together, and see that it is not about Christianity. It is about having the Spirit, the Great Spirit that helps me and takes care of me. Spirituality helped me when my sister passed away. I have never cried for her because, what I believe is I want to honor her life. I don't want to mourn her life because there was nothing bad about her life. She had a good life; she lived fully until she got sick. So I never cried for her. I want to honor that light.

Spirituality has helped me. It brought me back to my prayer life. I

Nancy, Heather, Christina, Naomi, Anji, and Breanne
waiting to enter Lock and Dam No. 2

us up. Upon his arrival, we would again begin the shuffle of boats and cars. It sounded as if it would be a while before he arrived so we continued to watch the river traffic entertainment. The girls went wading along the shore and encountered a little green snake that eventually disappeared under a log.

Occasionally the people at the boat launch provided comic entertainment. A couple was putting their boat in the water. Before she began backing the boat trailer into the water, he got into the boat along with a little auburn colored Yorkie. The tiny dog pranced precariously around the edge as if she owned the boat. Everyone on shore was watching the dog's performance. The woman gunned the truck a little more than she intended

Paddling team: Nancy, Christina, Heather, Naomi, Breanne and Anji

Grandmother Stories

never prayed to the dead. I guess I did but I never identified it. Now I talk to them and ask them to take care of us. I don't have the sense of loss. I guess I have what you call twinges of loneliness.

Elaine's Story

When I was little girl we lived in this old house on the south side of the tracks. A bunch of us would sleep in a bed together and my mom or my older sisters would always tell us stories. We would lie there in the dark and listen to these stories. It was just really wonderful. If my mom or my sister couldn't tell a story I would tell a story to my little sister. If there was no-one else to hear, I would tell a story to myself. They were good stories. My mom would tell us stories about Nanaboozhoo who was winter. My dad would tell stories about family members, but he would change the names. They would do crazy things.

Then there was going to school where our language was taken from us and we were introduced to a kind of silence. Where touch was taken away and we were hurt.

We would walk around and our eyes would be down. I always think about why our eyes were down when we could have been looking at all of this [indicating nature] around us, or looking at a real handsome man—looking him right in the eye. For a lot of us, when we got older if we wanted to be able to talk or sing or dance it was through drinking. I could drink and get all funny. I could dance. Even the men could get out there and dance at the bars. You could cry. You could cry as much as you wanted. You could get angry because you could not be angry without alcohol. And then you could fight. But it never took you anywhere. You could find a man. They could find a woman.

As soon as I graduated from high school, I took off because I couldn't stand what was going on at home. I thought I would go out into this world and would find something really different. But every where I went, I took my *using* with me. So everywhere I went, I found the alcohol and drugs. I found that kind of experience and did that kind of life. It is everywhere. There are unhappy people everywhere! There are oppressed people everywhere.

But you know, all the time I was traveling around, I would find myself up on a hill looking up at the moon and I would talk to her. I knew there were spirits. I had seen them. They had come to warn me at different times in my life when I was doing things I shouldn't have and it lurched backward. The Yorkie, who was poised at the very front of the boat, sailed off and disappeared into the water. Less than a second later she popped up like a fishing bobber and paddled furiously to shore. With the Yorkie's audience all laughing she emerged from the water looking even smaller. Her grinning owner quickly scooped up her tiny shivering body, wrapped her in a towel and placed her safely back on the boat.

We watched intently as a bright white tugboat pushed ten barges downstream. Just ahead of the tugboat, the river curves sharply to the left under the Highway 61 Bridge. It seemed impossible to maneuver that massive length of metal and its cargo around the curve without hitting the bridge pilings or the shore. The pilot of the tug approached the bridge slowly and then slowed to almost an indiscernible speed. At that speed the pilot maneuvered the entire mass of tug and barges and they magically pivoted around the curve and into a position that pointed the "barge train" down the center of the river. The process took about 15 minutes and they were underway again.

Waiting is not something I have ever done well and I had begun to feel like I was being held hostage. I had understood that the details of our ride had been arranged and we would be met at the landing or shortly after we arrived. I did not expect to wait and was antsy to get going. I tried going for a walk but was afraid the ride would come when I was gone. I got cranky and grew extremely tired of the constant noise of boats and camp talk. I tried to nap away from everyone in a shady spot but found myself covered in ants. I tried to keep my bad attitude from the girls, but my silence betrayed me.

At 6 pm when the ride came, Naomi went to get our car and returned 45 minutes later. We loaded the boats, said goodbye to our paddling companions and Naomi, Heather and I headed to the motel. Arriving at the motel we took our things into the room and then bee-lined to Subway across the street to get dinner. Then it was showers all around.

The TV came on like a loud intruder, irritating me. I grabbed Naomi's phone and headed outside to call Doug. I gave him the last on-the-river update, and vented my frustrations from the day so I would not carry them into the next day. He listened. Then we talked about the new deck he was working on at our home. I heard disappointment in his voice when he said it wouldn't be completed by the time I got home.

When I got back to our room, the TV was off, Naomi was in bed, and Heather was writing post cards. In moments I was fast asleep in bed.

Grandmother Stories

been doing. One would be behind me and I knew I was supposed to turn and talk or look at it. I knew it was warning me about this or that. And my mom had told me different things. I knew there was this Spirit life all around me. But I was just kind of numb to it because of the way I was living my life.

I came home because this is where my family is. This is where my people are and where I belong. I decided the day I came home I was going to quite drinking and using drugs. I just decided that day. I went up to the hospital that same day because I needed to get a cut repaired and stitched up. I had been drunk. I had broken a window so I could get in my house. I told the nurse, (her name was Roleen,) I am an alcoholic, and she said, *"I didn't know that about you Elaine, Why are you saying that?"* "Because I need to tell somebody this." They stitched me up and I walked across the street where Barb works and walked in and I said I need to talk to somebody. I said, "I am an alcoholic and I need to talk to somebody." He said, *"What are you doing here? Have you been sent here?"* I said, "No. I have come off the street. I just want you to know I am an alcoholic and I need some help here." They weren't used to anybody just walking in; they were supposed to be referred to that type of a program. So they gave me this book, called AA [Alcoholics Anonymous] and sent me home. We went to AA. Barb and I took off to Bemidji to a really good group. We would talk there. Oh, that was so hard.

I, [tears] it was so hard to talk. I would sit there and they would go around the circle and talk, *"Hi my name is so and so and I am an alcoholic."* Pretty soon it would get close to me and I would get sick inside. I would start coughing. I didn't want to cough because somebody might look at me. I was so full of fear when it was going to be my turn to talk. I finally got to talk. It was about crying. So I went to that group and I worked at talking and I did my crying.

Eventually my friend, Cathy, told me about this healing circle at the Women's Services Center. It wasn't about being an alcoholic, although a lot of people had those problems. I went to that healing circle and I gave up the AA group. We would go around the circle and she would talk. She would begin it with ceremony. That is what ritual and ceremony is for, to help us get through these hard things. I really needed to know those things. Each woman would talk. I would sit on this side of Cathy because I knew the circle would go this way. I knew everybody else would talk before me and I would be last. I knew I needed

July 15, Thursday, Day 41

We slept in. I awoke knowing the next day would be our last on the river. What would reentry into the world of cars, work, and family be like? The city traffic, noise, and chaos triggered anxiety. I didn't want to live with that racket. Listening to Doug on the phone the night before, I saw life at home as too complicated. Here we had a tent, kayaks, and food. At home, cars, house, work and a million related details awaited me. I knew when the time came, my frame of mind would need to shift.

We took our time getting onto the water, as if delaying would somehow postpone the end of our trip. Starting earlier probably would have been better, since the weather was already hazy and hot.

We crossed over many wing dams, approaching them with respect. We learned at this point in the river they offered little challenge. We passed Prescott, Wisconsin, where the St. Croix River joins the Mississippi River. Both of us were curious about any effect the St. Croix River might have on the Mississippi after watching what the Minnesota River did to the water. We noticed no change. We paused to float a few moments and looked back up into the St. Croix River. It appeared larger than the Mississippi from where we were positioned. The juncture of these two rivers is significant for Heather. It is where she grew up. She spent a great deal of time on them as a child. She said, "It feels good to see them together and to realize that I am paddling in water from both rivers." Just then we noticed bald eagles soaring in the sky above the mountainous bluffs on the east bank.

The heat of the day drained our energy. We were relieved to stop on an island to sit in the shade for lunch. Clouds drifted overhead, periodically providing relief from the sun.

Not long after lunch, we encountered a tugboat coming up stream with several barges; this one had more barges than any we had passed. We positioned ourselves at a safe distance and angled ourselves so we were aimed directly into the wake. It splashed high over the front of our kayaks. We bounced dramatically, but never worried about staying afloat. The number of barges directly affects the size of the wake, which kept coming for some time after the barge had passed.

The heat continued to sap our strength. Neither Heather nor I wanted to paddle, so we floated. Then Heather felt a breeze and decided it could aid in pushing us downriver. She fashioned a sail out of her shirt and paddle and held it high while I held on to her kayak. She was absolutely convinced the wind was pushing us along, but I could see by watching the

Grandmother Stories

to really, really listen to everybody. That eagle feather would come to different women and they couldn't talk. They would just sit there and hold it and they couldn't say a thing. They would pass it on because when your spirit is dull like that, when it hasn't been inspired, inflamed, it is hard to speak.

I admired her [Cathy], because whenever she started, *every time,* she would pray and pray. Everybody would go around. When it would come back to Cathy she would have really listened to them. She would pray for them again. She would say, well, so and so said this. She would reinforce that person. I thought that was so wonderful. I made myself sit on the end so I would listen. I think I cried for about 2 years in that healing circle.

When I am in a sweat lodge, when I am in a healing circle, if I am in a dark room or day lodge, everybody always gets a chance to sing, to dance, to speak. I am a very passionate woman! Some guy is really missing out! I feed my spirit. I feed it all of the time in different ways, acknowledging everything around me. I listen to other people. Through those relationships with their spirits I am inspired by them and everything else in creation.

I know really strong women. There are so many people in our community who are healing and have healed. But, in community it is the women who are doing things. It is the women who are sacrificing their time. They are *bringing along* their kids. They are making some important changes. My girls are 14 now. They can't remember me ever having a drink. That is a big change. When I was growing up I remember my parents drinking. My son, who is 19, he can remember some things, but he can't remember anything graphic. Times are changing. I think on our reservation we have some really wonderful things happening. For me it is about attitude—talking about Spirit, about feeling good. So many of us experienced hopelessness and fear, but we are growing out of that.

I work at the Leech Lake Tribal College and I teach history. I teach creative writing. We produce and direct a play that is about issues. Now the stories have good endings. I know how powerful we are. We are going to make those endings good. Our children are going through ceremonies with us now. They are finding voices. They are getting an opportunity to speak out. The kids get on stage and are making films. My daughter is a mentor. One of her films just showed in a film festival. She is 14. It was called, *Young Girls in the Director's Chair.*

bubbles on the surface of the water that we were still moving at the speed of the current. It was fun just the same.

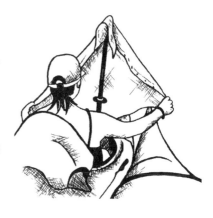

We came to the town of Diamond Bluff, Wisconsin and took a break. The town was smaller than we expected. It felt like we were in an old west movie walking through a deserted town in the scorching sun. Our search for a place with a cold beverage ended at a bar called The Gem. We sat at the bar, and ordered two pops and a frozen Milky Way bar. We arrived in time to catch the end of a TV movie about Houdini. The bartender humorously narrated as we and the other customer in the bar watched the end of the movie. It was entertaining. The air conditioning was a blessing. We were in no hurry to leave.

From Diamond Bluff we paddled only a half-mile downstream to our final campsite. It was mostly sandy beach and woods with a beautiful view of the cliffs on the opposite side of the river. The tent went up in record time and in moments I was down for a two-hour nap. Like our last beach campsite, the water traffic was loud and trains passed by regularly. But once again the wind befriended us and drowned out most of the noise.

Last campsite

Grandmother Stories

Our Pow Wows are phenomenal. We sit in the back and get goose bumps, because we feel so good. We get tears in our eyes because we are just so proud. We know the power and beauty of dance and those drums. What I am trying to say is that things are much better. We are moving. You know how they say when you step and the ground shakes? We are like that right here. We are going to make things happen.

Things are happening in the community. We did a garden. Now we are on our third garden. This one is dedicated to our young women because of a couple of deaths. Some of us women have organized around this issue. We got this guy evicted from his house where this young girl died. Now this guy is moving to the south side of town. So we are gong to have the reservation banish him. We are going to do a resolution and present it to the council.

I am really grateful to be here tonight and just to have some tears. You know, not to have to run away. I am grateful for this tobacco in my lap and this pop [soda] here. We are by the river. The wind is blowing. We've got tea and we can speak.

Mii Gwitch

[Thank You]

Later, we sat on the beach and relaxed until dinner. Searching for a way to celebrate our last night, we attempted to make chocolate pudding. It was either the heat or the way we put it together, but the pudding turned out like warm chocolate syrup. We tried to eat it but soon stopped. We were at a loss as to how to celebrate the end of such a significant trip. The mosquitoes came out in droves and forced us into the tent early. Through the screen door I watched a colony of bees that lived in the sand coming and going. I was amazed at how much sand a little bitty bee could kick up and move in a short amount of time.

We drifted off to sleep just as it was getting dark. Not long after falling asleep a bright light and loud explosion woke me. Startled, I bolted into a sitting position and looked out the screen door. To my amazement I saw fireworks in the sky on the other side of the river. I woke Heather. I could not believe she had slept through the loud bang. We watched the fireworks for a while and as suddenly as they started they stopped. A barge was coming. Heather lay back down to go to sleep. Then as the barge got even with us on the river, the fireworks continued. The boatman on the barge began to cheer as a grand fireworks finale began. In my wildest dreams I could not have imagined a better ending for our last night!

July 16, Friday Day 42—Last Day

Heather slept in while I enjoyed the amazingly cool crisp morning. I sang my morning song and made the last offering to the water. I took more time than usual to express my thankfulness for the trip, the safe travel and all of the wonderful women we met. I cleaned the mud and riverweeds out of the kayak's two storage compartments and cockpit. I felt respect and gratitude for the little craft that safely carried me so far. It had been a reliable companion and friend to me through our trip. I felt melancholy as I packed the gear for the last time.

Once on the water, we paddled slowly and steadily, making very good time. Few boats shared the river as we approached the fifth lock of our trip, Lock & Dam No. 3. Heather stayed at the beginning of the wall leading to the lock gates while I paddled up to pull the rope. Soon we entered the lock. The water level dropped about five feet and the gates opened. We paddled out, and found ourselves with boat traffic. The river felt more expansive here. We came around the bend into Red Wing, and a wave of sadness and joy engulfed me.

The bluffs along the banks were a lush patchwork of bare sandstone and dark green vegetation. Houses sat high atop the bluffs with views of the world. Marinas were plentiful. Each marina we passed seemed to be bigger than the last.

We pulled into the channel leading to the marina at Colvill Park. At the mouth of the channel I stopped paddling and took a long gaze downriver, knowing that I had to come back. I thought about the women downstream I had yet to meet, about the different cultures that touch the river on its way to the Gulf of Mexico, and how the river's personality changes during its journey. Now that I had seen this much, I would have to find a way to experience the rest. Reluctantly I paddled the channel to the boat launch and got out of the water. We unpacked the kayaks for the last time and piled our stuff in the shade. Heather hugged her kayak when she was done unpacking. We sat waiting for Naomi feeling conflicted.

Naomi arrived a while later with a Dairy Queen turtle blizzard—caramel, chocolate and pecans for me! Even though it was melted from the heat of the day, it was heavenly. Heather was thrilled about hers, too. We loaded everything and headed to the motel. When we got to our rooms, Naomi had already a set up a surprise. On the stand next to the bed were flowers and a framed collage of pictures. Each collage depicted the highpoints each of us had experienced on the trip. I gave her a big hug. We went down to Heather's room and found her ecstatic. She bounced over to Naomi and gave her a giant hug. After showers, we went for pizza, did a little browsing at the Red Wing Pottery complex, and then headed to the park to set up for the final gathering.

After we set up, forty-five minutes passed and no one came. We had just decided to pack it in when two women drove up: JoAn from the St. Paul gathering and her friend Mary O. Shortly after we started the gathering, Doug arrived with flowers for Heather, Naomi, and me. I jumped up to hug and kiss him. Then he drove off to find a coffee house. His plan to open a coffee house in Ely transformed every coffee house he passed into a tasty research project . . . an adventure with coffee.

Mary O. shared the bright joy and deep details of her life at the gathering. She told us she is Wiccan, a fact of her life she rarely shares with others but felt safe enough to reveal to us. When she said that Wicca's only creed is, "Do no harm!" Heather perked up as if she had found an important truth.

Mary O. told us about supporting a friend who is an abused wife.

I went through psychological and emotional abuse growing up, as did my mother. I also had physical abuse, so I have been there and come out of it. I am determined to help whomever I run into. I wish someone had stepped in and done more for me. I wish someone would have been a little more proactive. There were people who suspected abuse at various points and just sat back. I don't blame them, but I don't want to do that. We need to be a sisterhood and a brotherhood and watch out for each other. Otherwise, what is the point of being here?

I think one of the most interesting questions you ask is about the direction the river of life has taken you. Did it follow the path that you expected? I laughed when I read it. No. If you think the path is going to take you where you expected, just get that idea out of your mind. I can't think of a single woman whose path has followed what they expected. Most of that is good, some of it isn't. I think it depends on how soon you are aware of and fully embrace the fact that life is about the journey and not about a particular goal.

I was always yearning to find that "thing" that I was supposed to do. I went through a lot of different jobs. I took flack from people, because "You are just supposed to find a job and stay in it." It has probably taken me until this year to realize that I am a seeker, an adventurer. That is my job.

If you don't listen to the voice inside you, you can miss the message. The universe throws opportunities in front of you all the time. I wanted to move to San Francisco but I couldn't get a friend to go with me. There were so many dreams. I wanted to be a makeup artist in the movies. I went to school for that, but I didn't pursue it because it meant taking a leap. I missed a lot of leaps because I let fear stand in the way. There isn't anything more deadly on this planet than fear, except maybe apathy. Just get it out of your way. Eleanor Roosevelt said, and I am not quoting her exactly, "In order to conquer fear you have to look it in the face; you must do the thing you think you cannot do."

JoAn said,

I guess passion is the thing I think of the most. Find out what your passion is and do it. If you can't do the whole thing, do little parts of it. Always keep it in front of you, everyday. One of my mentors talks about making a mission statement of who you are and making it sensory-rich and emotionally laden. Be able to be there, smell it, hear the sounds and taste whatever is going on. Then repeat it every day. This is who I am and what I have.

One of the other things that was really big for me was knowing that decisions are not written in stone. I used to think that before I could make a decision to do anything or go anywhere, I needed to know exactly how everything was going to turn out. Once I made a decision, there was no changing it. That is not true. You make decisions, and if it doesn't happen to work out, then you make another decision to do something else.

All during this gathering we were presented with the challenge of hearing each other over the trains that barreled past on a track that traveled the edge of the park. We estimated the trains must be coming past us every ten minutes. At first the trains were annoying. Then they became just down right hilarious. In the middle of the sharing, Suzanne, a childhood friend of Naomi's, arrived and joined us as we ended with the usual ritual of the aspiration sticks. The girls and I participated this time. Soon it was dark and the bugs competed with the train noise to drive us away. Doug arrived, and we drove off to enjoy a late dinner celebration.

July 17, Saturday

Before everyone else was up, I started the day walking in a Red Wing neighborhood, looking at people's houses and yards, wondering what it would be like to be home. I could not shake the feeling that I didn't want to go back to my life as it was. I sang my morning song as I walked and leaned into the faith that had carried me throughout the trip. My role as mother never really changed with the girls as the trip proceeded. It is a role that has been there too long for me to expect that this experience would change it. But now there is a new aspect to the role. The girls and I have a deeper connection. In the future that connection will allow us to communicate on a new and more meaningful level.

Back at the motel, we sorted through gear for the last time separating it into piles by owner. We packed the vehicles, paused for a last muscle woman photo and parted company.

Naomi took Heather to a family gathering and headed home. Doug and I drove downriver to Lake Pepin to sail for a few hours with Bill and Melissa, Doug and Bill were clowning around as they usually do when they get together. It was delightful to watch. That peaceful morning sailing on

Heather and Nancy showing off muscles

Bill and Melissa's boat helped ease my transition. I said a quiet prayer, put Kinnickinnick in the water and tossed the aspiration sticks from the last gathering from the boat into the lake. I looked across Lake Pepin toward the Minnesota shore and wondered what it will be like paddling there on the next trip. Lake Pepin is so wide we will be but a speck.

From there, the transition home consisted of random realities of life away from the river. Doug and I met with our accountant. Then, we drove to cousin Pat's house and stayed for the evening. Her daughter, Mary, had birthed a stillborn baby while I was on the river. We listened to the heart-breaking story and looked at pictures of the baby. There were no words to express our feelings.

Settling into bed I pulled out Heather's journal. I had asked the girls how they felt now that the trip was over before we parted. Heather gave me her journal and told me to read the last entry. She wrote,

So here we are in Red Wing at the boat launch. We've paddled for 42 days (kind of), 560-plus miles. We're done. And my biggest concern at the moment is getting the red nail polish off my fingernails.

Before the trip, I was told more than once I would not be the same when I came home. I took that to mean, especially at the beginning of the trip, that I would come home obviously changed. I imagined me as someone new, an adventurer full of answers, overflowing with confidence, finally sure of my path in life. I was excited to meet this new person—this new me. I couldn't wait to be her!

But, as the days turned into weeks, and the number of days left began to drastically shrink, I slowly started to realize the new me wasn't going to make an appearance. Every day I woke up to find just the same old me. A part of me was bummed, another part of me was a little angry—it always turned out like this! I expected some big change and it never, ever came! When was it going to happen? How long was I going to have to wait?

Be who you are. This was a message I received on the trip. This is my answer. Strive to be you, the true you, in the most complete sense of what that means. Look deep into yourself and find who you are. Make this your goal. Make this your life's path.

Naomi had told me that she needed a little more time to process it. She shared the following with me later.

I didn't really think the end of the trip would be so hard or emotional for me. I was the car support, and I was with my family, whom I can see and talk to whenever. However, I discovered that when I was with Heather at her family's place, I didn't want to go because it would really be over. As I drove to her Mom's to drop things off, some tears fell. I realized I was unloading things from the car for the last time. Shortly after, I found myself driving home alone, without the two women with whom I had been so close the past month. More tears fell.

When I started this adventure, I had many open wounds that were healing. I was unhappy with who I was. I was terrified of what I had become and had given up over the past few years. I knew being on the trip was just what I needed. I would be forced to relax, spend time with myself, reflect on my life experiences, and have fun, while taking time to find myself. I was sure, when I said I would do car support, that I would face challenges, big and small. Surrounded by the support and guidance of the women, I always had help.

July 18, Sunday

I walked around Pat's neighborhood in Maple Grove and thought about how proud I am of my daughters Jo and Naomi and my son Wade. They take risks and work to stay true to who they are. Heather, too, had taken many risks on this voyage and I was proud to call her my paddling partner. I became aware that, like Heather, I had hoped for and expected a significant change in myself by the end of the journey. There is a significant change. I feel more confident than before the trip. Some self-imposed limitations have been removed or at least identified. But I return the same person I was when I left. Now it is about staying true to my truth.

I enjoyed breakfast with Doug and Pat. Then, with great anticipation, we were off to visit Auntie Chuck. She was sleeping when we arrived. Her nurse gave us an update on her health. When she woke she didn't recognize us and talked only with the nurse. Doug tried to tell her about my river trip, but she didn't understand what he was saying. She kept looking to the nurse as if the nurse's presence made her feel safe. When I spoke she appeared to be frightened by me so I did not say much. I was heartbroken for her, knowing how much she would have loved to hear about the trip and how she would have hung on every detail. This was not the Auntie Chuck we remembered. This woman was very thin and not as well kept as Auntie Chuck. She was barely there physically and even less mentally.

In a way, I was glad the Alzheimer's that had slowly crept into her life the last couple of years had made her life primarily a happy one. She was unaware of what the cancer had done to her. Auntie Chuck would have hated what was happening to her now. She was a very proud, distinguished 87-year-old woman who took great pride in her personal appearance as well as the appearance of her home. As much as I did not want to lose her, I quietly hoped the cancer would take her quickly. As we left, I was overcome with grief. I knew that would be the last time I would see her, and the loss hit me harder than I expected. Doug and I both sobbed as we drove away. I realized how much she meant to me. I knew deep in my heart she was a woman who believed in me. Who believed I could do anything. Waves of grief continued to wash over me as we drove home to Ely. Words she had shared with me just a few months before drifted through my mind:

Don't make life any fuller than it is.
You have got to enjoy this life while you can.

As we neared home we stopped by the local kennel to pick up Benny and Whisper, our dogs. When the dogs saw me they jumped and wiggled wildly. They found it difficult to sit still in the car during the ride to our house. When we pulled into our driveway, I spotted extra cars. Doug had called friends—Mark, Dianna, Rebecca, Becky, Pat, and Stacy—who gathered to welcome me home. It was wonderful to see them. Their anticipation for stories about the trip was evident, but I found it difficult to tell them much. I couldn't find the words that encompassed the enormity of my experience on this expedition, and my heart was still grieving Auntie Chuck.

I went to bed that night snuggled in Doug's loving arms feeling overwhelmed with what I had accomplished. The softness of the bed was comforting, but the firmness of the floor beckoned.

Every Long Journey

Words and music by

Ann Reed

Every long journey is made of small steps.
Is made of the courage, the feeling you get
When you know it's been waiting been waiting for you
The Journey's the only thing you want to do

We cannot know what you go through or see through your eyes
But we will surround you, the pride undisguised
In any direction whatever you view
You're taking our love there with you

In every long journey what drives you to go,
It's half what you know and half what you don't
The secret's been waiting your heart's got the key
The secret's the only thing you want to see(chorus)

Every long journey begins with a dream
A spirit with courage to make it all real
The dream has been calling, been calling to you
The dream is the only thing you want to do.(chorus)

Printed with permission from Turtlecub Publishing
Every Long Journeys words & music: Ann Reed
© 1986 Turtlecub Publishing/BMI
For further information on Ann and her music: www.annreed.com

These words and prayer closed each gathering.
I respectfully offer them to you.

Remember all women are wise women, a grandmother
or grandmother in the making.
Trust your heart and know you will make a difference.

May the gifts you have offered by your presence here today
circle back around to reward you.
May your head bless you with clear thinking.
May your heart bless you with love,compassion and joy.
May your feet always walk in honor.
May your hands always do good work and respect the things
the creator has made.
May your ears be sharp to hear the creator's voice.
May you be safe from inner and outer harm.
And may you be healthy and strong.

Nancy and Heather at celebration dinner

Route of the
Water Women Wisdom
Expedition

Mileage: Approximately 567 miles
Starting Sea Level: 1475 ft. above
Start Date: June 5, 2004
End Date: July 16, 2004
Length of Expedition: 42 Days
Total Dams: Sixteen
Total Locks: Five
Total Hours Paddling: 204
Modes of Transportation: Car, Canoe, Kayak

The Mississippi River wanders two miles for every mile of distance it gains towards the gulf. It loses half of it's sea level height before it leaves Minnesota.

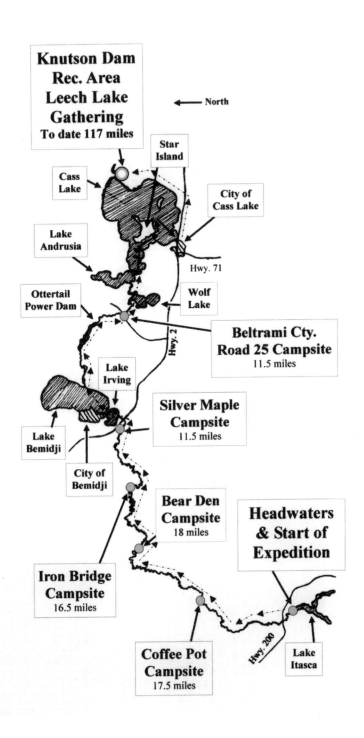

Knutson Dam Rec. Area Leech Lake Gathering
To date 117 miles

← North

Star Island

Cass Lake

City of Cass Lake

Lake Andrusia

Hwy. 71

Ottertail Power Dam

Wolf Lake

Beltrami Cty. Road 25 Campsite
11.5 miles

Hwy. 2

Lake Irving

Silver Maple Campsite
11.5 miles

Lake Bemidji

City of Bemidji

Bear Den Campsite
18 miles

Headwaters & Start of Expedition

Iron Bridge Campsite
16.5 miles

Coffee Pot Campsite
17.5 miles

Hwy. 200

Lake Itasca

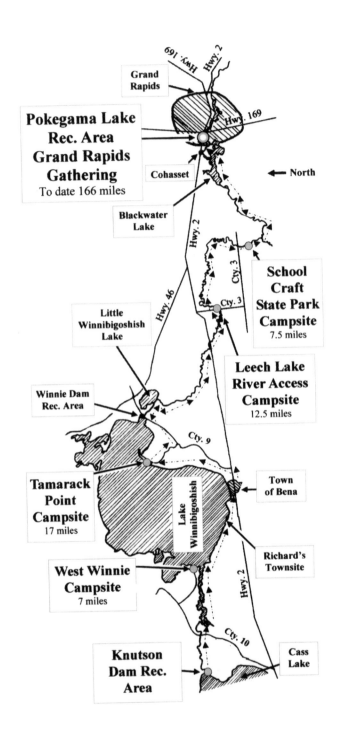

Grand
Rapids

Hwy. 169

Hwy. 2

Pokegama Lake
Rec. Area
Grand Rapids
Gathering
To date 166 miles

Hwy. 169

Cohasset

← North

Blackwater
Lake

Hwy. 2

School
Craft
State Park
Campsite
7.5 miles

Cty. 3

Little
Winnibigoshish
Lake

Hwy. 46

Cty. 3

Leech Lake
River Access
Campsite
12.5 miles

Winnie Dam
Rec. Area

Cty. 9

Tamarack
Point
Campsite
17 miles

Lake
Winnibigoshish

Town
of Bena

West Winnie
Campsite
7 miles

Richard's
Townsite

Hwy. 2

Knutson
Dam Rec.
Area

Cty. 10

Cass
Lake

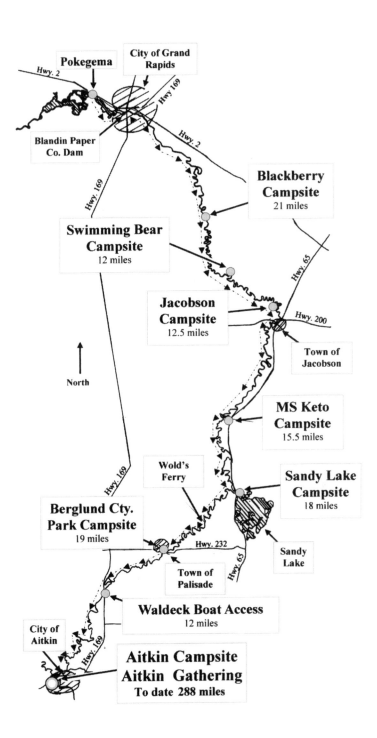

Pokegema
Hwy. 2

City of Grand Rapids

Hwy. 169

Blandin Paper Co. Dam

Hwy. 2

Blackberry Campsite
21 miles

Hwy. 169

Swimming Bear Campsite
12 miles

Hwy. 65

Jacobson Campsite
12.5 miles

Hwy. 200

Town of Jacobson

North

MS Keto Campsite
15.5 miles

Hwy. 169

Wold's Ferry

Sandy Lake Campsite
18 miles

Berglund Cty. Park Campsite
19 miles

Hwy. 232

Hwy. 65

Sandy Lake

Town of Palisade

Waldeck Boat Access
12 miles

City of Aitkin

Hwy. 169

Aitkin Campsite
Aitkin Gathering
To date 288 miles

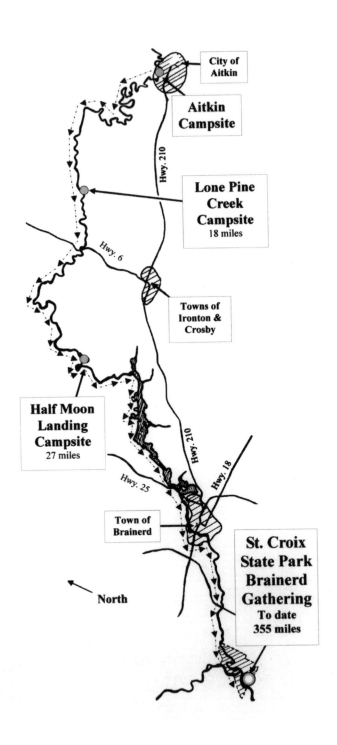

City of
Aitkin

**Aitkin
Campsite**

Hwy. 210

**Lone Pine
Creek
Campsite**
18 miles

Hwy. 6

Towns of
Ironton &
Crosby

**Half Moon
Landing
Campsite**
27 miles

Hwy. 25

Hwy. 210

Hwy. 18

Town of
Brainerd

North

**St. Croix
State Park
Brainerd
Gathering**
To date
355 miles

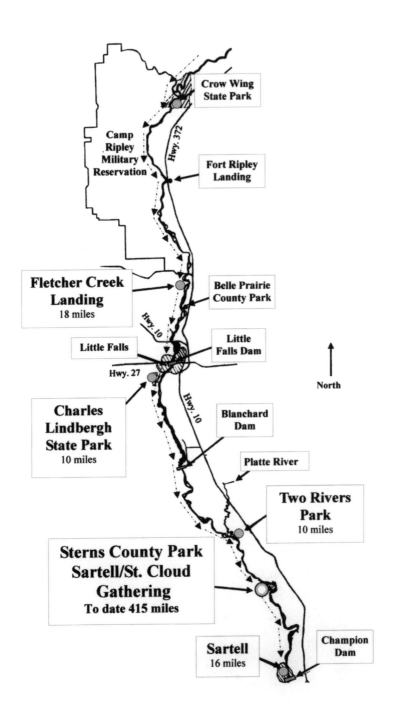

Crow Wing
State Park

Camp
Ripley
Military
Reservation

Hwy. 372

Fort Ripley
Landing

Fletcher Creek
Landing
18 miles

Belle Prairie
County Park

Hwy. 10

Little
Falls Dam

Little Falls

Hwy. 27

North

Charles
Lindbergh
State Park
10 miles

Hwy. 10

Blanchard
Dam

Platte River

Two Rivers
Park
10 miles

Sterns County Park
Sartell/St. Cloud
Gathering
To date 415 miles

Sartell
16 miles

Champion
Dam

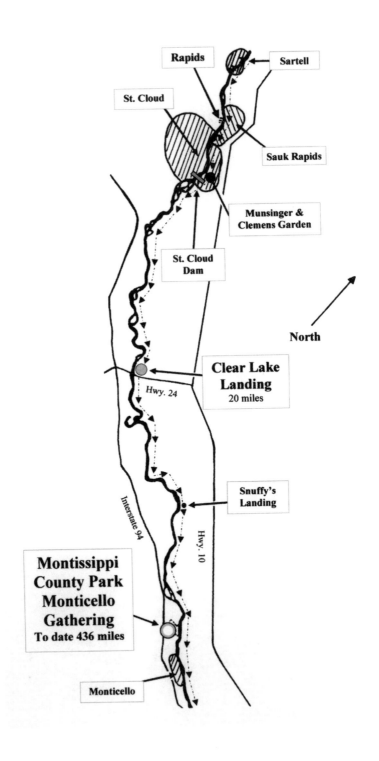

Rapids

Sartell

St. Cloud

Sauk Rapids

Munsinger &
Clemens Garden

St. Cloud
Dam

North

Clear Lake
Landing
20 miles

Hwy. 24

Snuffy's
Landing

Interstate 94

Hwy. 10

Montissippi
County Park
Monticello
Gathering
To date 436 miles

Monticello

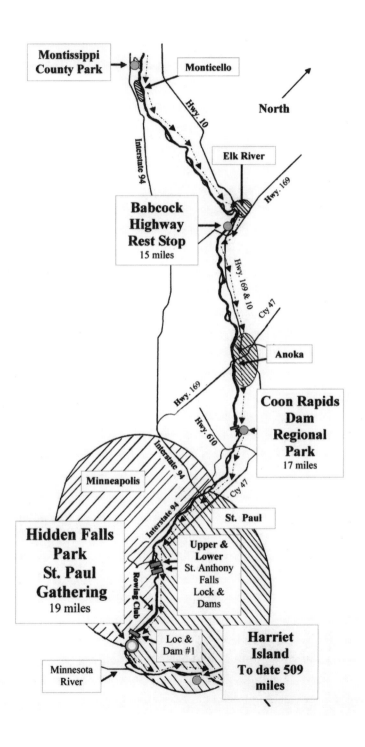

Montissippi
County Park

Monticello

North

Hwy. 10

Interstate 94

Elk River

Hwy. 169

Babcock
Highway
Rest Stop
15 miles

Hwy. 169 & 10

Cty 47

Anoka

Hwy. 169

Coon Rapids
Dam
Regional
Park
17 miles

Hwy. 610

Interstate 94

Minneapolis

Cty 47

Interstate 94

St. Paul

Hidden Falls
Park
St. Paul
Gathering
19 miles

Upper &
Lower
St. Anthony
Falls
Lock &
Dams

Rowing Club

Loc &
Dam #1

Harriet
Island
To date 509
miles

Minnesota
River

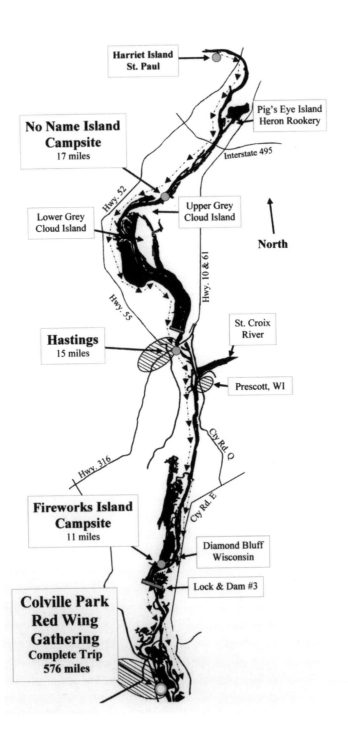

Harriet Island
St. Paul

Pig's Eye Island
Heron Rookery

**No Name Island
Campsite**
17 miles

Interstate 495

Hwy. 52

Lower Grey
Cloud Island

Upper Grey
Cloud Island

North

Hwy. 10 & 61

Hwy. 55

Hastings
15 miles

St. Croix
River

Prescott, WI

Cty. Rd. Q

Hwy. 316

Cty. Rd. E

**Fireworks Island
Campsite**
11 miles

Diamond Bluff
Wisconsin

Lock & Dam #3

**Colville Park
Red Wing
Gathering**
Complete Trip
576 miles

Women's Wisdom and Grandmother Stories Index

"You Go Girl"
Merchandise

Suppport future Water Women Wisdom Expeditions

All of the
"You Go Girl"
Merchandise
includes the
Water * Women * Wisdom
Logo

Tee Shirts

Tank Tops

Hooded Sweatshirts with full zipper

Bandanas

Mugs

Water Bottles

Thermal Mugs

To purchase
"You Go Girl"
merchandise go to:

www.waterwomenwisdom.com